INHERITANCE

The tragedy of Mary Davies:
property & madness in
eighteenth-century London

LEO HOLLIS

A Oneworld Book

First published by Oneworld Publications in 2021
This paperback edition published 2022

Copyright © Leo Hollis 2021

ISBN 978-0-86154-304-5
eISBN 978-1-78607-996-1

Illustration credits: All images author's own or Creative Commons
unless otherwise stated. With permission from the Grosvenor Archives:
image 3: Badeslade EM10; image 13: EM116.
From the Mary Evans Picture Library: image 8. From the Bridgeman
Picture Library: images 2, 14, 15, 16.

Typeset by Geethik Technologies
Printed and bound in Great Britain by Clays Ltd, Elcograf S.p.A.

Oneworld Publications
10 Bloomsbury Street
London WC1B 3SR
England

Stay up to date with the latest books,
special offers, and exclusive content from
Oneworld with our newsletter

Sign up on our website
oneworld-publications.com

Praise for Leo Hollis

'An enjoyable romp through the social history of a century from the Great Fire and the rebuilding of London to the Enlightenment, taking in discourses on midwifery, madness, child-rearing, burial practices, the birth and development of the London property market and the dangers of being a woman.'

The Times

'Genuinely gripping. Hollis tells a good tale... *Inheritance* is also a book about property... his knowledge shows here in confident and vivid descriptions of the capital at the start of the eighteenth century. But he comes at his subject from a novel angle.'

Adrian Tinniswood, *Literary Review*

'The story of an heiress whose patrimony lies at the root of a modern accumulation of a vast landed fortune, the Grosvenor Estate of the Dukes of Westminster... brilliant.'

Ian Bostridge, *Financial Times*

'A tale of lies, coercion and opium-laced strawberries... compelling.'

BBC History

'This wonderful book has many layers: the entwined stories of the men who stamped their names on the streets of London and, in their midst, one woman for whom a rich inheritance became an impossible cage. Leo Hollis knows the expanding city like the back of his hand, and brings a forensic eye and a deep empathy to the mystery at the heart of Mary Davies's tragic life. Combining biography and detective story with urban panorama and a thought-provoking exploration of the nature of property, *Inheritance* is a consistently enthralling read.'

Helen Castor, author of *Joan of Arc*

'Hollis expertly weaves together the human tragedy and high politics behind the explosion of one of the world's greatest cities. His scholarship and storytelling makes the seventeenth century seem so familiar.'

Dan Snow, author of *Death or Victory: The Battle for Quebec and the Birth of Empire*

'Leo Hollis combines meticulous research with his trademark style once again in this perceptive and humane book on one of modern London's most significant origin stories.'

Lucy Inglis, author of *Georgian London: Into the Streets*

'Identifying an authentic seventeenth-century mystery, Leo Hollis uses the form of the classic detective story to deliver a fast-moving and forensic account of the birth and development of the London property market. Here is a valuable addition to the literature of the city in another period of cancerous growth.'

Iain Sinclair, author of *The Last London*

'Leo Hollis has written a thorough and readable account of the Mary Davies saga, at times almost as a thriller, set in the glamour of Restoration London. We dodge from the plague and the Glorious Revolution into matrimonial rights, lunacy acts and 99-year leases. The life of this otherwise inconsequential woman is meticulously recorded, and all for the incubus of an inheritance which she barely seemed to comprehend.'

Simon Jenkins, *Oldie*

'An intriguing story of scandal, betrayal, law courts and corruption. It's a fascinating read.'

Who Do You Think You Are?

'Many men make no scruple to marry a woman they don't love, for the sake of her money; it may therefore be supposed, that women of fortune, are more liable to injuries of that kind than any other part of the sex.'

Sarah Chapone, *The Hardship of the English Lawes in Relation to Wives*, 1735

To Mum

Contents

Introduction   1

1   'The Way to be Rich'   13
2   'Lord, Have Mercy on Our Souls'   35
3   The Preparation of the Bride   59
4   'All the Trouble in the World'   87
5   'To Such a Mad Intemperance Was the Age Come'   112
6   'A Woman of Great Estate'   140
7   'Let Him Prove the Marriage'   166
8   'One Degree of Madness to Marry a Man Not
    Worth a Groat'   184
9   'For the Good of Her Family'   207
10 'An Amazing Scene of New Foundations'   225

Afterword   251
Acknowledgements   261
Notes   263
Index   277

Introduction

THE CARRIAGE ARRIVED at the Hôtel Castile, on Rue Saint-Dominique, deep in the night of Sunday, 12 June 1701. There was great activity as soon as the horses came to a halt, and as the party of English travellers uneasily stepped down to the street. This troupe included Lodowick Fenwick, a Benedictine monk. As a Catholic persecuted for his faith in Britain he often wore secular clothes in order to dissemble his true vocation. Beside him, looking frail and in distress, came Dame Mary Grosvenor, who was rushed into the house and her rooms on the first floor, with a view to the garden beyond. She was followed by a flurry of servants, who had accompanied her on the arduous journey. The owners of the hotel, Madame Dufief and her husband, had already prepared rooms and now busied themselves in settling the guests in.

Dame Mary, exhausted by the journey, took to her bed immediately. She had been ill when they had departed Rome a few weeks before and her condition had not improved despite a break in the itinerary for rest in Lyon. This respite included a succession of doctors' visits, and a regime of bleeding and dosing. There had been reports of her behaving strangely in Italy, of talking in agitation during a concert, and other unexpected conduct encouraging gossip and concern. Perhaps she was still in the depths of mourning, following the death of her husband eleven months before. Others interpreted her eruptions as something more disturbing: a mental instability manifesting itself in public. From the scenes that night and over the coming week, it appeared the days in a cramped carriage, exposed to the elements, had dramatically worsened her condition.

The exact location of the Hôtel Castile is unknown. It is not identified on the detailed Turgot map drawn thirty years later, illustrating each house, garden and churchyard in the city. On this plan, Rue Saint-Dominique sweeps into the city from the south-west, following the bend of the Seine, and emptying out into the bustling St Germain. Until the 1630s the route was known as the Rue des Vaches, a cattle path into the city markets. However, the establishment of the Dominican monastery and the elegantly baroque Église Saint-Thomas-d'Aquin demanded a more tempting identity for the emerging bourgeois neighbourhood.

It was a suitable location for respectable British travellers to find a resting place in the city. Fine stone buildings, in the latest modern styles, lined both sides of the street, making it a desirable enclave. More importantly, this was close to the exiled English community that clustered around the eclipsed star of the banished former monarch James II, at Saint-Germain-en-Laye. This court-in-exile attracted all sorts of Catholics, chancers and spies, which fixed an additional layer of intrigue to Dame Mary's story.

The rooms in the hotel had been arranged days before by Dame Mary's Paris banker, Mr Arthur, and Fr Fenwick's brother, Edward. Dame Mary had been in touch with Mr Arthur often to ensure her affairs were in order, and to share some gossip. On the other hand, Edward had met Dame Mary only twice before. During the previous summer, they had been introduced at the Fenwick family home in Essex, where the two seemingly made a connection; and then again a few weeks later in London, just before the group had set out on their travels. The brief encounters had made an impression on both.

That same summer, Michael Dahl, a fashionable portraitist amongst conservative grandees, painted Dame Mary in his studio on Leicester Square. Mary is in her widow's clothes, a simple black shawl and dress, a white lace collar and sleeves offering contrast. There is no background scenery, nor any object of contemplation in her hands. No rings on her fingers. It is as if she is looking into the future with nothing to guide her. She wears a white veil that frames her face; it appears like a Spanish mantilla with an intricate fringe. Her face is plain, without expression. Her eyes are heavily lidded. The portrait seems intended to display rather than record the person.

Michael Dahl's portrait of Mary Davies, 1700

Here was a woman who now faced the world alone. She was only thirty-five years old, a mother of four children – three boys and a seven-month-old daughter. As the child heir of an extensive plot of land to the west of the city, she had been marked out as an heiress of considerable fortune. As a child she had been a prize in the marriage market, the subject of negotiations with aristocrats and grandees. And finally a wife, married before her thirteenth birthday and, possibly, a mother still in her teens. As a widow, this inheritance was now hers once again, held on behalf of her children and future generations. She was already taking control of the management of the estate and, while in London, had signed a contract concerning a lease. This was the first legal agreement that she had signed in her own name. For reasons we will see, it turned out to be her last.

Something about those two short meetings in Essex and London had encouraged Edward Fenwick to follow on to Paris some months later. His cousin, Francis Radcliffe, had encouraged him to 'pursue his courtship', yet Edward had arrived in Paris three days after his brother and Dame Mary had left for Rome and he was forced to linger there for their return. In the meantime, he had taken a position as a tutor to a young aristocrat. However, once Dame Mary had arrived back in the city, Edward's attentions again turned to the ailing widow.

Over the next week Dame Mary kept to her rooms at the Hôtel Castile. Edward and other visitors were allowed to visit on Tuesday. There were solicitations after her health, as well as opinions sought and discussions on who were the best doctors amongst the English community in Paris. On the following day, Dr Ayres, recommended by Mr Arthur, was called for and Dame Mary was given an emetic to purge her malady. Despite the unpleasant vomiting, which weakened her body, the antimony did not seem to have had the desired effect. And on Thursday the doctor prescribed opium pills. By Friday, the symptoms had not altered and the doctor returned to bleed the patient as she lay in her bed. She was also dosed with opium. The bleeding was intended to release a surfeit of blood that caused the hot fever, but this only weakened her further.

On the following morning, Saturday 18th, gossip started to thread through the English community in Paris. Her name began to circulate with the news that Mary had woken up that morning with Mr Fenwick in her bed, and the widow had taken the sacred oath of marriage. There seemed to be no other witnesses than the couple, Fr Fenwick, who conducted the service, and two servants. Could it be true?

Immediately, whispers of foul play swirled. Mr Lewis, secretary to the British ambassador, noted that he had heard 'particularly in the chocolate and coffee houses, that Dame Mary Grosvenor had lately received ill-usage from Lodowick Fenwick, and persons about her'.[1] The ambassador himself contacted London in order to get word to Mary's family. He feared that she was being trapped, and that they might lose her estate through this misadventure.

Nearly three weeks later, Mary found her way back to London, and to her mother's house at Millbank, overlooking the Thames. Here, still in an anxious mania, she denied her marriage to Fenwick, swearing that it never happened. At the same time she wrote: 'I positively deny it, and so will swear, and shall never own any such thing, it being absolutely false; for I never saw book, nor heard marriage words, nor said any.'[2]

The close family were fearful that Fenwick might soon follow on from Paris to claim his property; and so he did. The supposed-husband arrived in the capital three weeks later and immediately started to behave like the rightful owner of Dame Mary's birthright. He began contacting the tenants who leased lands from her estate, demanding rents to be paid directly to him, while threatening eviction to others.

He then made his way to Millbank. When the widow's mother, his apparent mother-in-law, refused to receive him, he demanded that the servants show him to his wife. Instead, he was handed a note stating that Mary was not there and, furthermore, she was not betrothed. Forced to leave empty-handed, he was nevertheless not dissuaded from his course. And so on 12 August his representatives returned to Millbank and served Dame Mary with a legal demand from the Spiritual Court of the Dean and Chapter of Westminster that questioned why Edward Fenwick should not have 'the benefit of his conjugal rights'.[3] On the following day, 13 August, in fear that Fenwick now had the legal means to take control of his new wife, the family decided to send her away to the Grosvenor family estate in Cheshire.

These disputes culminated, over two years later, in a legal case in front of the highest court in the land in Westminster Hall. The building, over six hundred years old, had been the theatre for political drama, revels and regicides, and home to the court of the Queen's Bench. Above the hubbub, the elegant vaulted ceilings gave a sense of serene, structured order. Along the walls, fifteen statues of English monarchs stood in niches looking down upon the milling crowd below. A visitor or a petitioner might think that here, upon the flagstones, was the forum of the nation: where the law met power, and the business of the city. Within the throng, everything had its price, including justice. One side of the room, according to one contemporary observer, was 'occupied by the stalls of seamstresses, milliners, law stationers, and secondhand booksellers, and even publishers',[4] while in the west corner of the room sat the Queen's Bench, where Dame Mary's fate was to be decided.

This came to a head in the early hours of the morning of 4 February 1703, when, after fourteen hours of deliberations, pleas and cross-examinations, Lord Chief Justice Holt, the leading judge in the country, turned to the jury of twelve men and asked them to adjudicate upon a legal case that had scandalised London for the last two years. Witnesses had been called from across the Channel to bear testimony to what actually happened in that hotel on Rue Saint-Dominique on 18 June. Over the previous day and night of questions and witness statements, many disturbing tales were revealed in public about what had gone on. There were accounts of how the husband's family had laced glasses of wine with laudanum, and sprinkled strawberries with 'black grains' of salt prunello. Alternatively, the jury was informed that Dame Mary had fallen in love too fast, and then had had regrets. That she was turned against her new husband by her family who cared not for her heart, but only about her fortune.

Whatever the reasons, there was more at stake than the desires of a woman who had been treated as a commodity all her life. One can only imagine the gossip bubbling through the public gallery. What was a recently widowed woman doing, leaving her children behind for a reckless trip to Europe? Why was she alone with these men on that Saturday night? Was she drugged, and failed to remember what happened in that hotel room? Was the marriage legitimate, albeit unwilling? Or too hasty, and swiftly regretted?

Such hearsay and legal wrangling came to determine not only the lives of Dame Mary and her supposed husband, Edward Fenwick, but her whole family: her mother, Mrs Tregonwell, and her own brood from her first marriage. And, in time, their family, for many generations to come. Furthermore, it is fair to say that the future of London itself was also in the balance as the judge made his ruling on the legitimacy of the wedding:

> Gentlemen of the jury, it is supposed and admitted on all hands to be the estates of the Lady Grosvenor Mr Edward Fenwick does endeavour to make out his title to … On this account, that he was married to her (as he says), and that, Gentlemen, is the only question you are to try. If so be Mr Fenwick be [*sic*] the husband of Mary Grosvenor, then he hath a good title to the estate; if he is not married to her, that he hath not.[5]

The jury took only half an hour to make their decision.

* * *

I had not started out writing with this story in mind. I had begun with a completely different question: who owns London today? Researching the housing crisis, I soon came to recognise how often the question of land is overlooked. When we think about the modern city we look at the buildings and the infrastructural flows of the urban environment: stones, bricks, stairs, windows and kerbs. It is often assumed that when we consider the current housing crisis the debate is concerned only with the supply and distribution of houses. We should build more; open more space; construct taller; increase density. But this is not the solution in itself.

The question of land is indelibly linked to the question of the form and functions of the city. As radical geographer Brett Christophers notes, in London nearly eighty per cent of the price of a property is actually for the purchase of the land rather than the bricks and mortar that sit on top of it.[6] This has convinced me of the obvious, but ambiguous, fact that whoever owns the land has a disproportionate say in how the city is shaped and functions.

Having written one history of the seventeenth-century capital,[7] I realised that this period – so volatile, dangerous, transformative – was the crucible of the modern city. During the span of a single life, London went from a dilapidated backwater to the largest city in the world. It faced revolution, plague, fire, was the theatre for political ruptures and economic storms. Here, one finds the forcing ground of banking, empire, the Enlightenment. It changed the idea of what a city can be – in form, and as an idea. And in particular, what it was to be modern. This involves not just changes in technology and architectural style, but also a rupture in the economic system, a revolution in the understanding of value, time, work, and even a sense of self within an increasingly complex world.

It is therefore easy to overlook the birth of a young girl in the midst of these tumults, and the particulars of her circumscribed life afterwards. I was familiar with the story of Mary Davies's teenage marriage to Sir Thomas Grosvenor, and how this noteworthy union had set the future course of Mayfair, the most glittering of London estates. It appears in most history books as a fragment in time within much larger historical movements. For most narrators of this story there was a seeming inevitability between the wedding and the construction of Grosvenor Square over fifty years later.

The rest of Mary's life is less well known, although the subject of an idiosyncratic two-volume history in the 1920s,[8] and an essay by seasoned London chronicler, Simon Jenkins.[9] The events in Paris were even less well known, seemingly irrelevant to what happened afterwards. Surely there was something more to uncover here and something more to say? Not just to excavate the lives of the people involved but also to see how the activities and actions of this period formed our own. In order to understand what was happening today, one had to go back to see how the question of land and the form of the modern city intertwined.

Could something like the idea of private property have its own history, and what if it was less timeless than we commonly assume? What if we can see that, close up, a doctrine that seems to be solid and resolute is made up of contingencies, historical accidents and overlooked injuries? It was these questions that then set me on this course.

What did it mean to own something in 1700? We assume that private property has always existed, but both 'private' and 'property' are volatile notions that have evolved and mutated over centuries. Few in the seventeenth century had any concept of what private might signify as we do today. It was foremost the preserve of the king, who was advised by a privy council. Similarly, only the rich could afford to live separately from the rest of bustling society. The word was less an appeal to solitude than a barrier against the many. And as for property? This was also an emergent notion during this period. Who owned what? What freedoms and obligations did property offer? How was it to be protected, valued, or passed on? Charting these intellectual struggles through the story of the inheritance of Ebury Manor reveals the foundations of our own times to be based less on universal truths and more on anxious, historical contingency.

This is the story of an heiress and her inheritance, the Manor of Ebury, a plot of land to the west of the capital that became the compass of her life. It is a narrative of tragedy, leaseholds, marriage negotiations, long journeys across Europe, court cases, poisoning and accusations of lunacy. It is the story of a woman and her right to own property in a century when new ideas of ownership were formulated and the notion of private property was sanctified as the bedrock of modern politics. And yet, despite these seismic ruptures, the question of a woman's inheritance was constantly circumscribed by the men that surrounded her: father, guardian, husband, executor.

It is surprising how much of a life one can glean from a bundle of legal documents. Mary Davies's biography is written in deeds, covenants, leases and contracts. Other than that, there are only a scattering of letters written in her own hand. There is also a brief description of her life, written by her mother as a justification of her duty of care, rather than a true picture of the young girl's upbringing. A single painted portrait from the middle of her life, yet unfinished, shows the viewer how she wished to present herself. Court papers accumulate evidence of her tragedy, and offer another portrait. These are the raw materials at hand when attempting to restore Mary's story and the history of her inheritance. Each contract tells of a place, and an exchange of obligations, but also acts as the crystallisation of a moment. Together, these documents chart the pathways of a life like boundary markers along the route.

Property and marriage were the warp and weft through which Mary's tapestry is woven. Thus, the truth of her life, and much of the drama, was attached to the inheritance that weighed upon her every move, and informed the intentions of those around her – her mother, suitors, husband, confidantes and confidence men. In Grosvenor family histories, the episode at the Hôtel Castile in 1701, and the later court case, is blanketed over as 'the tragedy'. In almost every written portrait of her, Mary is brushed aside as a lunatic, whose irrational behaviour threatened the steady flow of dynastic destiny.

I want to claim Mary's life from such unpromising source material. For the life seeps through the pages of these documents. As a child, her inheritance was overseen by her family. After marriage, it became the property of her husband. Later in life, it was looked after by her guardians, and then passed to her children. A woman's life in the seventeenth century, it seems, was always someone else's property. A woman was not sovereign over her own domain: she could be portioned, sold, managed, improved and turned to profit. Yet the biography leaks out despite the legalistic jargon, the set phrases of 'bargain and sale', the dates of money due, bonds put down, the measurements of acres and fields. Furthermore, much can be interpreted through the silences, where a woman's voice is lost or misinterpreted. Desires remain unarticulated, or are diagnosed as unreasonable. Character can be read through points of negotiation between parties, weighed against more material gains.

But this is not just the story of Mary Davies and her inheritance. Another reason why Mary's story is often forgotten concerns the question of her legacy itself. When she inherited the Manor of Ebury, the fields, pastures and marshy riverbanks stood a long way outside the city. But as she aged, the city grew, until, in her sixth decade, this rural hinterland became some of the most valuable real estate in the metropolis, ripe for improvement. That scrub and fields became the squares, wide streets and elegant homes of Mayfair, and later Belgravia, Kensington, Pimlico – some of London's most exclusive neighbourhoods. In turn, the land made Mary's descendants one of the richest families in Britain, the Dukes of Westminster.

Property has shaped the destiny of the city; and whoever owned the land held the future in their hands. One can still find the delineation of the Great Estates in London today. The names of the distinguished landowners, who have made their fortunes from developing and speculating upon the ground beneath our feet, are etched into the urban spaces. Grand houses. Street names. Neighbourhoods. These enclaves have defined elite housing since the eighteenth century, and are still the most sought-after addresses amongst the world's Ultra High Net Worth Individuals. Some aristocratic landlords have risen, other have collapsed, but the overbearing power of private property has remained constant. It is London's lodestar.

But to tell that story, and Mary's, we need to start before her birth, with the formation of her inheritance: the Manor of Ebury, and the man who bought the land and then passed it to the Davies family.

I

'The Way to be Rich'

ON FRIDAY 23 January 1663, following a visit to a coffee house and a discussion on the state of trade with his friend Sir John Cutler, the clerk to the Navy Board, Samuel Pepys, found himself wandering by the Temple Bar, at the western end of Fleet Street. This was the place where, travelling out of the City, the main thoroughfare flowed westward into the Strand towards Westminster. Here, Pepys was at the meeting point where the two tidal currents – the commercial and the courtly – of Restoration London swelled and churned.

To the east, the route rolled downwards to Ludgate and the Fleet River, a slow roiling sewer that disgorged its refuse into the Thames. And, up the other side of the fetid gap, stood the dilapidated hulk of Old St Paul's Cathedral. This was the City of London, the merchants' capital. To the west, past the churches of St Dunstan's and St Clement's, stood the old aristocratic houses that hugged the Thames along the Strand. They were decidedly down at heel, hard to distinguish from the slums that clustered within the gaps, signs of the disorganised expansion of the city. Beyond, the road followed the curve of the river past the newly established Covent Garden and the open space of the King's Mews towards Whitehall and Westminster, the centre of the recently revived royal court.

From here Pepys observed urban life in all its variety. This was a place of exchange: along Fleet Street tradesmen, craftsmen and retailers took advantage of the continuous passing traffic to sell their wares, and this main thoroughfare was home to some of the finest purveyors in the capital. Each outlet could be identified by its unique signage, so that the street became a sea of 'Lions blue and red, falcons, and dragons of all colours, alternated with heads of John the Baptist, flying pigs, and hogs in armour'. Shopping intermingled with fancy, and danger. It was a place for riots and protests, as young people gathered for entertainments and wonders. The playwright Ben Jonson wrote of seeing a performance of 'a new motion of the city of Nineveh, with Jonas and the whale, at Fleet Bridge'.[1] Here also stood St Bride's Church and Bridewell Gaol to remind the traveller that the distance between salvation and the fall from grace were never far away.

From 1500, when Wynkyn de Worde set up his first press at the sign of the Sun on the south side of the street, this was also home to booksellers and printers that serviced the demands of the educated City elite. It was from one of these booksellers that Pepys picked up, as he later noted, 'a serious pamphlett and some good things worth my finding'.[2] The item was an anonymous thirty-two-page broadside with the full title: 'The Way to be Rich, according to the practice of the great Audley, who begun with two hundred Pound, in the year 1605, and dyed worth four hundred thousand Pound this instant November 1662, etc.'[3]

The publication acted as a brief eulogy to Hugh Audley, who had indeed died in November the previous year and, as Pepys noted, had 'left a very great estate'. Other obituaries noted that he was 'infinitely rich'. Later historians accepted the definition without scrutiny and Audley became the emblematic image of the early modern moneylender, living alone with his fortune in his rooms in the Temple. Yet Audley could not be reduced to an archetype.

No portraits were painted of this unique Londoner, so the pamphlet that Pepys picked up that January morning will have to suffice. One imagines a man in sober dress, 'grave and decent'. 'He wore a Trunk Hose with Drawyers upon all occasions, with a leather Doublet, and plate Buttons; and his special care was to buy good Cloth, Linnen and Woolen, the best being best cheap, and to keep them neat and clean.'[4] He avoided taking sides where possible, either religious or political. He was wary of taking high office or becoming too close to the grandees of the city. As he noted: 'He that eats Cherries with Noble men, shall have his eyes spitted out with the stones.'[5] Thus, as he rose, he did not become part of the elite but remained apart, a new class: the so-called 'masterless men'.

Today, his likeness appears caught between that of the medieval usurer and the protean capitalist. In truth, his life's work encapsulates the transitions eddying through in the city, as it evolved from a citadel of obligations and hierarchies to a metropolis of speculation. As London lurched fitfully towards becoming the first modern city, Audley became adept at riding the turbulence. His eulogy presents him as a thoroughly modern man: 'He went on as in a labyrinth with the clue of a resolved mind, which made plaine to him all the rough passages he met with; he with a round and solid mind fashioned his own fate, fixed and unmoveable in the great tumults and stir of business, the hard *Rocke* in the middest of Waves.'[6]

Amid such choppy waters emerged the story of Mary Davies's inheritance.

Audley was born in the heart of the Elizabethan capital, in January 1577, the tenth child of the wealthy merchant, John Audley, and his wife, Margaret. From a young age he was encouraged to learn his letters at the Temple, and was made a lawyer's clerk. He swiftly proved himself to be a prudent and intelligent student, who learned thrift as well as guile. At this stage of life, his parents may have hoped for a position near to the source of ultimate power, the Crown. To become a councillor was the ideal route for a well-educated citizen, a Thomas Cromwell, giving advice to the monarch, pulling the threads of state, and reaping the profits. However, the queen was not the only master in the city. Money itself was a bright star by which many merchants navigated.

As he learned the law, Audley scrimped every penny where he could, and rather than remain in chambers he became a judicious moneylender. At the time usury was considered a pursuit of ungodly profit, but the negotiations of debt and credit were the grease that lubricated the city's economy. Banking, as we understand it today, did not yet exist, so all borrowing was on an intimate level and Audley soon gained a reputation as a shrewd but fair creditor.

He placed himself close to those who could push business his way, and stepped forward when the right time presented itself. Despite what later historians have claimed, he did not gouge his debtors, but offered a reasonable interest rate of six per cent. However, as his obituary did note, he lived by his wits: 'his High-way is in By-paths, and he loveth a Cavil, better than an Argument; an Evasion, than an Answer. He had this property of an honest man, That his Word was as good as his Bond; or he could pick the Lock of the strongest Conveyance, or creep out at the Lattice of a word.'[7]

In time, Audley gathered a fortune of £6,000, but this was just the first act in his accumulation of 'infinite riches'. Next, he chanced his hand in the Exchange, moving from usury to investments. In the first decades of the emergent English Empire, he put £50 into each of four ships that sailed from the Thames to find new trade. One sank, but the other three returned, and he tripled his ante. After similar successful ventures, once again he needed to diversify his portfolio. Such high-risk speculations demanded to be hedged and Audley then ploughed his surplus into the procurement of lucrative offices, and the safest investment of all – land.

In 1619, he spent £3,000 to purchase the clerkship of the Court of Wards and Liveries, based in the Temple, where he once again took chambers and remained for almost the rest of his life. The Court of Wards was a remnant of a bygone way of the world, a reflection of the feudal obligation of the landowner to his king and a reminder that the Crown was still the final judge on all property.

All property belonged, and still does to this day, to the Crown, obtained through the Norman Conquest. Therefore, property was an idea that originated from, and was imposed from, the top down. This system during the feudal period was structured through the division of the land, and the obligations that went with it. The king gave estates to his barons, who further divided the lands amongst knights, who leased to tenants, and then down to the lowest level of villeins. The donation of land always came with duties going back up the hierarchy: political obedience, military service, a portion of the crops, taxes, rents or mandatory agricultural labour.

Thus, the social order of the agrarian economy was regulated and made rigid by the control of access to, and use of, land.

A complex lattice of regulations and customary rights evolved across the centuries. Land moved from one generation to the next by means of primogeniture, the first son taking control of the whole estate on the father's death. This practice was encouraged, and later enforced by law, to prevent the division of the estate. These feudal rights and customs soon enough became encoded in statutes and contracts. This enshrined in clause and codicil the tension between the king who wished that all property be in his gift, and the landowners who wished to hold on to their property as a legal right.

Initially, common law was encouraged by the Crown as it offered a process that appeared to centralise power, enshrined in the three courts of Exchequer, Common Pleas and the King's Bench, taking priority over local jurisdictions and manorial traditions. But as the major landowners grew powerful, they too used common law for their own ends. For example, the 1215 Magna Carta was a set of commands to protect the barons' rights as property holders, in opposition to the Crown.

However, this system was in flux. Slowly, land transformed from the site of customs and obligations, into a legal, and then a commercial, instrument that could be quantified and exchanged. As a consequence, these measurements and transactions needed to be managed, and the professions of lawyers, judges and surveyors, and places of the law, like the Inns of Court, soon blossomed as the proving ground for the new doctrines of private property relations. Most significantly, Parliament emerged as the meeting place for the interests of the emerging landowning classes. In this manner, British law and economy was founded in the adjudication of land disputes and the primacy of property over all other considerations. At the heart of this was the question of the protection of ownership, the mechanics of exchange and the management of inheritance. Often this was in conflict with the interest of the Crown.

But for a market to grow it needs not just a ready demand, the codified rules of exchange, and the offices to oversee it, but also the steady supply of land itself. The 1530s–40s saw the largest exchange of property in British history, that radically transformed the complexion of the nation. It is estimated that in 1531 the Catholic Church owned fifteen per cent of all English land, about twenty per cent of all farmable property. At the time, Henry VIII wanted to break with Rome and was in need of cash to fund his wars. The Dissolution of the Monasteries and the sale of Church lands provided him with a solution to both problems.

This newly acquired land was to be turned to profit. The vast transfer of land heralded a revolution in the law to describe ownership: not for purposes of sufficiency but the production of surplus. Here, English law grew increasingly complex as it sought ways to protect land and empower landowners. This was personified in Parliament itself. And, at the start of this revolution, these tectonic shifts between power, property and privilege set up the inevitable contest between the Crown and the Commons to establish who had power over the regulation of property.

This dispute is illustrated in the strange case of the true mile. In the contest about who had the final say about the laws governing land, measurement became increasingly important. Since the thirteenth century most land was measured by the 'perch' or the surveyor's rod, traditionally marked at 5 1/2 feet. But this only makes sense if the inch itself was also regular. At the time, it was measured by 'three grains of barley dry and round'. However, Henry VIII decided to reduce the size of the rod by 1/11th, in order to plump up his tax revenue. In response, Parliament refused to comply and maintained the old measurement. This may not have mattered much on a small scale, but when it came to distances like miles, which were also calculated as a multiple of the rod, this created disparities that were to cause serious problems. This dilemma was not cleared up until the 1593 Weights and Measures Act that defined an English mile as 5280 feet. From now on, the measure was to be strictly regulated and policed. Places became defined by their dimensions and boundaries.

Yet there was an alternative system of ownership, in contrast to private property, and one that was regulated from the bottom up: the commons. Common land had traditionally been reserved for the community for their free use. It was often poor soil, but here the poor were able to eke out some kind of subsistence.

However, in time, the commons were increasingly deemed unproductive; in the words of Thomas Fuller: 'the poor man who is monarch of but one enclosed acre will receive more profit from it than from his share of many acres in common with others.'[8] And so the commons were enclosed and the poor were driven away. Fences and hedges were raised in order to stop the use of common lands, and despite the powerful history of disputes where boundaries were torn down again, and enclosure challenged, in the end, the interests of private property won, and the fences stayed up.

A good example of this was in the fields close by the Manor of Ebury in Westminster, enclosed in 1592 with ditches and hedges, presumably to be converted into land for livestock, or gardens to produce food for the ever-hungry city. By custom these lands were called Lammas Ground, which is to say that they were commons that anyone could utilise from the day after the harvest, around the beginning of August, to Candlemas, in early February. But when the parishioners were confronted with fences that year, they gathered on 1 August, Lammas Day, with pickaxes and other instruments to rip the hedges out, and break the gates. The evidence given by a local constable, Ralph Wood, offers an account of coming across over 100 protesters breaking fences. In the following trial, the tenants and landowners made their case, saying that the rioters should face the full force of the law. As expected, the state took the side of the landowners, and to make this loss concrete, some accommodation was made with the arrangement of Lammas money that was given to the parish in place of common grazing rights.

As a consequence, the poor became wage labourers, their rights reduced to a financial transaction. This drove many of them away from the village towards the city, where they became absorbed into the cash nexus. The land they left behind that once grew the grain to feed the village was now turned to pasture, and England became a country of sheep. As Thomas More exhorts in a famous line from *Utopia*, the transference of common land to sheep fields was devastating: 'Your sheep … that commonly are so meek and so little, now, as I hear, they have become so greedy and fierce that they devour men themselves. They devastate and depopulate fields, houses and towns.'[9] As Ellen Meiksins Wood notes, therefore,

British capitalism 'was born in the countryside', but it was converted into cash in the city.[10]

These systemic paradigm shifts were coming to the fore as Audley acquired his new position. In the midst of this maelstrom, however, the anachronistic Court of Wards remained a cash cow that could not yet be sacrificed. It was formed by the warmongering Henry VIII who needed cash wherever it came from. For a payment or fine, a guardian could be found to look after those unfortunate orphans who needed the king's protection against untrustworthy relatives. The court further arranged for safeguards to preserve estates. It policed the role of executors and kin who might want to take advantage of the situation. All this for a fee, and the chance of plenty of graft to the officers who took advantage of the situation. It delivered a steady stream of coin into the Royal Exchequer without the interference of Parliament.

But this antiquated system was coming unstuck during the seventeenth century. James I and then Charles I were both determined to rule without parliamentary interference and, desperate to find any new source of income outside the normal tax levy, they turned to the Court of Wards, amongst other schemes. During the 1630s, Charles I attempted to rule without MPs, and he floated his venture on fines, extra-parliamentary taxes and customs, the sale of knighthoods and monopolies, and the Court of Wards. Revenue from the Court went from £49,069 in 1627 to £83,085 in 1639. No wonder, according to the Earl of Clarendon, the landowners were displeased: 'all the rich families of England, of noblemen and gentlemen, were exceedingly incensed, and even indevoted to the Crown, looking upon what the law had intended for their protection and preservation to be now applied to their destruction.'[11]

Audley entered this circus and 'gained money by doing a good Office, viz. in hindring some great persons to make a prey of young Heires, for some fees allowed him by the Heirs relations, and therefore he was the father of the fatherless.'[12] Furthermore, there was money to be made, bribes to pocket and influence to buy. Audley continued to find profit where it lay. This also allowed him access to a wider range of aristocrats and property owners who, on occasion, needed financial aid, which he was well placed to provide.

During this period, Audley rose in reputation but refused to forget where he came from. As he noted, 'I am loth to rise higher, for I fore-see my Fall.'[13] He had few friends, preferred the company of serious men and shunned folly. He sounds like a Puritan but was a confirmed Anglican who believed in the established order of king, Church and bishops, as much as a well-ordered investment. For this reason, despite his skills in making his fortune in the courts or the bourse, he saw the value of putting his money into land rather than impressing princes. There were few better places than the courts to hear the distressing news of estates on the brink of collapse, or noblemen and heirs on the rocks. And Audley was always there to offer advice and respite, as long as it was to his own advantage. Hearing of one woodland estate that was mortgaged to the hilt, Audley bought the obligation for £13,200, cut down the timber for £4,000, and sold the land in thirty-two parts and made an overall profit of £8,000 in a year. He also bought estates in Norfolk, Lincolnshire and Wiltshire.

His next purchase, the Manor of Ebury, came out of a scandal that embroiled his superiors in the Court of Wards. Lionel Cranfield, like Audley, was a London-born son of a merchant who, unlike his fellow, had set his compass towards power and the court of James I. He became Surveyor General of Customs, in charge of raking in taxes for the king from the goods arriving at England's ports from around the world, as well as receiving other honorific titles such as Keeper of the Great Wardrobe, Master of the Court of Wards (becoming Audley's superior) and, in 1622, Lord High Treasurer. He had climbed the greasy pole and that year was named Earl of Middlesex.

But, as Audley himself might have warned, those who seek reputation must suffer the consequences. Only two years after his elevation, in 1624, Cranfield clashed with the Prince of Wales and his favourite, the Duke of Buckingham, over whether England should go to war with Spain. That same year, the new Earl was accused of corruption by the House of Commons, and the Lords stripped him of all offices. In a desperate attempt to stay afloat,

Cranfield sold his assets including a collection of estates that he had been slowly accumulating to the west of the city: the Manor of Ebury, Hyde Manor and Neate House. Audley picked up this motley collection of farmland, marshes and waterfront for £9,400 in 1626.[14] Cranfield had made a small profit on the sale, but still opined that Audley had driven a hard bargain.

The history of the manor lands reflects the complex history of ownership reaching back to the era of the Norman Conquest. Originally called Eia, the estate was entered into Domesday Book as a farm of arable, pasture and meadow. It was gifted by the king to one of his knights, Geoffrey de Mandeville, but in time the fields had passed into ecclesiastical hands and, after the Dissolution of the Monasteries, the royal estate.

Cranfield had bought the land in two plots in 1618 and 1623, but even within these deeds there were ancient obligations, exemptions, leases and complications. For example, some fields belonged to other estates: a strip of waste land that later became the exclusive site of the Dorchester Hotel on Park Lane was held by the Dean and Chapter of Westminster Abbey. Another plot, where Buckingham Palace now stands, had been retained by James I, who had planted a series of mulberry trees here, in the hope of inspiring a home-grown silk industry to rival France or Italy. It was an abject failure. Elsewhere, the Crown had sold off long leases on some plots, so there was to be no new revenue until the contracts expired in the 1670s. It was a tidy investment for Audley, if not the crowning jewel of his portfolio.

However, at the time he had other, more urgent issues close at hand. Despite his attention to the business of business, it was impossible to divorce these machinations from what was happening beyond the Inns of Court. As events were escalating in the Palace of Westminster, Audley was not immune to the political tumult that swept the city. For many Parliamentarians, the work of the Court of Wards went in direct opposition to their interests. To finish Clarendon's remark from above: 'and therefore (the great and the good) resolved to take the first opportunity to ravish that jewel out of the royal diadem.' In the Grand Remonstrance of 1641, a list of the MPs' grievances against the king, there was an explicit criticism of the Court that had 'been grievous in exceeding their jurisdiction'. And the further complaint that 'The estate of many families weakened, and some ruined by excessive fines, exacted from them for compositions of wardships.'[15]

This did not toll the end of the Court quite yet. By January 1642, the divisions between the king and his Parliament had become so hot that Charles I fled his capital and, later that summer, declared war. London had been, so far, the forcing ground of revolution, but now the violence spread across all four nations of England, Wales, Scotland and Ireland. Nevertheless, back in the Temple, the power of the Court of Wards, based as it was on a received notion of royal power, was under existential threat; but the ready funds it produced proved too alluring to both sides.

Late in 1642, Charles I set up his new centre of power in Oxford, where he attempted to open a reconstituted Court of Wards. He needed the money, and many of the existing officials were willing to travel to the royal camp and pledge their loyalty. Audley, despite having been openly in support of Charles, was ordered to stay in London and Parliament jealously coveted the income that his work might generate, while ignoring the ironies of its origin.

Eventually, in 1645, the Court collapsed under its own contradictions. Nevertheless, Parliament was still keen to chase up any funds it could, and when it was later revealed that Audley had sent money to Charles in Oxford, the MPs demanded the moneylender pay a £10,000 bond to them. Parliament were determined to have a figure like Audley close to them, and in 1649, after the execution of Charles I, he was forced into service as Sheriff of Norfolk. Despite his reluctance to leave the capital, he was threatened with another fine of £1,000, and so did as he was told. In time, he returned to his chambers at the Temple and settled back into his life's work of bonds, credit and contracts.

No matter who sat on the throne, or took the king's seat, there was always a place for profit. When Cromwell started to penalise leading Royalists who remained in their estates with a fine called the compound, which was usually calculated as one-tenth of the estate but sometimes went up to one-third, Audley was there to give support at his usual rates. As many of his borrowers faced lean times, he was also able to add to his property portfolio with significant lands across the counties.

In 1660, on his Restoration, Charles II confirmed the extinction of the Court of Wards and Liveries alongside the end of Feudal Tenure laws. The old systems of knight service and feudal ownership were over. The fates of widows and orphans were no longer the gift of the Crown, but the subject of wills and testaments, courts and common law. This marked a watershed in the question of private property.

* * *

Hugh Audley died on 15 November 1662, in the house of Dr Dukeson, rector of St Clement Danes, on Milford Street, only a few hundred yards from his old lodgings in the Temple. Dukeson was related to Audley through his daughter's marriage to Audley's great nephew, Alexander Davies. Dukeson had been rector here since 1635, except during the Wars, when he had been punished for his loyalty to Anglican orthodoxy. Following a 1648 petition from his own parishioners, Parliament had forced him out of his living. They claimed that he was a gambler and had raised funds for wounded Royalist soldiers. Furthermore, he promoted Anglicanism, including – scandalously – refusing to preach on Christmas afternoon.[16] He had been reinstated to the parish on the Restoration, and by 1662 was settled back in the Rectory.

Audley, now in his eighties, had in recent years become the victim of sharp practices from those who were supposed to be looking after his interests. In 1654, he had taken on a new assistant, John Rea, who had swiftly got on top of Audley's complicated transaction records and took control over other aspects of his master's life. Rea became indispensable and Audley started to treat him like a potential heir, bestowing profitable leases and legacies upon him and his family. But it soon became clear that Rea was cooking the books. Furthermore, during the summer of 1661, the clerk had shipped his master off to his own family in Richmond for care. During Audley's absence, his property was raided, with a loss of gold, silver and jewels and the account books. However, unusually, the locks were still intact. The family was forced to act, either out of a sense of duty or in fear of losing their own legacy. Alexander Davies, trained as a scrivener, became the old man's confidential clerk, while other members of the family took charge of his businesses.

Davies's father, John, a draper from Old Jewry, had married Audley's niece, Mary. The family had struggled during the Civil Wars, and the father had died in debtors' prison in Blackfriars in 1652. Alexander was born in 1634, educated at Merchant Taylors' and by the time of Audley's death was living with his own wife, Mary, in Southampton Buildings near Gray's Inn. Working in Audley's office meant that he was at the heart of a major financial corporation, where he did more than draft contracts and take notes, and was as adept at the law and finance as estate management.

And thus Audley's affairs were settled before his death. In his will, he asked to be buried in the Temple chapel and for attendants to the funeral to come 'without any blacks or mourning weeds'. He gave a large bequest of £333 to his faithful servant, Marie Lockwood, 'towards a satisfaction of her broken sleep and pains taken with me in my sickness'.[17] A series of funeral rings were struck for family members. One was recently found by a treasure hunter in Norfolk. It is 24 carat gold, with a skull engraved on the outside and the date of Audley's death on the inside of the band.[18]

The rest of the vast wealth was to be divided up amongst the moneylender's kin, the descendants of his three sisters. Before his death, there had been much speculation about how he was going to share it out. There were five recipients and executors: Thomas Bonfroy, Robert Harvey, Nicholas Bonfroy, the scrivener and his older brother, Thomas Davies, a successful bookseller, with a stall at the sign of the Bible in St Paul's Churchyard. Thomas had already started to climb the tiers of civic government. He was to be a sheriff and was knighted in 1667, Master of the Guild of Booksellers the following year, and the Lord Mayor in 1676. In a later report, he was called 'A mean spirited person … He seldom appears in any business but his own'.[19]

On 14 April 1663, five months after the funeral, it was decided that all the beneficiaries were to meet at the Mermaid Inn by Gray's

Inn to settle their shares, and to sort out Audley's affairs. There was a paper tower of unsettled debts and mortgages from all quarters – grandees returning from exile, Royalists who borrowed against their lands to raise troops, nobles who suffered during the Interregnum, merchants and former Roundheads, Papists who had to cover the fines for their delinquency, and dukes who needed ready cash for lavish entertainments to catch the attention of the restored monarch. It was agreed that all these bills were to be placed in a trunk that was then kept in an agreed place. Three keys were cut and shared amongst the five.

The Agreement between the executors now resides in the Westminster Archives.[20] The vellum document is heavily water damaged, and the surface ranges in tone from dirt to bone white. In places the text is illegible. From the bottom of the page hang what remains of the seals of the executors: the two Bonfroy brothers, Harvey, Alexander and Thomas Davies. Looking at Alexander's signature, it is most likely that the whole document is written in his hand, reflecting the scrivener's duty always to be legible. There are gaps in the main body of text due to wear and tear, but sewn in are three long strips: the Schedule of debts and the Schedule of legacies. Each line begins with a dash and **Item** in bold; then a list of Audley's mortgages, loans and possessions, from a small black box to debts of thousands of pounds.

The executors hoped that by organising Audley's affairs in this way, they might not fall out amongst each other. Undoubtedly, the sharing out of Audley's fortune 'made a great many poor familys rich', and no such good luck comes without divisions and squabbles. The estate was to be shared five equal ways, but how to measure this? Biographer Charles Gatty estimates that legal cases concerning the legacy continued for another forty years, 'when all the parties originally interested had left the world and its goods behind'.[21] The division of Audley's property portfolio lay at the heart of these disputes. Some of the moneylender's estates were to be sold immediately to pay for any outstanding debts and for the division of bequests. Others were to be passed to members of the family. Who would inherit the Manor at Ebury was a revealing case of Audley changing his mind over the years. This plot was not the most prized amongst his estate, but rather it illustrated how he kept his family in check, balancing interests, and affections.

In 1647, when Audley was at the impressive age of seventy, and at the end of the first Civil War, he settled the farm on his nephew Robert Harvey 'for the consideration of the actual love and affection which he did bear unto him'.[22] But this affection only lasted so long. For in 1656, the estate was then resettled on another nephew, Nicholas Bonfroy, and his family. Harvey was given other lands in Lincolnshire in recompense.[23] No reason is given for the change of mind, and it could have been solely a matter of convenience: Harvey lived in Godmanchester in Huntingdonshire and the new estate was nearby; meanwhile, Bonfroy lived closer to London. However, the bequest was changed again the following year, when the estate was promised to the malevolent assistant John Rea. This gift was withdrawn when Rae's crimes were unveiled in 1660, and then finally in 1662, just before his death, all the properties within the Manor of Ebury were settled on Alexander and Thomas Davies.[24] Thomas was given the land close to the Thames, the Market Meadows, while Alexander was promised the rest. That Alexander was Audley's scrivener and the old man spent his last days in the house of the young man's father-in-law, Dr Dukeson, surely played some role in the generosity of the settlement.

* * *

As the question of private property became more important, so too did the map. Here the literal representation of the lie of the land became the essential method of charting and measuring land. And so, as soon as Alexander Davies inherited the Manor of Ebury, he set out his new property in a comprehensive surveyor's chart that now resides in the British Library.[25]

The numerous maps of the city during this period are testament to this growing fascination with measuring the exact dimensions of the city, the limits of ownership, the designation of the metropolis's boundaries. In 1653, one new map advertised itself as 'A guide to countrymen in the famous city of London by the help of which plot they shall be able to know how far it is to any street. As also to go unto the same without further trouble.'[26] This functional street map came with a directory of street names covering the walled city and liberties around, running across the bottom of the chart, each marked by a number, symbol or letter. This was clearly an attempt to anatomise and label every corner of the city. Another version, at the end of the Commonwealth years, in 1658, by Newcourt and Faithorne, illustrates a growing commitment to scientific accuracy. Yet still individual houses are imagined, inconvenient spaces ignored. There are rowing boats on the Thames as tall as churches! Nonetheless, it offers insight into the dimensions of the metropolis (a word first used to describe London that year). To the west, the map reaches as far as the orchards at Millbank, which delineates the end of the city, and a collection of houses to the north.

A section from Hermannides's 1661 map, showing Westminster and the Horse Ferry at the very western fringes of the city

Similarly, the map *Londinum London*, made in 1661 by a Dutchman, Rutger Hermannides, attempts to encapsulate the Restoration city. In order to do this, it is almost as if he has flown high above the city, and looked down – an angel's view. There is no perspective, or idiosyncratic inclusion of watermen on the river, or stags gambolling in the park. This is as mathematical an approximation to real life as possible, as shown by the sea captain's pincers and the scale bar in the bottom right-hand corner. From this altitude, the individual buildings have lost their identity unless they are palaces, livery halls or churches. What one notices immediately is the expansion of the city to the east. The docks are now drawn in, as well as the houses of Whitechapel, Shoreditch, Wapping and Limehouse. To the north, the fields of Moorgate are being filled in with new neighbourhoods. To the west of the walls, Lincoln's Inn Fields and Covent Garden, both now near completion, set a new boundary. To the west, however, there has been little change. One can still find the Horse Ferry and beside it the orchards of Millbank. Following the road north from Westminster Abbey, one finds a windmill, just north of where Piccadilly Circus now stands, and a few houses, dotted throughout the heath and hunting grounds.

During the sixteenth century, London grew from 50,000 inhabitants in 1500 to 140,000 on Elizabeth I's death in 1603, and was close to 250,000 by the time of Hermannides's map. There had been few attempts to manage this rapid increase. London was staggering out of the tumults of civil war and the Commonwealth years of Oliver Cromwell's rule, into the uncertainties of Charles II's Restoration. While statute books could be redrafted, a new age heralded and a reconstituted political settlement celebrated, the city could not be refounded. In the words of one historian, the city in 1660 was 'not much more than a collection of monumental buildings with a slum attached'.[27]

In October 1661, the diarist and intellectual John Evelyn had been aboard a ship with Charles II, when the monarch bemoaned 'how good building was now very rare in England comparatively to other countries'.[28] In the hope of further gaining the attention of the king, Evelyn wrote *Fumifugium*, presenting London as a uniquely situated city, 'the most considerable that the earth has standing on her bosom', but that had been allowed, through a lacking of planning, to become 'a suburb of Hell'.[29] The use of coal choked the city, ruining the architecture, allowing fruit to wither on the branch.

Charles himself could do little about it: he was not rich enough to build palaces or act as a patron. Instead, the king was reliant on aristocrats and cultural influencers such as Evelyn, architects who desired to be praised for their innovation, as well as speculators such as Davies who made plans for the new projects hoping to attract the most tasteful and distinguished residents. The market determined the innovations in British taste rather than royal patronage.

The aristocrats who returned in 1660 with Charles II from Europe not only wanted to mark their restoration with the latest architectural projections, they also wanted to do it in a completely new place, on the western edge of the city. This drift had, of course, started before the Wars. The tailor Robert Baker was the first speculator to build on what came to be known as Piccadilly, supposedly named after the trendy collar ruffs that made him his fortune. Next to the windmill, where Great Windmill Street stands today, he rented land on the back of the King's Mews 'at the Town's End'.[30] In time this became the site for a gaming house and a bowling green; a tennis court was added. The neighbourhood soon gained a reputation for hijinks and dangerous behaviour. There was at least one crime of passion across a dicing table. In 1664, the estate was bought by the gambler Thomas Panton who was said to have won £1,500 at the tables one night, bought the freehold, and never put down a bet again. Panton developed a series of housing schemes over the next few years, expanding the city westwards from the new Leicester Square.

The city was ripe for improvement, and it was men like Alexander Davies who were planning to transform the capital. On the settlement of Audley's will, the creation of a surveyor's map was the first act of defining the extent of the estate and its legal standing. This was the best way for the new owner to understand the size and form of the holding, as well its complex legal status.

The whole estate was made up of three manorial plots – the Manor of Ebury, Hyde Manor and Neate House – that had been gathered together by Lionel Cranfield and sold to Audley. (In describing the estate, I will overlay the modern city in order to give a sense of proportion as well as to chart the peculiarities of various boundaries and plots.) It appears on the map like two flaps of land that narrow in the middle, like a badly skewed bow tie, meeting at what is now Hyde Park Corner. To the north, the main portion, the Hundred Acres, starts at Oxford Street (then called Tyburn Road), and runs from Marble Arch to just beyond Bond Street station. The western edge is Park Lane, to the east the course of the River Tyburn, the boundary with the neighbouring estates. The river rolls westward until it cuts across Piccadilly near Shepherd Market.

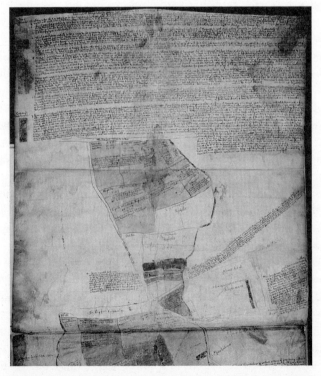

Alexander Davies's surveyor map of his new inheritance, 1662

South of Piccadilly, the estate widens out again to include the lands of Goring House (which later became the site for Buckingham Palace) and leads towards the Thames at the Horse Ferry, west of Westminster. The western boundary of this portion took in the lands of Neate House. This was a property separate from the Manor of Ebury, but both had been owned by Westminster Abbey and so came into the possession of the Crown at the Dissolution of the Monasteries and were passed on as a single property. It was named after the Abbot's house that was close to the river (south of present-day Victoria station).

Here, at the hinterlands of the city, only a short coach ride from the metropolitan fug, one could find open fields. The physician Dr Everard Mainwaringe observed that such places were much sought after as 'there being country air, pleasure and city conveniences joined together'.[31] Yet the Market Meadows did not quite have the aspect of other fashionable locales such as Bloomsbury. It was marshy ground, open to flooding. Following the 1651 Battle of Worcester, Cromwell had imprisoned some four thousand Royalist prisoners on these fields before they were sent abroad. Many died due to the wretched conditions.

Returning to the surveyor's map: the fields within the maps are divided and coloured, and filled in with annotations. Each field has its own name. So present-day Belgravia is recast as More Gardens, Allen's little meade and Allen's great meade, Broadmore, Doggesmeadow, Little Horseleyes. Alongside, notes on the tenancies: 'Allen's Great Meade 5:1:0 5:3:12 [the name and the proportions of the field] Child once Tenant. 20 Dec. 12 Jac [the date of the original tenancy: 20 December 1615] Let by Hayes to Doubledayes. In 37 let by Foster. 53 let by Ashton. 58 let to Calaway'.

Even with this level of detail, disputes were likely to occur as tenants claimed precedents and rights, while others challenged the size of the grounds or the measurement of the boundaries. This is the accumulation of facts, contracts, precedents, court papers and rulings upon which our current understanding of how the system of property is built. For Davies as he inherited this estate, this brought in an annual income of approximately £1,200, but some of the land did not offer any sort of income, as it was tied up in historical leases that did not expire for another decade. However, Alexander saw a new harvest to be made from these fields.

Next door and close by the river stood the Market Meadows that had been given by Audley to Thomas Davies, rather than Alexander. Because of its proximity to the river and the royal court at Westminster, this plot had the most potential: it was land that could be improved. And so as soon as he was able, Alexander made an offer to his brother to take this marshy farm off his hands.[32] It is highly probable that the deal was done while the executors were still shuffling through the moneylender's papers. Thomas, the bookseller, was not interested in becoming a landowner, seeing his future in urban politics. They signed the deal on 28 May 1663, but Alexander had already started work on leasing out the plot. A month later, Thomas was complaining that the remainder of the price 'was not then nor is paid'.[33] This debt hung over the family for years to come.[34]

The scrivener had turned into a developer. Before building, therefore, the ground needed to be irrigated and the river held back. On 14 January 1664, Alexander leased out portions of the river front and wharf to the carpenters John Goodchild and Robert Stawker.[35] There was a down payment and a yearly rent folded into the agreement, but also these craftsmen were expected to improve their plot with building.

To the south, work started on the Market Meadows as soon as Davies was able. He had had to borrow more, and was often slow in paying. The houses that ranged west of the Horse Ferry were large enough to accommodate respectable families. Davies clearly liked to deal with a small team of speculators; a tip he may have learned from Audley. Stawker was leased further land to build two houses on 13 April and three houses on the following day.[36] John Goodchild also started speculating by buying up a lease for more land in March 1665, and then again the following month.[37] According to another cartographer of the region, this was 'a very good row of houses, much inhabited by gentry, by reason of the pleasant situation and prospect of the Thames',[38] although it was damp and somewhat bleak in winter due to being surrounded by low, marshy meadows.

By 1664, the hearth tax returns for that year showed a cluster of new houses. While there were a number of dwellings that only reported one hearth, which were clearly poorer houses, there were eleven that reported over ten fireplaces, which indicates a sizable and respectable home. Notably, John Goodchild had chosen to live in one of the new houses, while Stawker was not listed, although there is a 'Stocker' that sounds very similar.[39] The Davies name was not yet recorded as a leaseholder as the house was still a building site.

The plans included a new family home for Alexander and his wife, Mary. The new house was to face out towards the Thames with a large garden to the north. An etching exists that originated from a drawing of the house in 1666. It is purported to have been built by the first Earl of Peterborough, and was for a long time named Peterborough House, but this is an oft-repeated mistake. However, the house was of elegant proportions, in brick with simple fenestrations and pilasters, offering a modern touch without being too exclamatory. The house was designed in the latest style, fit for an urban grandee.

In other areas of his life, Alexander was also thinking about the future. In August 1664, he noted down a settlement for the estate that would give security to his wife and, as Mary was now three months pregnant, their forthcoming child. Three months later, Alexander and the now heavily pregnant Mary took a lease on a house in Lincoln's Inn Fields. It was a short distance from their previous home, but while that former address had been perfectly respectable for a scrivener, the new dwelling was a residence for a respectable man in town. By this time, Lincoln's Inn Fields had established itself as the home for the well-to-do. In 1664, according to the rates book, the square appeared to be ideal for a new family on the rise, with twenty-two peers and forty-two gentlemen as neighbours.

Planning for the future of the family was important, because on 17 January 1665, a baby was born; a girl, called Mary, after her mother. Three weeks later, on 3 February, her name was registered in the baptism records of St Giles in the Fields. Mary Davies's first mark on the world was, predictably, a ledger.

'Lord, Have Mercy on Our Souls'

O N 16 JANUARY 1665, the day before Mary Davies was born, an eclipse momentarily covered the face of the sun. At the time the city was in the grips of a bitterly cold winter. There had been no rain since October, but a blizzard in January brought frost and ice. Conditions were so grim that coal was hard to find and the price of bread had to be regulated so that the poor did not starve. The astrologer William Lilly saw more than economic precarity in this situation and predicted 'the sword, famine, pestilence and mortality or plague'.[1]

Despite the omen, Alexander Davies continued his scheme at the Market Meadows. In November, he rented out two new houses to John Cook.[2] In February 1665, he negotiated mortgages on three more houses to Emery Hill, William Watts and Bryan Barnaby.[3] He was moving ahead with his expansion project. The fields by the Horse Ferry were now being dug up and turned into a construction site. This was to be a community of families, workshops and stores where once had stood an old mill, fruit trees and pasture. At the western end of the site, work continued on the new home for the Davies family itself. The new home was not yet ready, and Alexander, Mary and the baby remained in the house they had rented in Lincoln's Inn Fields, so Mary was registered at the church at St Giles in the Fields. However, at the moment of celebration, disturbing news was starting to emerge within the parish.

Over the winter, the local Bill of Mortality started to register unexpected data. In December, there was the unexplained death of two Frenchmen on Long Acre, the main thoroughfare running north of Covent Garden. The area was poor, ramshackle and overcrowded, exposed to the churn of urban life; more shanty town than planned suburb. It was said that the Frenchmen had just arrived in London and brought the disease with them. Others said that their family had attempted to conceal their affliction, but the authorities caught wind of it and recorded the first notice of the return of the plague. According to Daniel Defoe's fictionalised account, *A Journal of the Plague Year*, two physicians and a surgeon were sent to the house to inspect the bodies and found the tell-tale signature of the distemper.

Yet there was, for the moment, no need to raise the alarm. And as was often the practice, the symptoms were put down as the less panic-inducing 'spotted fever'. For the first few months of the epidemic, this diagnosis was used by officials to hide the full extent of the crisis.

The plague was a blight that had regularly visited the city. In 1603, it had struck at the same time as the nation was lost in mourning following the death of Elizabeth I. During the febrile months as James I travelled to the capital and was named king, the disease bit hard, and by the time the new monarch was able to take measures to curb the epidemic, it was too late. Over 33,000 deaths were recorded, nearly ten per cent of the population. There was another major outbreak in 1625, when nearly twenty per cent of the population were struck down and ended up in the specially dug pits placed at the city's edge.

The plague visited the city thirty-six times over the following forty years. It appeared the distemper was embedded into the fabric of the city; in the words of apothecary William Boghurst, 'the earth, the seminary and seedplott of these venomous vapours'.[4] Alternatively, it was reported that the disease had arrived from Holland, bundled up in a roll of cloth that arrived at the Norfolk port of Yarmouth. Too late, the ports were shut and shipping banned from disembarking from the Low Countries.

The disease itself was spread by fleas, carried by the rats that scurried through every corner. The bacterium *Y. Pestis* was transferred to the infected body by a flea's bite. Over the course of the first week, the victim started to feel flu-like symptoms: headaches, fever, cramps, vomiting. At the same time, the infection moved towards the lymph nodes that are spread throughout the body but mainly around the armpits, groin and throat. The fingers, toes and nose might also start to blacken with gangrene as the limbs were deprived of oxygen. In time, the infected started to lose control of their bodies and to stagger; speech began to slur. The lumps that had formed at the lymph nodes bled, creating large black buboes, hard lumpy bruising under the skin. Finally, blotchy red 'tokens' covered the body, before it took its last breath.

While physicians could diagnose the symptoms of the disease once it had entered the body, it was less well understood how the disease spread. Leading medicine men placed their faith in the theory of the humours, and that the infection could be purged through emetics or bloodletting, in order for the body to rediscover its balance. The physician Nathaniel Hodges, who worked throughout the summer and yet remained unaffected throughout, swore by a dose of nutmeg and honey at breakfast, and in the evening a glass of wine with walnuts. (Both nutmeg and walnuts turn out to be surprisingly good flea repellents.) Even more still put their faith in 'charms, philtres, exorcisms, amulets and I know not what preparations'.[5] Meanwhile, other physicians, such as Thomas Sydenham, suggested that doing nothing might be the best cure: let the body regulate itself, and sweat out the fever.

The disease was delivered around the city by animals, and so a call was put out to slaughter 'hogs, dogs or cats, or tame pigeons, or conies'.[6] For others, there was no cure for the city's sins except repentance. The Puritan doctors, such as the preacher Thomas Vincent, warned: 'Now Death rides triumphal on his pale horse through our streets, and breaks into every house.'[7] Vincent believed that it was the nature of a man's soul rather than his social station that determined his fate. Whatever the cause, the effects were devastating, and the death toll high. Close to seventy per cent of those afflicted died, but the disease wrought the most havoc within the poor communities rather than among the rich. It was a symptom of a city that was beyond control, overpopulated, straining at its edges. It began in the suburbs and later entered into the City, and it was only at this stage that the authorities decided to take action.

During the week of 19 January 1665, days after Mary Davies's entry into the world, twenty-three died of the distemper in the parish. There were also instances of the disease in the neighbouring parishes of St Andrew's, Holborn, St James's, Clerkenwell, and St Bride's, on the western fringes of the City walls. Yet the city did not seem to stir through the cold. In March, the Thames was frozen and there was a single rainstorm in April but conditions did not change. On 15 April, the king travelled to the Royal College of Physicians and made enquiries into 'the seat and causes of infectious diseases'.[8]

Then, on 27 April, news reached the king's council of more deaths on Drury Lane, east of Covent Garden. This turn of events could no longer be ignored and the authorities commanded that the family of the dead be quarantined in their contaminated home. This edict was a death sentence by any definition and the neighbourhood rose in a 'ryatt'. The crowd overpowered the guards that were stationed in front of the dwelling, and the door was ripped open, releasing the family sheltering within. In another version of the story, the baby of the household was passed through the window and bundled away through the city to safety. The next day, the council declared emergency measures across the infected parishes. Condemned houses were closed up, and the front door daubed with a cross and the prayer 'Lord, Have mercy on our souls.'

As April turned to May, summer arrived with a burst of heat after so many inclement weeks. It also brought the disease inside the walls of the City itself. On 9 May, the death was announced of another Frenchman on Bearbinder Alley, by St Mary's Woolchurch. It was later revealed that the victim was formerly from St Giles and had moved into the City to get away from the danger, but instead became its messenger. At last, the City government decided to act: this was not just a local disturbance, but now a London-wide crisis.

An official commission of physicians was set up to conjure medical solutions, where none were to be expected. Was it airborne?

In that case one needed to avoid fetid air. Bonfires were lit to clear the air. Aromatic posies and herbs were burned inside affected houses. Streets were cleared of the filth that gathered in the gutters. A series of pest houses were constructed on the outskirts of the city to nurse the dying. Accounts of these hospitals give a picture of a near hell: the floors swilled with putrefaction; beds were crammed together to accommodate the sick; there were no medicines; and the staff were as likely to fall ill as cure the afflicted. Otherwise, it was planned that whenever a house was found to be infected, a guard was set up outside and a woman found to tend to the condemned inside until they died or were cured. There were tales of the nurses hastening death, and stealing whatever they could find in the closed-up houses. After their passing, the bodies were collected at night and taken to the pits that started to fill on the city's edge.

By the end of May, those who could do so took leave of the city without hesitation. This began with the court. Charles II prorogued Parliament and headed to Oxford. As a Puritan divine coolly noted, 'The great orbs begin first to move; the Lords and gentry retire into their countries; their remote houses are prepared, goods removed, and London is quickly on their backs.'⁹ From his house on Broad Street, Aldgate, one of the main thoroughfares out of the city, Defoe's protagonist observed: 'nothing was to be seen but wagons and carts, with goods, women, servants, children etc; coaches filled with people of the better sort, and horsemen attending them, and all hurrying away.'¹⁰

Then departed the physicians, churchmen and merchants who could no longer trade without a ready market. The lawyers left next, and the courts were closed for the summer. All that was left was the Lord Mayor, four physicians under the management of Nathaniel Hodges, and two generals, Lord Albemarle and Lord Craven, to keep the peace. The city was abandoned to its fate.

In June, according to the Bill of Mortality, the death toll continued to rise. On 6 June, forty-three deaths were recorded; on 13 June, this number was 112; and by 20 June, it had escalated to 168. London was now a neglected city. Many of the shops were shut and the customers departed. Gardens were left to the weeds:

'roses and other sweet flowers wither in the Gardens, and are disregarded in the market.'[11] The theatres had staged their last performances in mid-May. The food markets remained open, as the poor could not store up provisions and hide themselves away from public contact. In order to avoid unnecessary interactions, shopkeepers asked for coins to be dropped into a pot of vinegar to avoid the horror of human touch.

Despite this, the city was still a cacophony of unusual sounds. According to Defoe, on his walks around the city, he encountered 'persons falling dead in the streets, terrible shrieks and screeching of women, who in their agonies, would throw open their chamber windows and cry out in a dismal, surprising manner.'[12] In Cripplegate, the church bell that was commanded to toll for each announced death broke. In other parishes, the chiming of the bell became incessant.

Yet, in parts, the city attempted to be at work. There is a lease for a land deal signed by Alexander Davies on 20 June for a brick house, garden and yard near the Horse Ferry for a Thomas Osbourne.[13] The scrivener and his family moved out from Lincoln's Inn Fields at some point during this season, settling into the new dwelling at Millbank. The house was still unfinished, lacking a roof, but whatever state it was in, it offered a haven outside the city for the young family.

But even here, no one was safe from the distemper. On 20 June, the parish of St Margaret's, Westminster, recorded thirty-one deaths. The slum neighbourhoods that encircled the Abbey and the Palace of Westminster offered a juddering contrast between the Gothic grandeur and the dilapidated surroundings. And this chaos rubbed up against the new works at the Horse Ferry only a few hundred yards to the west. Alexander still had business in the Temple, even if many of the lawyers had departed, and he probably returned to his old neighbourhood on a regular basis. Such diligence may have proved a fatal error.

In early July, the weather turned again, delivering a heatwave, 'most extraordinary hot', that continued throughout the summer. On the third of the month, an obituary was issued: 'Alexander Davies, Scrivener, died in Westminster, suspected (not returned)

THE HOUSE OF EARL GROSVENOR ON THE BANKSIDE WESTMINSTER.

Peterborough House, the original home of
Mary Davies near the Horse Ferry

of the plague; his mother Mis Davis in Old Jury died there.'[14] The
cause of death was confirmed later in a court case, but one can
understand why the family might not want to confirm or deny the
visitation of the plague to the new home. However, Davies went
from being a father, a husband, a son, to a statistical point in the
Bills of Mortality, one of the 470 that had died across thirty-three
parishes in the city that week.

Did a watchman stand outside the Davieses' house as a nurse
tended Alexander inside? Did the guard ensure that no one, not
even his wife, Mary, and the baby girl, was allowed to leave the
house until the infected patient was cured or carried out to the
cart under the cover of night? Or did the family separate in order
to protect the child? Did Mary find refuge at her father's rectory
on Milford Street? Did Alexander's mother tend to him and catch
the distemper herself? The record tells us nothing but the speculation is heartrending. Sometimes, the number of the dead and the
historical distance allow us to forget the deeply intimate, visceral

impact of the plague upon those who were close to the dying and the departed.

Without knowing where the disease came from, and how the contagion spread, it was almost impossible to protect oneself. Afflicting the poor first, it forced the most vulnerable to risk hunger or contagion on a daily basis. Imagine that moment when the family discovers that one among them has been infected. Do they notify the authorities immediately, or do they ensure the safety of those who can get away? How do they tell their family not to come near? Do they call a surgeon who might cut, purge, bleed and, more likely, cause more pain than good? Or do they rely on home medicine, or on rumour, or fall into despair?

When the officer was then called, and the signs identified, the machinery of the state took over: a watchman was called, one for the daytime, one for the evening. A nurse also came to visit to check on the progress of the disease's signatures. Was there a physician who could offer succour? Had the lumps around the throat and groin gone black? Had gangrene started to creep up the limbs, turning the fingers and toes into bloody pus-ridden stumps? Had the red spots, the final signal of impending death, started to spread? Were there any priests left in the city who would come and offer a final prayer?

Defoe writes of the despair and mania that overcame many as they faced the unknowable horrors. Walking around the abandoned streets, he watched impotently as citizens faced their end:

> raving and distracted, and often times laying violent hands upon themselves, throwing themselves out of their windows, shooting themselves etc. Mothers murdering their own children in their lunacy, some dying of mere grief as a passion, some of mere fright and surprise without any infection at all, some frighted into idiots and foolish distractions, some into despair and lunacy, others into melancholy madness.[15]

Alexander was buried at St Margaret's, Westminster, under the eastern buttresses of the Gothic abbey. Thankfully, he did not suffer the ignominy of burial in one of the pest pits that gaped open at the end of the city over the course of the summer. When the death cart collected the dead, the bodies were usually wrapped by a sheet; sometimes nothing at all. By August, the number of bodies had become so great that the carters could not carry them away fast enough. There were often sixteen or seventeen corpses bundled together and carried to the nearest parish pit. These too started to fill up and, in the summer heat, swell and stink as the bodies decomposed. Once the pit was filled, the bodies were covered in lime and then buried over. By the end of the year, over 100,000 had died; that is, one in three of everyone who remained in the city. Alexander was fortunate to find a resting place in a churchyard, with a tombstone to mark his death; many were not so lucky.

* * *

How many wives were made widows over the course of that summer? How many children lost their parents? In August, the month after Alexander's death, the city was possessed by the dead. On 2 August, a national fast was called to 'deprecate God's displeasure against the land'.[16] The week after, the Lord Mayor called for a curfew, demanding that all healthy citizens stay indoors for a day while those who were ill were able to leave their homes, and feel the sun one more time. In a desperate need to mourn, families came together to form funeral processions to mark the last days of their kin. The dread of damnation was so grave that the chapels started to fill up. On some occasions they were so full that the preacher was forced to clamber over the pews to get to the pulpit to deliver his sermon.

Thinking of a more material future, many of the poor had little property, and bereaved families faced a precarious existence. For Alexander's widow, Mary, his sudden death, and disorganised affairs, raised the dangers of unfinished schemes and an uncertain inheritance. Supposedly the diligent scrivener, in April 1663, Alexander had put together a trust agreement that directed his brothers, Thomas and William, to look after the business of the estate. There was £100 a year to be put aside for his wife, 'beyond her dower or right of Dower in the premises, or any other her customary or other share or portion of in or to real estate or personal of the said Alexander'.[17] There was no mention of the future heir in the agreement, girl or boy. But there was no final will and testament, and so Alexander died intestate. The future of the estate was in jeopardy.

Mary was expected to be left 'in great plenty', but Alexander had died with huge debts. His investments at Millbank had not yet borne fruit. He still owed his brother Thomas for the sale of the Market Meadows. There were outstanding court cases on various property deals. The scrivener had left a twenty-one-year-old widow, with a six-month-old child, in an unfinished house. Meanwhile, outside, the city was paralysed by the plague. No court could adjudge the legal standing of the estate. There were no lawyers who could offer resolution amongst the parties. Parliament had fled and therefore was unable to legislate. What was to be done?

The widow in early modern England holds a unique grip on the imagination, even when, as on this occasion, she was still in her youth. She was, on the one hand, the luckiest of women. Widowhood liberated a wife despite her grief. She was once again a legal subject, able to own property, represent herself in court and answer to no man. She could sign contracts and therefore conduct her own affairs. Outside of any specific arrangement set out in a will, she was expected to demand a 'reasonable portion', a third of her husband's land or goods, for the length of her lifetime, in order to keep heart and soul together. This is most likely why Mr Peachum in John Gay's *The Beggar's Opera* is able to identify that 'the comfortable estate of widow hood is the only hope that keeps up a wife's spirit. Where is the woman who would scruple to be a wife if she had it in her power to be a widow when ever she pleas'd?'[18] Even a poor widow with few prospects of inheritance was to be celebrated: 'she was her own woman and could run her life as she saw fit.'[19]

On the Restoration stage, the widow was a well-rehearsed comic turn. More tellingly, the stock character was portrayed as either a litigious shrew, consumed by deeds, contracts and profits; or the victim of covetous suitors, who sought advantage over the unworldly dowager. One gets the impression that Mary Davies was something of the former, and she spent much of the rest of her life fighting and defending her family's legacy with passion and guile. Here, she shows a steely, albeit not always admirable, determination to keep her husband's estate together, whatever the cost, or whoever got hurt, including her daughter.

By the same common law that gave Mary her widow's portion, the rest of the estate went to the only offspring. Obviously, baby Mary's legacy was to be looked after by the mother as well. These rights were confirmed by the Court of the Dean and Chapter of Westminster that outlined Mary's intention 'to administer the goods etc of the deceased'.[20] And of the rights of the daughter? Since the Court of Wards and Liveries had been closed down in 1660, the protection of orphans, like land, was moving from the statement of customs into the codified realm of law and the market.

The relationship between land and the body of the heiress was a complex one: in the seventeenth century both were properties that should be turned to profit. If baby Mary had been a boy, there was a simpler story to tell, hardly worthy of notice. But Mary's sex dictates an alternative history; one of disavowals and silences, of others speaking and dealing in her name, of an identity formed between the spaces of others.

In common law, women had few rights before the law. According to the King James Bible, translated at the beginning of the century, wives were told to be 'in subjection to your own husbands'.[21] And accordingly, 'that which the husband hath is his own ... that which the wife hath is the husband's.'[22] The system of couverture, the transition of property rights from a woman to her husband on marriage, had become common law since 1542. This occurred, unsurprisingly, at the same time as the vast transfer of property following the Dissolution of the Monasteries. As land gained commercial value to be bought and sold, it was important that the estate was protected. These rules were more forcefully regulated in England than any other country in Europe. According to Amy Louise Erickson, 'The English husband covered his wife's legal identity completely.'[23] This is the reason, for example, why married English women took their husband's surname and lost their own family name. This condemned women to what a later writer called 'civil death'.

But how accurate was this? Throughout the century there are powerful examples of women owning and inheriting their own property, managing businesses, living independent lives. The invaluable work of feminist histories has shown that the social and economic picture was more complex than the statute books and commonplace assumptions suggest. Mary inherited her estate because there were no other heirs. And her sex defined her relationship to the land, and to the people around her, at each stage of her life onwards. But even here, her life does not adhere to the presumed conventions of what a woman should be, and could do.

The norms, set out in common law precedents and contracts, were a testimony of deprivations. As historian Christine Churches notes:

> a woman inherited property only if she had no brothers, on marriages surrendered all personal estate and control of her real estate, while married she could not sue, obtain credit or sign a contract in her own name, or write a will without express permission from her husband, and if he died before her, she was entitled to only so much of his estate as had been reserved to her.[24]

But there are enough examples of families that wished to protect the property of daughters and wives to show that there was space within the legal framework for flexibility.

Women made up at least half of the population and were deeply involved in all different types of transactions and, as Amy Erickson calculates, the situation was never clear cut. At any one time, most women were not married, being either unmarried or widowed, and so were legally entitled to hold their own property. Only sixty per cent of marriages produced a son who was likely to be of age, so property tended to wander to the mother for her care. By the laws of dower, the widow was expected to take her portion, at least a third of the property for her lifetime. Twenty per cent of all families had only daughters, so the land went to them, either the eldest heiress or to all the siblings equally. These percentages stack up to a large number of examples contrary to the norm. And thus, it was not so strange that Mary Davies, now only five months old, was therefore a legal heiress. But this did not necessarily provide the desired security that property was supposed to bestow.

Nevertheless, the sure future of infant Mary's inheritance depended on her mother's ability to navigate the treacherous waters of the courts, the conflicting demands of family and convention, and possibly the fate of London itself. Mary merely needed money to shore up the creaking, overextended schemes that Alexander had left incomplete. Nonetheless, she was not yet able to sell the land, which may have seemed the most plausible option. After all, who was buying during a plague? Those who may have been interested – the nobles, merchants, speculators – were far from the city; and did not start to return to the capital until autumn, and even then sparely. Parliament reconvened from 3 October but then broke at the end of the month for nearly a year. In February 1666, it was considered safe enough for the king to return at last and survey the horrors that he had hastily abandoned. By that time, 'the streets were as full, the Exchange was much crowded, the people in all places as numerous as they had ever been.'[25]

Instead, Mary looked to the marriage market as a safe harbour. And in February 1666, it was announced that Mary was to marry Mr John Tregonwell, an MP from Dorset. It may have been a love match, but it is also recorded that he was selected by Mary's friends as 'a man of honour and good understanding'.[26] He came from a distinguished family from the south-west. His grandfather had been close to Henry VIII and had gained Milton Abbey as a reward in the Dissolution of the Monasteries. His father had raised a regiment on the Royalist side during the Civil War, but saw no action. The son was suspected of being involved in the anti-Cromwell Penruddock uprising in 1655 that raised the Royalist banner in Salisbury but was swiftly stamped out by the New Model Army. Nonetheless, in 1659, he was made a Member of Parliament, where he sat for much of the rest of his life, gaining the reputation as an aggrieved landlord, constantly seeking advantage for his and his new wife's estate. The new family split their time between Dorset and Millbank. Thus, Mr and Mrs Tregonwell took over management of the widow's portion, as well as the inheritance of the infant. They were soon at work to make the legacy secure.

They swiftly discovered that the reorganisation of lands at Ebury Manor was not going to make a difference. Most of these fields were still bound up with agreements that had another ten years to run. Instead, they had to look at plots that they might sell and reap profits that way. At the western end of St James's Park, Goring House was situated in a marshy bowl of land, and was the last significant dwelling on the westerly edge of the city. It had been the subject of litigation and contestation during Alexander's brief supervision of the estate. Frankly, it was a mess, and the Tregonwells were happy to be rid of the plot, and to use some of the cash to keep their creditors at bay, if only they could just sell it.

In November 1666, Thomas Davies felt the need to go back to the courts to chase his £2,000. There were also the workers, carpenters and builders who were waiting for their wages after their work at Millbank. Unfortunately, a sale of land as significant and complicated as Goring House needed to be approved by Parliament, and so a Bill was introduced into the House of Commons. At the same time, the politicians demanded scrutiny 'to inform themselves of the Debts and Value of the Estate; and to summon and hear all Parties concerned: And to send for Persons, Papers, and Records'.[27]

Goring House itself had an unusual story. The land had been part of the sale of royal lands when Cranfield bought the rights to Ebury Manor. James I held on to a few acres and hoped to kickstart the British silk industry. He had looked with jealousy at what Henri IV had done to encourage fine silk workers to come to Paris. And so, James wanted the same beside the Thames. Since the arrival of Huguenot refugees in the 1580s, the city had acquired the skilled weavers needed, but there was still a lack of home-grown raw materials. In 1607, James I sent out a request to his nobles to plant ten thousand mulberry trees. Plantations of trees were plotted in the new colonies in Jamestown, Virginia. And the king himself attempted to grow the trees in the damp soil by Goring House. The project was a failure, however, and was allowed to decline. The wrong type of tree was planted, or the weather was not conducive.

(There are still some mulberry trees on the same site, in the garden at Buckingham Palace, but these are not descendants of those Jacobean originals.) Despite this, on the Restoration, the Mulberry Gardens were put to good use as pleasure gardens for young gallants. The rendezvous became so notorious that it featured in many of the more scurrilous plays and broadsides of the period.

The estate also came unstuck when it was used in a convoluted circus of arbitrage. At the same time as the silk venture, a Sir William Blake enclosed the neighbouring field and built a substantial house. When Blake died in 1630, the land, now owned by Audley, was then leased to Lord Goring, first Earl of Norwich, who extended the house and gardens to include a terrace, a fountain and outhouses. Goring also leased some more land from Audley for his extension programme. A price was agreed, but Goring only paid a portion. Goring had been a significant Royalist general during the Civil Wars, and avoided execution by only one vote in the House of Commons. He spent the rest of the Commonwealth years in exile, and so the grounds of his house went into decline. For a brief few years, the estate was requisitioned by Parliament and given to the Speaker of the House of Commons, and sometimes used by the French ambassador, but was restored to the family on the Restoration.[28]

Exile was expensive and the ambitious aristocrat borrowed some more money from a third party and put the house up as a principal against the debt. Goring also borrowed elsewhere in the city, leveraging his assets as collateral. On the Restoration, he returned to power, but not to fortune. By the time the estate had moved to Alexander Davies, Goring's business dealings had become byzantine, and even the king made certain claims on the land. These needed to be cleared up before the Tregonwells could make their sale.

This chicanery was part of the reason why any sale of the house had to go through Parliament, scrutinised by MPs and passed as a private bill on the statute books. This took nine years and was not to be completed until 1674, partly as a result of Tregonwell's failure to bootstrap the process. He had been able to get a Bill read in 1666 but failed to get it finalised at committee stage. There was also some resistance from the wider Davies family over selling off the family jewels so quickly.

However, in the meantime, Goring House was leased to Lord Arlington (and in time was renamed Arlington House). Pepys visited often, and found it 'a very fine house and finely furnished';[29] in contrast, his rather more snobbish friend John Evelyn found it 'ill built'. At the time, Lord Arlington was Charles II's favourite, leading the maritime efforts during the Second Anglo-Dutch War. Clearly, Goring House was a suitable enough address to attract a rising courtier, close to the new developments at St James's Palace and Piccadilly. And as Charles II continued to develop St James's Park, which swept in front of the house, it swiftly gained a reputation as one of the most coveted locations in London.

What this proved was that the Davies inheritance was gaining in prestige, even if value could not yet be extracted. The aristocrats continued to move westward, hoping to create new neighbourhoods outside the old parts of the city; either driven by fear of the plague or dedicated to new ways of living that the cramped old streets and ramshackle houses could no longer provide. As a result, the seemingly unprofitable meadows and pastures, now belonging to the infant Mary Davies, started to accumulate into an enviable legacy, even if the family could not yet get their hands on these benefits.

After the devastations of the dreadful visitation, when the city was reduced to a graveyard, events during the following year not only made the land even more valuable, but transformed the shape and history of the city itself.

* * *

On the morning of Sunday, 2 September 1666, the schoolboy William Taswell, standing in front of the Abbey at Westminster Yard, described the scene before him. He saw 'some people below me running to and fro in a seeming disquietude and consternation'.[30] As he moved towards the commotion down by the river's edge, he caught a disturbing rumour of fire in the city. By the time he had reached the Thames, he saw the first victims: 'four boats crowded with objects of distress ... Scarce under any other covering except that of a blanket'.[31] The tide had brought these refugees up river and they were hoping for safety.

Also on this tide came Samuel Pepys, who had travelled from his home at the eastern fringes of the walled city. He had been woken by his maid in the small hours of the morning with news of a fire nearby. He had travelled to the Tower in order to see the extent of the damage. By then, the fire had moved from a baker's house on Pudding Lane, where the first flames had got out of hand, towards the river and London Bridge, where he saw 'the houses at that end of the bridge all on fire, and an infinite great fire on this and the other side the end of the bridge'.[32] What he saw gave him enough trepidation to take a boat straight to Whitehall in order to awaken the king and stir him into action.

On that morning in Westminster, the fire still seemed distant; only the debris on the easterly wind bore evidence of the destruction. The faces of those victims who clambered ashore acted as heralds for the terror stirring downriver. But over the course of the next three days, the entire City was consumed by the conflagration. The first the family at Millbank knew of the fire, a few hundred yards further west from Westminster Yard, probably came with the thickening smell, the blackening air blowing up the river from the east. The wind had picked up the sooty debris and distributed it across the gardens and fields to the west. There were soon reports from Windsor, thirty miles away, of charred paper and silks covering the town in a ghostly black snow.

Then, on the tide, they saw bundles of goods that had been thrown into the river in panic from the Bridge or the northern banks. Next, they started to see the people escaping from the flames, taking whatever they could and finding refuge in the fields beyond the city. At the same time, the militia started to muster on the same fields, hesitant to enter the city, but charged with the task of fighting the flames with squirts and buckets, hooks and dynamite to pull down houses.

On that first day of the fire, the flames had crept west from Pudding Lane. Overnight, London Bridge had fallen victim, as the storehouses and quays of Thames Street were torn open and the goods – hemp, tar, barrels of beer, coal, resin and straw – became fodder for the ravenous invader. In a burnished arc, the fire also moved northwards, along Gracechurch Street, towards Leadenhall Market, where an alderman stood with his cap filled with coins, imploring his fellow citizens to save the ancient marketplace. The wind was his friend, and the flames bowed towards the west and saved most of the market as well as nearby Gresham College. By the end of the day, Pepys was back on the water, having persuaded the king to take action. He had seen the Lord Mayor appear like a 'fainting woman' unable to command the attempts to rescue the city. Pepys sat in his boat, watching the tableau of destruction in front of him, and wept.

The next day, Monday, the flames continue to ravage the huddled thoroughfares of the walled city. On Lombard Street, as Thomas Vincent noted, the more elegant houses collapsed, 'tumble, tumble tumble, from one end of the street to the other with a great crash'.[33] The sound of the conflagration was like a stampeding herd of horses upon the stones and cobbles. The flames also broke into the Royal Exchange and it was said that the perfume of burnt spices hung over the broken towers for weeks afterwards. Only the statue of Sir Thomas Gresham stood resolute. The fire then raced westwards up the main thoroughfare, Cheapside, at a pace so fast that fire-fighters were not able to pull down the houses in advance of the galloping flames. Reaching the ancient church of St Mary-le-Bow, the fire scaled the spire like ivy and attacked the bell, which crashed to the ground and melted in the heat.

Panic filled the streets as people started to evacuate the city: 'for the first rank they minded only for their own preservation; the middle sort so distracted and amazed, that they did not know what they did.'[34] The streets started to fill with carts laden with valuables, chaos everywhere, according to the merchant Nicholas Corsellis: 'the goods [were] thrown into the streets and the crowds of people so that ye carts could not possible bee brought in ye lane, what little which here be saved was carried on men's backs to London Wall and then thrown over.'[35]

The schoolboy, William Taswell, did not remain on Westminster Yard for long. On the Monday, he gathered with his classmates and master, John Doblen, and together they marched towards St Dunstan-in-the-East, where the troop attempted to halt the flames with buckets of water. But as Vincent noted, if the fire 'be a little allayed, or beaten down, or put to a stand in some places, it is but a very little while; it quickly recruits, and recovers its force'.[36] By the end of that day, the flames were visible from Millbank. While the bend of the river meant that they could only see as far as Whitehall across the water, the tumult of flames and smoke was visible on the horizon above Lambeth. That evening, John Evelyn travelled from his house to the south at Deptford to Bankside, where the Tate Modern now stands. He noted that during the day the sky had been black, but in the evening it appeared like an oven. He described the scene of Hades in front of him: 'the noise and the cracking, and thunder of impetuous flames, the shrieking of women and children, the hurry of people, the fall of towers, houses and churches, was like a hideous storm … The ruins resembling the picture of Troy.' He summed up his pain and anxiety with a valediction to his city: 'London was, but is no more.'[37]

The fire raged for two more days. On Tuesday, it encircled St Paul's Cathedral. A single fiery brand fell upon the roof of the dilapidated building and the flames started to run across the exposed beams. In time, the six acres of lead covering started to sizzle and melt, dripping into the body of the cathedral itself. Those who had hoped the vast nave was a refuge were forced to flee. Taswell had been here the day before, and had watched as the local booksellers and residents had 'raised their expectations greatly concerning the absolute security of that place upon account of the immense thickness of its walls and situation. Upon this account they filled it with all sorts of goods.'[38] But the great piers that once held up the spire started to sheer and fall, breaking the floor and tearing into the crypt below, and the flames followed after. Taswell watched the destruction from the safe distance of London Bridge, and noted how the building 'blazed so conspicuous' that he was able to read his Latin primer by the light.

On the final day, the fire had made it across the city wall, and started to roll up Fleet Street. Yet by the time it had reached the

Temple, the easterly wind had died down and the flames started to peter out. Here were stationed a series of fire barriers, manned by militia as well as city worthies, and even the king. By the time the final blaze had been quenched, the city was on its knees. As Edward Atkyns wrote: 'there is nothing but stones and rubbish, all exposed to the open air so that you could see from one end of the city to another.'[39] Over the course of four days, 436 acres had been reduced to ash, including 400 streets and over 13,000 houses, eighty-seven churches, and all the places of trade and government, including the Guildhall and fifty-two livery halls. Prisons, courts, gates and bridges. The fortunes of merchants went up in smoke – cloth, spices, luxury goods and foodstuffs. The workshops of the craftsmen turned to rubble. The historical records of the city were lost. Over 100,000 Londoners were made homeless.

After the fire had subsided, Taswell wandered the blasted heath of the city. Making his way along Fleet Street, he observed that he could still feel the hot coals beneath his feet. By the walls of St Paul's Cathedral, he was lucky to avoid being crushed by a large boulder that crashed to the ground as he walked by. He was also able to pick up some of the melted bell metal that had run across the churchyard and turned solid. Finally he came across a body of an old woman caught under the east side of the building: 'parched up as if it were with the flames … Her clothes were burnt and every limb reduced to a coal.'[40]

Those that had made it out of the city waited in trepidation. Alarms went up when rumours circulated that the French or the Dutch were about to invade. But the king delivered a proclamation on 6 September to say that there were no foreign threats to be feared, and that the fire was an accident rather than a military assault. Next, the king came to the crowd on Moorfields and set out how to put the city back in order. Food needed to be found and more permanent shelter organised. Four days later, Charles II wanted the crowds to clear. Yet those who returned to the city, hoping to find what they could salvage from the wreckage, scanned the rubble for their old lives. Others saw what was once their homes and turned away, never to return again. However, in time, the capital started the process of clearing up the debris.

A ceremony to give thanks to God was scheduled for the following Sunday and the whole city prayed either in gratitude for the cataclysm's end or to ask a vengeful deity for forgiveness. A few weeks later, on a day of formal fasting, the Dean of St Paul's preached a sermon called 'Lex Ignea'. Like the destruction of the Temple of Jerusalem, he intoned, this fire was not to be judged a punishment for the city, but a test. What kind of new city might emerge from the ashes?

The conflagration affected everyone in the city, from the king to the still infant heiress, Mary Davies. Even at Millbank, the fire made its presence felt. At nearby Kensington, one writer observed that 'you might have thought … it had been doomsday … my walks and gardens are almost covered with the ashes of paper, linens etc and pieces of ceiling and plasterwork blow thither from the tempest.'[41] In the longer view, the fire of September 1666 influenced Mary's destiny as much as the plague, and the loss of her father, the year before.

Who was to blame? This was an important question because the answer determined how the city was to be rebuilt. Within six weeks of the final embers, a Frenchman, Robert Hubert, was tried for starting the fire, having confessed to dropping a fire-bomb into the house at Pudding Lane. On 27 October he was taken to Tyburn and hanged. Once his body was cut down, the mob tore it apart until there was nothing left. However, while the execution performed some kind of civic catharsis, it was clear that Hubert was not the cause of the conflagration. He was physically incapable of doing the job, and mentally deranged. Furthermore, it became apparent that if a Frenchman had started the fire, this could be legally construed as being an act of aggression by a foreign party. As an act of war, the burden for reconstruction therefore fell on landlords rather than their tenants. Parliament soon realised that, as the representatives of the landowning interests, this state of affairs put them on the hook for all the costs of rebuilding.

Therefore, after the execution, the MPs set about confirming that the fire was an accident, a verdict that they delivered in a report in 1667. This meant that the city was to be rebuilt by the renters rather than the owners. A series of Fire Courts were set up to adjudicate on property rights and how to share the costs of reconstruction fairly. However, this process made clear that the interests of private property were to be defended above all else. Secondly, as a consequence of this, many tenants decided they wanted to move out of the city. They looked to the new suburban territories as a refuge away from the huddled and chaotic city centre. By 1673, over 8,000 plots within the burned city had been rebuilt, but 3,500 of these remained empty. In addition, there was unclaimed ground for another 1,000 homes left open. Many of these families were now looking at the fields of Bloomsbury, Spitalfields, Soho, Westminster and beyond, for a new home. This process, in time, brought the city to the edge of the fields of Ebury Manor.

The primacy of private property also tolled the death of any grand scheme for the rebuilding of the city. Within days of the fire, some of the leading urban thinkers and architects, including John Evelyn, the then-astronomer Christopher Wren, and Robert Hooke, produced new plans for cityscapes 'far superior to any other city in the habitable world for beauty, commodiousness, and magnificence',[42] in Evelyn's words. Almost all of these plans took the best examples of baroque planning as seen in Rome and Paris and aspired to bring such order and modernity to the blasted landscape beside the Thames. It was not to be. Such ambitious plans would take time and money; more than that, they demanded the king taking control of the city, overriding the interests of the landowners and the city administration. That was never going to be popular with Parliament, who debated the various plans, dragged their feet and in the end let the schemes get lost in the discussion of other more pressing matters.

The resolution that London rebuild itself nonetheless came with calls for regulation. If private property was to be preserved, then its materials had to be safe; such a catastrophe could never be allowed to occur again. New standards of planning and building were needed to take in health and safety, as well as beauty. A committee of surveyors, the arch measurers, was convened with the task of devising a new set of rules for construction and planning. The group was made up of two surveyors selected by the king, Roger Pratt, the architect of Clarendon House, and the scientist Christopher Wren, who had recently shown some interest in design; and two on behalf of the city, Peter Mills and Robert Hooke. The commission visited the damaged sites and started to consider some general principles that might determine the future for the metropolis.

The commissioners devised the rudiments of what became the February 1667 Rebuilding Act, the very first set of urban planning regulations in British history. The first rule stated that no street should be so narrow that flames could jump from one side to another, also allowing for a cart or carriage to pass without hindrance. There was also a systematic programme for street widening, according to four types. In addition, there were to be four types of standardised housing. Every house was to be built from stone or brick, rather than wood. There were to be no overhangs such as 'bulks, jetties, windows, posts, seats or anything of any sort'. Finally, the Act set out the system for checking that all new houses followed the new street plan and the construction regulations. Surveyors set out each individual ground plan and recorded it in a series of master documents held by the Guildhall. Subsequently, quantity surveyors inspected the building work, ensuring that party walls and materials were up to scratch.

And so the city started to be born again. In March 1667, despite 'great frosts, snow and winds',[43] the commissioners put a map of the city in front of the king with a new street plan. Then, on 27 March, Hooke, alongside a team of surveyors, started to stake the first road, Fleet Street, out of the ashes. Piling the markers into the ground every one hundred feet, the team set out the plan for eleven miles of new thoroughfares in the first week. Where the new streetscape infringed on private property, the Fire Courts adjudicated upon compensation. Between 1667 and December 1671, 8,394 plots of private property were measured and recorded and, after that, work was allowed to start on rebuilding. In the last month of 1667, an advertisement was placed on the front wall of the Temple Exchange Coffee House, at the far end of Fleet Street, near to where Hugh Audley once lived; it read:

You see before you
The Last House of the city in Flames
The first in the City to be restored; may this be favour-
able and fortunate
For both the city and the House.[44]

London survived, albeit transformed. The terrors it had faced with the plague and fire forced the metropolis to rebuild. But this reconstruction was not just in the fabric of the city but in every aspect of urban life. This, in time, came to have an impact on the life of the infant Mary Davies. But as she started to grow up, it was impossible to keep her cocooned from the wider world outside. She was a young woman in possession of an inheritance that was gathering value every year. How would her inheritance determine the course of her childhood? What kind of woman might she grow into? When would she take possession of her destiny?

3

The Preparation of the Bride

I F WE ARE to understand the daughter, we must first see the mother. History overlooks women like Mrs Tregonwell. There are no portraits in public galleries. Nor are there entries in the *Oxford Dictionary of National Biography*. According to the records, she was first a cleric's daughter, then one man's wife, and after that, another's. We are forced to make general assumptions about her life by the events around her. She had seen first-hand the fragility of a woman's estate in a time of turbulence.

The year she was born in the rectory of St Clement Danes, London became the forcing ground of the Civil Wars that started, as lore tells, with the smashing of glass on nearby Fetter Lane.[1] Growing up, she had known adversity when her father was persecuted and driven out of his church. In this way she learned how fortune can turn at a moment. How the affairs of great men have an impact on those less in control of their fates. Did she suffer when she saw her father accused of great crimes and dispossessed of his office, and the family home? How insecure did she feel when the family was forced to rely on the hospitality of others? Could she ever imagine that the world would turn upside down, and back to normal again? She may have thought that once she had sworn her oath to Alexander Davies in 1659, a year of extraordinary uncertainty on the London streets, her future was finding its ballast. With the return of the king, coinciding with the first months of joyful matrimony, one imagines there was hope that her situation might finally find peace after such upheaval.

The expectation that the Audley inheritance, in whatever form it came, offered an anchor to those aspirations. A few years later, once the legacy had been settled, the work at Millbank made these hopes real, culminating in the establishment of the new family home.

It was to these empty, incomplete corridors that the twenty-one-year-old widow returned after the death of her Alexander. It was here that the young woman decided it was no longer wise to leave her destiny to the capricious winds of the age. She did not just have her own welfare to protect; it was her maternal duty to craft the fate of her family out of the debris.

What kind of mother was she? We may not recognise her mode of motherhood, but it appears that the compass that guided Mrs Tregonwell was the determination for security. To create a protective bulwark against the uncertain waters that flowed around her and her family. And at the heart of this, to safeguard Mary and her inheritance. At times she may have appeared wilfully distant from her daughter, who was left in the care of an aunt, Mrs Mason. At other moments, Mary was seemingly played like a chip at the gaming table, with little consideration for the young girl's happiness. The harshest critics might suggest that Mrs Tregonwell was willing to sacrifice her daughter for the sake of the inheritance; that the land and her daughter's body were interchangeable commodities. However, as a woman who had experienced a maelstrom during her own childhood, the young mother understood clearly that the ability of a woman to control her destiny was circumscribed. Baby Mary's future security from the outset was overwritten with the preservation and skilful management of the Manor of Ebury.

Many years later, in 1705, the mother was forced to quantify her duty of care to her daughter. In a quasi-*apologia,* Mrs Tregonwell outlined how she gave her daughter everything that she was able to give, in order to prepare the child for her future. She argued that no mother could have done more. Even if, to us, it appears a strange way of showing her love.

Philippe Ariès, one of the first historians of that most slippery idea, childhood, proffered that before the seventeenth century, it did not exist at all.[2] The child was an unformed adult that needed to grow. Look at any family portrait of the times, and once the baby has turned into a child, they dress as miniature versions of their parents. Ariès argued that this attitude was changing across the early modern period, as Mary Davies was growing up. Rather than a small adult, the child was a separate type of person, one that needed raising. Education therefore became a central question, in terms of the role of both the family, which offered spiritual and social guidance, and the classroom, which cultivated the intellect in preparation for the world of work.

Here, many recent historians question Ariès's conclusions. Rather than ask what the child was in society, they ask: how did a Mrs Tregonwell treat her Mary in order to mould an adult, primed for the wide world? Was the babe a sinner to be saved? A blank slate that needed to be inscribed with instruction? Furthermore, as a daughter, determined by her sex, how was she to be prepared for a life of obligations? Some of these debates may appear surprisingly contemporary, others bizarrely alien.

By no means a Puritan household, the Davies family nonetheless had probably absorbed Calvin's exhortation that the child was stained by Sin: 'their whole nature is, as it were, a seed of sin, and, therefore, cannot but be odious and abominable to God.'[3] Therefore, a child should first be taught discipline, and right from wrong. This was typified by the way the child approached their parents. The family itself was a social form that reflected the spiritual order, with a God-like father at the apex of the hierarchy, and therefore the child needed to know its place. According to the not-so-catch-ily-titled 1654 primer *A fruitfull and Usefull Discourse Touching on the Honour Due from Children to Parents, and the Duty of Parents towards their Children*, a child should 'stand up when they speak to their parents', bow when meeting them, and definitely no 'gabbling, laughing or flouting' in their presence.[4] The spiritual education also demanded that the child not be too 'coddled'. At one extreme of this argument was the odious notion that 'if you spare the rod, you lose the child.'

More commonplace, one hopes, was the affection that John Evelyn's wife, Margaret, showed in a letter to her fifteen-year-old son in 1670:

Much is to be wished in your behalf; that your temper were humble and tractable; your inclinations virtuous, and that from choice, not compulsion, you make an honest man ... You are not too young to know that lying, defrauding, swearing, disobedience to parents and persons in authority, are offences of God and man: that debauchery is injurious to growth, health, life and indeed to the pleasures of life; therefore, now that you are turning from child to man, endeavour to follow the best precepts, and choose such ways as may render you worthy of praise and love. You are assured of your father's care and my tenderness.[5]

The formation of the soul in the home was as important as the development of the mind in the classroom. Again, such considerations were shaped by what thinkers imagined the newborn child brought into the world. In the years that Mary Davies was growing up, London was also home to the philosopher John Locke, residing at Exeter House, on the Strand, a mile down the Thames from Millbank. At the time, he was deeply involved in political questions, but he was also concerning himself with the question of knowledge. How did we know something? How did we learn about the world? He later expanded these ideas in his work *An Essay Concerning Human Understanding*, writing that the answers to these questions were rooted in the notion that 'If we will attentively consider new born children, we shall have little reason to think that they bring many ideas into the world with them.'[6] In short, the mewling infant was a blank slate, and experience was the stylus that wrote the individual character upon life's parchment.

Education, therefore, was meant to prepare the child for the world, in whatever circle they were expected to turn. John and Margaret Evelyn's first son, who died as an infant, was clearly a prodigy: 'at two years and a half old he could perfectly read any of the English, Latin, French, or Gothic letters, pronouncing the three first languages exactly ... The number of verses he could recite was prodigious ... He had a wonderful disposition to mathematics, having by heart divers propositions of Euclid.'[7] In contrast, the more modest Dr Morris, a West Country physician, also invested in his son William's education. At seven years old, he was sent to a local tutor for a year. At eight, he went to grammar school as a day scholar, where he also learned the violin. At thirteen, he moved away to a boarding grammar school, where he was instructed in Greek and Latin. His father paid for extra lessons in writing, arithmetic and drawing. Eventually, he ascended to university at eighteen.

Education was determined by social class, however. The rich learned from a tutor, or were sent away to school, while an apprentice was taught by a master, and the labourer in the field. It was also determined by gender. Mrs Tregonwell might have wanted the best for Mary, as befitted the family's elevation into London society, but that was limited by Mary's sex. It was, after all, Eve's curiosity that had driven the first family from the Garden of Eden and so, for her own sake, an inquisitive daughter was not to be encouraged. Instead, according to the educational thinker Comenius, 'women should not be admitted to education because of curiosity, but because of virtue and modesty.'[8]

Therefore, female education was not rare but it was limited. There were fewer apprenticeships for girls, and many daughters had to be satisfied with learning domestic chores. Higher up the social ladder, there were more opportunities for girls, but it often appeared that education was more focused on the preparation of the bride than the intellectual formation of the woman. Grace Sherrington was taught by a governess, Ms Humbly, until marriage at fifteen, later noting:

> She would sett me to cypher with my pen, and to cast up and prove great sums and accepts, and sometimes cowrite a supposed letter to this or that body concerning such and such things, and other times let me read in Dr Turner's Herball and Bartholemews Vigoe, and at other times sett me to sing psalmes, and other times sett me to some curious works.[9]

Back in the West Country, the daughter of Dr Morris, William's sister, went to day school at seven. At nine years old, she started the violin and singing lessons. At eleven, she went to boarding school, where she learned French, dancing and violin, and even had a teacher to instruct her to dress, 'to encourage her care'.[10] However, her education, unlike her brother's, ended at thirteen.

Mrs Tregonwell goes into few details about Mary's education except to say that she had 'nurses, servants and an aunt as an inspector or governess and all things else in proportion to the fortune she was suppos'd to be born to', not for her own sake but in the expectation that 'in some years ... she would be marriageable'.[11] So when we ask what kind of mother Mrs Tregonwell might have been, in the circumstances presented to her, her choices were limited. In finding a new husband, in holding on to the house at Millbank and shoring up the work, now that she owned the widow's portion of the estate, she looked after her own future. In addition, she was determined to make safe the Davies inheritance, and this included marrying off Mary as advantageously as possible. The childhood of Mary Davies, therefore, was primarily dedicated to the preparation of the girl's bride-hood.

The first task was a question of appearances. The family was in deeper straits than their well-orchestrated simulation of a contented, up-and-coming family portrayed. Alexander Davies had died leaving unpayable debts across the city, to his brother, lawyers and builders, amongst others. The family home at Millbank had proved to be more expensive than expected, and his widow was forced to borrow £200 from her father, Dr Dukeson, to put a literal roof above their heads. The marriage to the MP John Tregonwell was a strategic marriage 'the better to disentangle the Estate and prevent the buildings falling for want of finishing and make them produce some rent'.[12] It was a seemingly contented and judicious marriage. The new Mrs Tregonwell understood the importance of maintaining a front amidst calamity. In a time of turbulence, the family brand was paramount. They were 'look't upon to bee in great plenty', and 'it was no one's business or interest to contradict such reports'.[13]

Meanwhile, the young Mary became the family mascot. Alongside the nurse, servants and constant attention of Mrs Mason, Mr Tregonwell kept 'six horses to his coach which [Mary] was to have frequent use to take the air and all things were carried on with an air of greatness answerable to the fortune she was supposed to have.'[14] Furthermore, she was always dressed to the nines. Family accounts audit the costs of 'lustring hood and scarfe', 'a flowr'd tabby coate', as well as eighteen shillings and sixpence for 'comb, gloves, stockings and shoes'.

The child probably spent some time with the Tregonwell step-family in Dorset where, in time, she was joined by a trio of stepsisters. Back in London, however, what might the young Mary have seen as she rode out by her well-appointed horse-drawn coach into the city from the house at Millbank? The metropolis in the early 1670s was still recovering from the devastation of the Great Fire. The coach and six first may have exited from the house grounds facing the river and followed the Thames northwards until it reached the Horse Ferry and then headed west then north along Market Street, to avoid the bustle and congestion of Westminster.

Within minutes the coach would have found itself on the road skirting the west of the city; the fields to the left, as far as Mary could see, were her own. To the east, she saw the Abbey towering above everything, the slums as well as the gardens of the larger houses at Tothill. At the New Chapel, they turned up James Street, heading northward.

After a few hundred yards, the coach skirted the front of Goring House, surrounded by the hunting grounds of St James's Park on the right. There were still disputes about this property rumbling on in the House of Commons and among the lawyers of the Temple about who owned what, and who owed whom. Such machinations would not have bothered the young girl as she continued past Pall Mall and up Constitution Hill. It would have felt like she had travelled from city to farmland and now ornamental parkland in a matter of minutes. This land had been recently improved as the grounds of Charles II's St James's Palace. A picturesque canal ran through the centre of the landscape that was now planted with walks of elms and lindens and was home to clusters of red deer and herds of grazing cows. This was a place for social circulation and the art of being seen. Constitution Hill itself was named after Charles II's passion for taking walks as he conducted business. Ned Ward noted that in the evening 'the court ladies raise their extended limbs from their downy couches and walk in to the Mall to refresh their limbs with the salubrious breezes of the cooling evening.'[15]

The coach may have rested awhile at the top of Pall Mall, home to a variety of sports, including *paillemaille*, a fashionable game similar to croquet – as well as for sportsmen, such as the libertine Earl of Rochester, who took advantage of the cover of varied foliage of St James's Park for more carnal pleasures. It was unlikely Mary came this way on Sundays, as that was the day that the park became destination for 'whole shoals' of ordinary Londoners.

As the road turned, Mary was still travelling along the edge of the city. Once she had reached Hyde Park, the western fringe of her inheritance, she might alight from the coach at the Ring, another exclusive pleasure spot for the capital's most well-to-do citizens. Set among unploughed pastureland and ponds, the Ring was where grandees came to exercise their horses and to show off. It had first been opened by Charles I, and then enclosed by Cromwell, who attempted to charge Londoners to visit the park during the 1650s. Here, also, the local militia were drilled upon a hastily created muster ground. After the Restoration, it once again became a popular space for urban pleasures.

The inveterate social climber Pepys writes in his diary of the moment when he was finally able to afford a coach of his own and so took his wife to the Ring to ensure the appreciation of his peers. On another occasion, he saw horse races, and even a foot race between 'an Irishman and Crow, that was once my Lord Claypole's footman'.[16] While some spectators bought 'milk from a red cow' from a wandering milkmaid, the better sort supped on boozy tidbits. Mary may have stopped off at the fashionable Lodge, or Cake House, for 'a cheesecake, a tart, or a syllabub'.[17]

There was a perfectly timed lyric that appeared in 1671, called 'Hide Park', in a publication called *Westminster Drolleries*, that seemed written with Mary Davies in mind:

> Here come the girls of the rich city,
> Aldermen's daughters fair and proud
> Their jealous mothers come t'invite ye,
> For fear they should be lost in the croud

> Who for their breeding are taught to dance,
> Their birth and fortune to advance:
> And they will be as frolick and free
> As you yourself expect to see.[18]

Climbing back into the coach, and heading into the city along what later became Piccadilly, someone may have pointed out to Mary that the land to the north was hers again, all the way until the coach encountered the new aristocratic *hôtels*, along the emerging street: as she travelled eastward, Berkeley House, Clarendon House and then finally Burlington House.

The Lord Chancellor, the Duke of Clarendon, was one of the foremost of the king's favourites who had shared exile in Europe, and on his return to the capital had recently come into money, and thus decided to move from his old house on the Strand to a more suitable location. In 1664, 'in consideration of his eminent and faithful services', Charles granted Clarendon a lease for thirty acres here to the north of Portugal Street.[19] This took in a collection of small estates including Stonebridge Close, which sat on the easterly banks of the Tyburn, and then heading towards the city: including the sites named Penniless Bench and Stone Conduit. As soon as the letters patent were signed, Clarendon disposed of a lion's share of the land, passing it on to two other aristocrats: Lord Berkeley and the Earl of Burlington, who wished to build new homes there too.

Clarendon then set out plans for his own grand *hôtel* that looked southwards to St James's Palace (where Albemarle Street now stands). He commissioned the architect Roger Pratt to draft designs. Pratt had travelled in Europe with John Evelyn and picked up the latest styles. On his return, he had written his own history of architecture, *Certain Heads to be Largely Treated of Concerning the Undertaking of Any Building*, and claimed himself the heir to Inigo Jones, England's first modern architect. Clarendon intended that his house surpass any royal palace. It was so vast that critics and political enemies claimed he must have stolen stone intended for St Paul's Cathedral to complete the behemoth. The design mixed French, Italian and English motifs in an achingly modern show of bravura. To the north, John Evelyn set out the new gardens in the finest European styles.

To the south, it was impossible not to notice the work that was going on at St James's Square. Here Henry Jermyn, Lord St Albans, was developing his vision of a thoroughly Frenchified enclave for London's fashionable grandees. It was the first large-scale project in what has become known as 'aristocratic capitalism', the system whereby landowners started to develop new forms of speculative housing in the suburbs that would dictate the growth of the city until the modern day. By the early 1670s, St James's was starting to appear like a 'small town', built around the central square, lined on all sides by the grandest of houses, with more modest dwellings for lesser sorts set behind, a market place and a parish church to be completed by the nation's rising architect, Christopher Wren.

Each plot was leased by Jermyn to speculators, who undertook building until the basic 'carcase' of the house was in place, which was then sold on to the owner, who chose the decoration of the interiors and added fittings as they desired. The scheme had attracted some of the leading designers and builders of the era. By 1676, the square appeared on the official ratings records, presenting itself as the finest address in the capital. New residents included lords and ladies, an earl, a viscount, two knights of the realm, the French ambassador, and supposedly at least one royal mistress, as well as Jermyn himself in the grandest house on the piazza. The 1676 rate books also include a property, no. 21, belonging to a Ms Mary (Moll) Davies. However, this turns out not to be our heroine but the sister of Nell Gywnne, whose theatrical antics were enough to make Pepys's heart race and his wife to proclaim her 'the most impertinent slut in the world'.[20]

Where else in London might Mary be allowed to wander in her coach? She may have gone to watch her stepfather, Mr Tregonwell, at the Palace of Westminster, when Parliament was in session. She would have visited her grandfather at the rectory off the Strand. Here she would have seen the rebirth of the city out of the ashes of the Great Fire. Dr Dukeson's church stood on the edge of the burned city, and the scene, even five years after the conflagration, might have seemed desperate.

The year before, John Evelyn had dreamed that the capital 'might doubtless be rendered as far superior to any other city in the habitable world for beauty, commodiousness and magnificence'; he would thus far be disappointed by the pace of resurrection.[21] By 1670, over 1,600 private homes had been rebuilt, but there were plenty of broken-toothed gaps on the streetscape where no one was willing to rebuild, or inhabitants had upped and left, never to return. This exodus was one of the reasons for the growth of new neighbourhoods of housing outside the city, in the suburban areas of Holborn, Bloomsbury, Soho, Spitalfields.

Elsewhere, the trading floor of the new Royal Exchange had been in business since 1669, and was now a temple to capital. This had been completed at a breakneck pace by the City architect, Edward Jerman. Samuel Rolfe called it 'one of the greatest glories and ornaments of London', despite it nearly bankrupting the Mercers' Company, who paid for the reconstruction, and who were desperate for the city to get back to business.[22] Despite the cost, it soon came to symbolise the revived capital. Many of the livery halls had now also been restored in stone.

There was work on the Customs House by the river, as well as the standing column, the Monument, that marked the fire with a golden, burning urn at its summit. This was not the wholesale reinvention of the baroque (read foreign) metropolis initially envisioned by Charles II and Christopher Wren, but it was a haphazard, pragmatic, thoroughly English response to the calamity, with a scattering of modern motifs. London was pulling itself up by its bootstraps, with only the occasional flash of architectural flair.

In 1669, an agreement was made on the rebuilding of the numerous parish churches in the city. Parliament had passed an act that allowed a levy to be made on all coal coming into the city, to pay for the fifty-one churches and chapels. It was at least another thirty years until the London skyline was pinpricked by Wren's idiosyncratic steeples and towers. St Paul's Cathedral remained a broken hulk at the centre of the wretched scenery. The bishops and chapter were still trying to find ways to patch and make do. It took until 1668, when a falling piece of masonry narrowly missed the dean, that it was decided that something had to be done, and Wren was given the task of developing new designs. Yet work on the site at Ludgate Hill did not start until 1674.

What the child Mary may have thought of the scenes in front of her is impossible to guess. Except that over time such a diorama of chaos and transformation became the familiar backdrop to her childhood, and the dramas of her everyday life. Aren't all cities in perpetual motion – caught between collapse and completion?

* * *

As Mrs Tregonwell later confessed: from birth, Mary was raised so 'she should be marriageable'. And it seemed to work: for even as an infant, since the widow took control of her daughter's fate, 'several matches were proposed', despite Mrs Tregonwell protesting vehemently that her intention was never 'in selling her daughter at a certain price, and make several unfair advantages of her'.[23]

There is plenty of confusion about the bridal age during the early modern period. Because Juliet Capulet was fourteen when she first eyed Romeo Montague across a Veronese celebration, it was taken for granted that many couples were in their teens. The truth is more nuanced – Shakespeare had intended to scandalise his audience rather than reflect the norm. It is not just the age of matrimony that is in contention; there is also a difference between the classes, as well as a debate on consent.

For most families, an exchange of words in the church porch was sufficient. The wheres and whats of who could and could not get hitched were seen as the concern of the Book of Common Prayer, and politicians were happy to stay out of it. In 1653, Oliver Cromwell had made compulsory the registration of all unions in parish registers in the Marriage Act, which added some formal legal standing to the spiritual union. The Act stated that participants should have reached 'the age of discretion' – approximately fifteen for boys, fourteen for girls. Any couple under twenty-one years old needed their parents' permission. Nevertheless, the records show that the average age for newlyweds was closer to twenty-five for men, and twenty-two for brides.

Despite this, arrangements became more complicated when marriage combined with property. While most weddings were between two willing, and adult, partners, the higher up the social ladder one went, the younger the betrothed. This was because the agreement was a meeting of families, rather than two individuals. As previously noted, nearly twenty per cent of all legacies were in the hands of an heiress. The decline of the ward courts meant that previous means of getting hold of an inheritance, by becoming a legal guardian of the orphan, put added impetus on the marriage market as the place to change a family's fortunes. Thus, the exchange of power and property went in hand with nuptial tokens.

Love had little to do with it, although some parents – such as Mrs Tregonwell – allowed for the question of consent from Mary once she reached her majority. Love might be something that came later, but that was not yet seen as a prerequisite to the wedding. 'I was never infected therewith', reported the inestimable Duchess of Newcastle. 'It is a disease, or passion, or both, I know only by relation.'[24] Love could come and go, the wedding bells appeared to chime, but land was permanent.

Marrying for love was for a future age. Instead, this was a financial exchange: the wedding created a new household that needed to be floated with sufficient funds to flourish. Here, the dowry, or portion, from the wife's side was met by a jointure, an annual income, from the groom's family. This was traditionally calculated at a ratio of one to ten; so that when the dowry was £1,000, the husband could guarantee an annual income of £100. This was often the basis of further negotiations that covered inheritance, land and other property, then codified in a marriage contract signed by both parties. Such arrangements could override tradition; a father ensured his daughter's security with substantial promises from the groom; clauses defined the priority of inheritance and the itemisation of moveable goods that were to be exchanged, and returned on the death of one partner.

In 1680, the Tory essayist Sir William Temple in his *Popular Discontents* recalled that it was in recent memory that 'the first noble families ... married into the city for downright money'.[25] There were other examples than Mary Davies that he could have chosen, but it fits. Many Royalists had returned to London with empty pockets, having lost out during the Civil Wars. They had to make their fortunes at court or in the marriage market. There was a concurrent rise of the wealthy merchant class, masterless and landless, looking to convert their profits into social capital.

In December 1672, therefore, as Mary Davies was now seven years old, her parents began marriage negotiations with Lord Berkeley of Stratton on behalf of his ten-year-old son, Charles. It was to be a union that might seal the Davieses' elevated status – from scrivener to aristocrat in two generations – as well as bring some desperately needed cash to oil the creaking estate.

In recent years, the Tregonwells' attempt to shore up the inheritance had not been so successful. The legal cases surrounding the Goring House estate were still trundling on. In March 1673, the family had been forced to move out of the family home on Millbank and rent it to Lord Peterborough, Henry Mordaunt.[26] The aristocrat had recently been governor of Tangiers, but had returned to London and was given the title of Groom of the Stole within the court of James, Duke of York, the king's brother. This meant that he was the intimate keeper of royal secrets, and with such great responsibility came significant power. It may have been through Peterborough that the Tregonwells were first introduced to Lord Berkeley, who was also a close associate of the Duke of York. Another reason why the two families may have connected was because they were neighbours: Berkeley House, marking the most westerly limits of the city's expansion so far, looked out towards the undeveloped Davies meadows.

Berkeley was an aristocratic second son, and despite his privilege a lack of inheritance forced him to become master of his own destiny. Some may say that his life was a sequence of heroic gestures that inevitably led to further elevation: others might mutter that he possessed the talent of the already privileged for failing upwards. He sought fame first at arms, and in 1638 fought bravely enough against the Scots to gain Charles I's attention and a knighthood. The campaign itself was a disaster. On his return to London, he was involved in a military plot against Parliament, jailed in the Tower and only saved by the outbreak of the Civil War. During the conflict, he became Royalist governor of Exeter, and fought, according to Pepys, 'more set fields than any man in England'[27] but was once more defeated. More famously, he helped the wretched king escape from incarceration at Hampton Court in 1647, failing to get him across the Channel, instead only to be imprisoned again on the Isle of Wight.

In exile in Paris, he turned his adversity to good fortune. He became the governor, then master of the household, of the teenaged Duke of York. He continued his pursuit of martial fame on the Continent but with few rewards. On the Restoration, he held on to the Duke's rising star, converting his loyalty in exile into offices and bountiful incomes once in power. He was made a privy councillor, took high office in the Admiralty and in 1670 was named Lieutenant of Ireland.

He was worth £50,000 but was not universally admired. Notes from a meeting between the king and his advisors suggest that he was given the prestigious role of lieutenant as a means of getting him out of London. Charles confessed 'the being rid of him doth incline me something to it.'[28] He was considered intemperate; Pepys calling him 'the most hot, fiery man in discourse, without any cause', and a weak political strategist.[29] But he did not seem to stop winning, and planted his new status in London soil.

In 1664, Berkeley had gained a large tract of land in America, later New Jersey, that he hoped might put him in the highest rank. Therefore, he needed the kind of dwelling that might reflect such esteem. The following year, he bought an eight-acre plot from Lord Clarendon and started to build his own *hôtel* alongside Clarendon House on Piccadilly. For architectural guidance he looked to his friend John Evelyn, who recommended the architect Hugh May.

May was a good choice of architect. In 1662, he had worked with John Evelyn on a translation of Fréart's *Parallel of Architecture*, and he was seen as one of the leading proponents of the European style in English. His own particular signature was more Dutch than French, since he had spent his exile in Holland during the Civil Wars, inspired by recent baroque innovations in Amsterdam and the Hague. Returning to London, May used his contacts to gain commissions including Eltham Lodge in Kent, which he had completed before he started work on Berkeley House. Seven years into the building project, Evelyn reported on an evening spent with his friend:

> It was in his new house, or rather palace, for I am assured it stood him in near £30,000. It is very well built, and has many noble rooms, but they are not very convenient, consisting of but one corps de logis; they are all roomes of state, without clossets. The staircase is of cedar, the furniture is princely, the kitchen and the stables are ill plac'd, and the corridor worse, having no report to the wings they joyne to. For the rest, the forecourt is noble, so are the stables, and above all, the gardens, which are incomparable, by reason of the inequality of the ground, and a pretty piscina. The holly bushes on the terrace I advised the planting of. The porticos are in imitation of a house described by Palladio, but it happens to be the worst in his book, tho' my good friend Mr Hugh May, his Lordship's architect, effected it.[30]

It appeared the perfect match: seven-year-old Mary was to marry the future Lord Berkeley, ten-year-old Charles. The City was to be united with the court. Two neighbouring estates to merge into a single plot of land that ran along the western edge of the capital. And so negotiations began in December 1672. Berkeley had just returned from Ireland that summer, and having suffered from some illness, was thinking about his legacy as well as a means to shore up his financial situation.

The 12 December contract between Mr Tregonwell and Lord Berkeley appears like the written equivalent of a gentleman's hand-shake. It was barely more than a receipt for £5,000: 'Then received of the Right Honble John Lord Berkeley, the sume of five thousand pounds of lawful money of England.'[31] The deal was later explained by Mrs Tregonwell: the agreement was based on Mary giving her consent at the age of twelve; but in the meantime, Berkeley paid Tregonwell £5,000 upfront in compensation for all the money the stepfather had spent on Mary and the upkeep of the estate. Meanwhile, Berkeley promised to settle a jointure on his son that was worth at least £3,000 a year. This suggests that Mary's estate was estimated at over £30,000.

For all intents and purposes, it seems the young girl was bartered for a fast £5,000, with all propriety as befits the times. Sir William Temple, of another opinion, put such business thus: 'These contracts would never be made but by men's avarice and greediness of portions … our marriages are made just like other common bargains and sales by the mere considerations of interest and gain, without any of love or esteem, of birth or of beauty itself.'[32]

Except that Berkeley did not have the money. Whatever embarrassment he had got himself into, after paying £5,000 upfront as agreed he could not secure the annual jointure of £3,000. And so the wedding was abruptly called off. The truth was that Berkeley was in dire straits that he had hoped to disguise with the prospect of the Davies fortune. In 1675, he sold his interests in west New Jersey to a group of Quakers for £1,000. The house, at £30,000, was clearly a money pit. And his work in Ireland had turned out to be frustrating and unremunerative. As Mrs Tregonwell noted: 'things not succeeding with Lord Berkeley at Court as he expected, he found himself altogether unable to purchase the £3000 per ann. which he had undertaken to have ready and therefore honourably gave timely notice of it.'[33]

It turned out that the marriage alliance was like two exhausted dancers maintaining their balance by leaning into the other, but at one turn, twisting and collapsing into a jumble. On top of their standing debts, the Tregonwells now owed Berkeley his £5,000 and interest. More pressing, the family needed to return to the marriage market.

Lord Berkeley died in August 1678, never having recovered his payment. His son, Charles, joined the French Army at the age of fourteen, hoping to repeat the valour of his father to better fortune. Two years later, he was recruited by the British Navy, and at nineteen was in command of the frigate *Tiger*. Sailing through the Straits of Gibraltar, chasing pirates, he contracted smallpox and died at sea. His body was preserved in a barrel and brought back to the family graveyard in Twickenham. He was twenty years old.

* * *

According to Mrs Tregonwell, following the debacle with the Berkeleys there were plenty more offers to consider for Mary's hand. She positively had to bat away the young, wealthy grooms. However, the family were so fearful that some young chancer might kidnap and elope with the young girl that they decided at one point to send her to France with her Aunt Mason.

Such threats were rare but very real. There had been a law against abduction of young heiresses, 'for the lucre of their substance', since the reign of Henry VII. In 1637, the fourteen-year-old orphan Sarah Cox was abducted by her schoolfriend's brother, Roger Fulwood, who rode up to her on Newington Common and snatched her away by coach to the house of the Bishop of Winchester. The next day, she was led to the chapel where she was forcibly married by a priest. She was then led to a bedchamber and stripped. However, at this point, help came, and she was saved. When the Lord Mayor heard of the scandal, Fulwood was arrested. The king also got involved, and heard a plea for clemency from Lady Fulwood. In the end, Roger was not released from prison until he agreed to annul the wedding himself, and forgo any future interest in the girl's inheritance.

In the meantime, work continued on putting the Davies estate on a sound footing, ensuring the prize of the bride's hand was ever more attractive. The pool that Mrs Tregonwell was fishing in was wide. There were the sons of merchant adventurers that had started to make profits from international ventures in America, Jamaica and the East. They came with cash, but wanted to turn that into land. To them, Mary might have seemed a good investment. There were also the sons of aristocrats who had returned from exile and were now hoping to establish their position at court. They had land, but had lost money during the Interregnum and might have hoped that a young Mary could pay off their debts with her dowry. Ironically, this shoal was somewhat depleted by the marriage market itself. Between 1650 and 1675, there was an unusually high level of child mortality amongst the peerage, beyond the ravages of the battleground and exile. At least one historian blames this on the demands of the London season, when all the worthies came to the capital to socialise, and suffered exposure to the city's infectious maladies, sometimes with fatal consequences.[34]

Such machinations proved that the economy had already crept into all corners of everyday life. Property was starting to define the relationships between all things. But how did one define ownership? At the very same time as the agreement between the Berkeleys and the Tregonwells was being thrashed out, only a few miles away on the Strand the idea of property itself was under debate. Here, the philosopher John Locke, while interested in questions of education, was also considering the question of who owned the land in the newly established colonies.

At the time, Locke was part of the household of the Earl of Shaftesbury, who was the Lord Chancellor between 1672 and 1675. Before this, in return for his support during the first years of the Restoration, Charles II made Shaftesbury one of the Lord Proprietors of the new colony of the Carolinas in the Americas. The philosopher, as the aristocrat's secretary, became the principal draftsman of the *Fundamental Constitutions of Carolina* that was produced in 1669. This document attempted to set out the laws of the new colony but also justify the possession of the land, despite the acknowledgement that it had clearly been used by natives before the arrival of the Europeans. Ownership could not therefore be defined by who got there first. Furthermore, emerging rules of private property ensured that this new land could not be shared in common. The New World was to be the property of the settlers, but how could this imperial venture be legally described, without admitting robbery or conquest?

Locke proposed that the native populations did not own the land. This was not, as in the reasoning of the Spanish Conquistadores, a question of religion; rather it was based upon how one used the land. As Locke set out: the land was given by God to everyone, but ownership was determined by who worked the earth. He later put it thus: 'Though the earth and all inferior creatures be common to all men, yet every man has a property in his own person; this nobody has any right to but himself. The labour of his body and the work of his hands, we may say, are properly his. Whatsoever he removes out of the state that nature hath provided and left in it, he hath mixed his labour with, and joined it to something that is his own, and therefore makes it his property.'[35] The natives were hunter-gatherers, who moved across the land and hunted on it, but they never settled, nor ploughed the soil. They could not, therefore, be the legal stewards. In contrast, the property owner ended their migrations, set up a house, tilled and sowed. They made the land productive rather than just harvesting Nature's bounty. This work justified the privileges of landlord-ship. The *Fundamental Constitutions* became one of the original texts of the British Empire, based on the notion of improvement of the land as a definition of property rights: the world was thus enclosed.

Where did this leave Mary, who clearly had no intention of getting her hands dirtied by work? Was the harvesting of rents a requisite definition of productivity, even if she did not actually produce anything at all? It seems the definition of improvement was expansive enough to include the development of techniques in husbandry to increase crop yields, the enclosure of rural commons into fenced property, the transformation of fields into streets and squares, or the reaping of rents from tenants. This form of rentier capitalism was only just germinating, and as a result the relationship between Crown, Parliament, landlord and tenant was working itself out anew.

When first inherited by Alexander Davies in 1663, many of the farms within the estate were discovered to be on extant long leases, sold when the land was owned by the Crown. Also, the fact that Alexander had died intestate meant that the ratification of the inheritance had to grind through the legal gears at a frustrating drag. There was little the family could do except wait.

Finally, at the end of 1675, there was a rash of contracts. This came as a result of Tregonwell finally getting legislation through the House of Commons that acknowledged the change of ownership of Davies's estate and the power of the trustees to work on Mary's behalf. That such matters had to be decided by MPs rather than the courts was a reassertion of the power of Parliament as the institution founded on the interests of the landed, above the interests of the Crown. Tregonwell had to navigate through an increasingly fractious Parliament that was beginning to fray and split. He was forced to throw his lot in with the anti-court faction to see the Bill across the line and into law. But needs must, and his parliamentary career seemed to fizzle out at this point.

But now, once the Bill had passed, the Tregonwells could start turning the legacy into profit. Between November and December 1675, the family signed thirty-seven new lease contracts for plots across the estate: Stone Bridge Field, Ebury Farm, Mulberry Gardens, Goring Gardens, Neate House and so on.[36] In addition, the Act allowed the trustees to start to sell some of the property. Goring House was once again put out to sale, and finally acquired in 1681 by Lord Arlington. A few acres were sold in Knightsbridge, which were bought back by later generations of the family. Nevertheless, the family's most valuable property remained Mary.

Of all the offers that were considered by the Tregonwells, Sir Thomas Grosvenor's caught their eye. Aristocratic. Youthful. Educated. Monied. A burgeoning political career. The family name went back to the Normans, with valiant origins. Legend has it that their first lands were a gift from the Conqueror for bravery during the Battle of Hastings. The first records of Robert le Gros Venour appeared in the 1160s; the 'Gros Venour' refers to the Great Huntsman. Stories continue of knights' valour at home as well as in the Crusades. By the fifteenth century, the family was settled at Eaton Hall, on the outskirts of Chester, and through the sixteenth century they accumulated extensive properties. From then on, the family reputation was based less on acts of bravery than management of the estate, local power and judicious business dealings. By the 1630s they had added significant mining interests in Denbighshire and Flintshire to their property and, in 1622, Sir Richard was made first Baronet Grosvenor for his support of James I.

Despite such social standing, the family also faced calamity over the coming decades. The first Baronet was a leading local politician and represented Chester in the House of Commons during the 1620s. He did not appear to distinguish himself. His diaries of his time at Westminster are recorded as being 'very dreary reading, [having] the dullness of a narrative which has no particular point or reason for being told'.[37] Nevertheless, he got in some hot water when he attempted to impeach the king's favourite, the Duke of

Buckingham. His political career came to an unexpected halt when, having stood as guarantor for his son-in-law, Peter Daniell, who defaulted on a loan, he spent the following decade in the Fleet debtor's prison. The surety was not paid off until 1638, when Daniell made some money from his own son's marriage agreement, and Grosvenor returned to Chester. At the same time, the first sparks that set the Civil Wars aflame started to flicker and catch, which put the family into further jeopardy.

The first Baronet attempted to remain outside the affray, seeking the peaceful middle path between the Crown and its enemies. His son, the second Baronet, also called Richard, was less timid. As High Sheriff of Chester in 1643, he outlawed from the city any parliamentary soldier who fought in the Battle of Edgehill. He was punished by the new regime with a fine, the 'compound', of £1,250, and lost his annual tithe of £130. This was a fate suffered by many loyal families across the nation, but was no less debilitating. This goes some way to explain a union with a supposedly rich bourgeois family like the Tregonwells thirty years later.

The second Baronet was also a supposed co-conspirator in Booth's Uprising in August 1659. This laughable coup was a reaction to the uncertainties that emerged following the death of Oliver Cromwell. Royalists desired to turn fate to their advantage, but could not get their act together. Gathering a small band of insurgents, they took Chester, but were dismayed when the hoped-for risings across the country did not emerge. The band was easily squashed by the parliamentary army, and the leader, Sir George Booth, attempted to escape to France dressed in women's clothing. Hiding in a tavern in Buckinghamshire, he was caught in his dress, and put in the Tower amid much hilarity and satire. Grosvenor went unpunished as the king returned to London in a matter of months.

However, tragedy and farce combined again in 1661 when Sir Richard's heir, also Richard, was killed by his own cousin, Hugh Roberts, in a duel over a running race. According to one account, the day before the race, Grosvenor had sworn 'if any man was to ride near his footman ... He would kill him, or be killed by him.'[38] Some offence was duly taken and the challenge was arranged, and

Grosvenor met Roberts at four in the afternoon on the road to Claverton, near Chester. Grosvenor attacked as Roberts moved away to avoid the lunge. Roberts then drew his rapier in defence and, according to the later royal pardon, stuck it into his cousin's stomach. Sir Richard took a day to die, meeting his end at the family home at Eaton Hall.

He left a child, the four-year-old Thomas, who became the third Baronet on the death of his grandfather in 1664. So, like Mary Davies, the young boy became master of a huge inheritance at a tender age. Also, like Mary, his mother quickly remarried. Unlike his future wife, however, he was allowed to grow up, gain an education and see the world without the burden of impending marriage vows determining his every step. The estate was managed by trustees, including close family, until he reached his majority.

In 1670, Sir Thomas went with a tutor, M. Gaillard, on a three-year grand tour of Europe. At the time, the idea of a continental education was in its infancy, and the young Grosvenor was a pioneer. Many of the previous generations had spent time abroad as Royalist exiles and so the encounter with the strangeness of Europe was now seen as an essential classroom for the young student. Furthermore, compared to the first half of the century, there were fewer wars, so it was safe to travel. Even the East was opened and Sir Thomas made it as far as the Levant on his voyage.

He saw the Bourse of Amsterdam, Louis XIV's Paris, Geneva, Papal Rome and maybe even the wonders of Constantinople. From Lyon in 1673, he wrote to his stepfather concerning a trunk of things he had procured along the way: 'there is nothing forbidden in it, the books much less than anything else. There is nothing against the Church of England, or against the King, only they are in Italian; and as for the little box which cannot be opened, there is nothing in it but stones of Florence.'[39] Sir Thomas collected artefacts at every stop and had them sent back to England. The books, art and objects harvested during these adolescent travels would fill the storehouses of the nation's country houses for the next three centuries.

On his return, Sir Thomas presented himself as a cultured man who wished to bring home all the lessons in style, design and beauty that he had encountered abroad. How London looked in comparison to Louis XIV's Paris! How small and pokey his family home might have appeared beside his memories of the Palladian villas of the Veneto. In his pocket book in 1675, he listed over 330 books that he had bought in recent years, at least 130 on his travels. The library ranged over old volumes and new, from the rare Atlas of De La Haye bought at Geneva to Milton's *Paradise Lost*. There were plays and more practical tomes on *Free Trade, or the Meanes to Make Trade Flourish*, the *Art of Gardening*, a 1636 argument against the use of coaches, as well as military and mathematical treatises.

His notebook also contains the accounts for 'Nicholas Mercator … Begun with me the 15th of Febu att £1.10 0 for the month'.[40] This high price was suitable remuneration for time spent with the famous German mathematician, who was already a fellow of the Royal Society, had built maritime chronometers for Charles II and would go on to push the boundaries of early work on logarithms. Five years later, Mercator was invited to Paris to work on the design of the palace fountains at Versailles. Whatever Sir Thomas learned in these tutorials, it was clear that he was determined to be a young man in the front rank of learning and taste: he was to be a modern man.

What better way to display this learning than transforming the family estate at Eaton? The old family house had suffered through the wars, and Sir Thomas desired to start again with something that was new, exciting, reflecting the best of the age. The former home remained standing, renamed the Villa. He made arrangements with the architect William Samwell, a distinguished gentleman architect who deserves to be as well remembered as Hugh May or Roger Pratt, but unfortunately most of his creations have not survived. His first designs following the Restoration were at The Grange in Hampshire, and the remodelling of Ham House for the Duke of Lauderdale. Like his contemporaries, Samwell was interested in the classical templates that were first introduced by Inigo Jones in England before the Civil Wars. These were to be augmented and adapted using more recent innovations from France or Holland. There is no record that Samwell went abroad to see these for himself, but he would probably have picked them up from publications and discussions with know-alls such as Evelyn. He then worked on a set of stables for Charles II at Newmarket.

During the summer of 1675, Sir Thomas paid Samwell £15 to come to Chester and survey the site and then, back in London, to conjure up some designs. Although Samwell's work at Eaton Hall was demolished long ago, a picture of it can be found in Campbell's *Vitruvius Britannicus* from the 1710s. The house was made of brick with stone dressing; much of the stone brought from the ruined Holt Castle in North Wales. The frontage had nine bays that ranged around a wide courtyard. It was simple, well proportioned and elegant: setting out what would become the standard for the English country house.

Work continued into the 1680s and was said to have cost over £1,000 a year; less than Berkeley House, but still a huge sum. Unfortunately, Samwell never saw the final edifice as he died in 1676. Sir Thomas took personal interest in the progress. He wrote to an agent in Italy, 'You are to bargain with your lead Marchants to bring your blockes of Marble from Genoa, every blocke is to bee 8 foote long att least 2 foote beded and 18 inches high.'[41] He also laid out exact measurements for two million bricks, the dimensions for sawn timber from the estate, as well as the arrangements for the stone blocks. His attention to detail was admirable.

The following year, seemingly in a hurry to make an impression, the twenty-two-year-old Sir Thomas had his first portrait painted by the leading court painter in London, Sir Peter Lely. He stands in a heroic pose; his left arm is raised and pointed to his chest, his right is resting on his hip. He is, for some reason, wearing a breast plate despite never having seen battle. The rest of his dress is luxurious: red silks and fashionable lace. He wears red pantaloons with gold piping. His perruque is fulsome and flowing, framing his pale, expressive face. He has full red lips. A weak chin. Heavy-lidded eyes that look at the spectator not quite with disdain but youthful insouciance.

It may be unfair to notice but Sir Peter Lely painted the same year a portrait of John Wilmot, the second Earl of Rochester, in almost exactly the same garb and pose. Was the most famous

Sir Thomas Grosvenor, master of Eaton Hall, painted by Sir Peter Lely

portrait painter of the age churning out that season's 'look' *en masse* for the leading bachelors? As a lonely hearts advertisement, it might be saying: 'sensitive, educated but not to be underestimated'. The portrait placed the young buck standing within untamed Nature but in front of the cultivated and tempered gardens of the as-yet-unrealised Eaton Hall. This was an artist's impression of his ongoing work, of transforming the family home.

In the same year, Sir Thomas had also made his first lurch up the greasy pole of politics when he was named an alderman of Chester. The Chester seat in the House of Commons was the next step, which he achieved in 1679. He was on his way. And, as universally acknowledged, must be in want of a wife.

First, the negotiations. The officials needed to be notified, and so permission was sought from the body that oversaw the protection of the orphans of the City of London. Also, because of Mary's age – she was still only twelve years old – permission was needed from the Bishop of London, who settled a licence on 8 October 1677. Next, the two parties had to make their own agreement. As with all mergers and acquisitions, a certain amount of due diligence was necessary. Sir Thomas may have wanted to know the income and value of the Davies inheritance. It was made clear that he had no right to any of the income that had come to the estate during the eleven years since Alexander's death. Furthermore, the groom was to settle the debt with Lord Berkeley: the initial sum of £5,000, alongside a further £1,500 in interest. An annual income of £50 was to be given to Aunt Mason, who had looked after Mary so diligently. And finally, while Mary was still a child, it was agreed that she should stay at home until she reached her majority at fourteen. For the intervening two years, Sir Thomas must provide £500 a year for her upkeep.

The day before the wedding, there was a series of agreements. This document, signed by Thomas Grosvenor (lawyer), Thomas Myddleton (trustee), Sir Thomas Cholmondeley, Mary Tregonwell, John Tregonwell, and (Mary's grandfather) Richard Dukeson, folds out to the size of a small table, and goes across four sheets.[42] It is also an elaborately decorated article. In the top left-hand corner of the front page, the letter T has been transformed into an insignia, containing an intricately inked lion and unicorn. The text goes into exhaustive details of the union. A date was set, before the Feast of St Luke the Evangelist (18 October).

There were also scenarios of what was to happen if Sir Thomas died before Mary reached twenty-one. The estate was to be looked after by a set of trustees. Also, what would happen if the marriage produced only daughters. Five days after the wedding, another agreement between Thomas Grosvenor and Mr Tregonwell was signed for 'Bargain and sale of reversionary interest in two-thirds of the Bailiwick and manor of Ebury', that recorded the transfer of the Davies lands to Sir Thomas, apart from that third that remained with Mrs Tregonwell during her lifetime.[43] And it was only in July the following year that a full understanding of the financial settlement of the union was concluded.[44]

The marriage was sealed by Crown, law, Church and family. When all these matters were agreed, signed and sealed, the bride and groom were able to meet at the altar rail of St Clement Danes. And so, on 10 October 1677, when she was just over twelve-and-three-quarter years old, Mary travelled once more to her grandparents' parish. At the altar, where her elderly grandfather undoubtedly stood, she took the hand of Sir Thomas Grosvenor. He was nine years older, an aristocrat, a rich heir and by now a man of the world.

According to the 1662 *Book of Common Prayer*, Sir Thomas vowed 'to love (Mary), to comfort her, honour, and keep her in sickness and in health; and forsaking all others to keep himself only unto her, so long as they both shall live'. Mary, on the other hand, repeated her vows and was urged that she 'submit to your husband' and 'to be in subjection'.[45] What the twelve-year-old girl might have felt, standing at the railing, is left silent.

4

'All the Trouble in the World'

S IR THOMAS AND Mary were wed, but they were not yet man and wife. It was not until two years later, at least, after Mary had reached her majority at fourteen, that she arrived at her nearly finished home at Eaton. It was a long way from London to Chester. While it was unlikely that she took the stage coach with other passengers, nonetheless the journey ensconced in a private carriage might still have taken five days. Before she left Millbank for the last time, what advice had her mother given her about her future? She had been used to the bustle of the capital; now she was going to the north of England, a part of the nation she had never visited before. And what of her duties, both to her lord, as well as mistress of a huge estate? What fourteen-year-old girl was prepared for such a life change?

Sir Thomas and his lady were to be married for just under twenty-three years. From October 1677 to Sir Thomas's death in July 1700, they lived much of the time away from London. They came to the capital when he sat in Parliament and Mary was occasionally in contact with her mother on matters of the estate, which was now the property of her husband. The record of Mary's life during this period, as she became a teenager, moved into young adulthood and then found herself a widow at thirty-five, is thin. The archive holds only a few notes in her own hand, often in pale ink and a rushed hand. She, the daughter of a scrivener, was now the wife of an important man in local politics and of noble standing.

During this time she became a mother – six times over. But before that she became the mistress of the house.

She spent most of these years outside History. And while little of Mary's life was noted down, this is not because she was of little note. The moments of her life that have been recorded are like bright pinpricks within the darkness, from which we must construct a constellation and so, like an astrologer, divine some determination about her life. Even with what little evidence we have, one can see a portrait of a woman finding a place in the world, struggling towards subjectivity, building herself out of the things, people, ideas and barriers that she finds around her.

The vast literature on female etiquette that proliferated during the seventeenth century dictated the many ways a woman should be. This library of directions and moral observation located the woman as 'being made of the softest mould', needing protection and guidance, but conversely at the moral, nurturing centre of society.[1] A woman was a mother, and bearing children was seen as a penance, but also she was the mistress of the household. There were as many books teaching practical skills as there were exhortation to spiritual purity. Many were taught to read, but fewer to write, enforcing the rule that 'silence is a woman's glory.'[2]

But how are we to judge the gulf between the literature and the reality? There was clearly an ideological desire to suppress women's actions and identity, but there is plenty of evidence to show that early modern women sought to identify themselves beyond the restrictions of the prayer book and husbandry manual. In 1696, Judith Drake, one of a group of London women intellectuals, wrote *An Essay in Defence of the Female Sex*, that argued that it was custom and language that defined the weakness of women. And like a natural philosopher she set about burning down traditions and received wisdom in order to see the truth more clearly. Women's history had been erased from the record because 'Time and the Malice of Men have effactually conspired to suppress 'em.'[3] Similarly, ancient 'logic' could not deliver anything but a repetition of the past. Instead, 'nothing but Discouragement, or an idle uncurious Humour, can hinder us from rivalling most Men in the Knowledge of great Variety of things.'[4] Nonetheless, in the present moment, women 'are born slaves, and live prisoners all their lives'.[5]

Despite this, throughout the century there are powerful examples of women owning and inheriting their own property, managing businesses, living independent lives. The seventeenth century started with a queen, Elizabeth I, admittedly weaker than she appeared, and ended with Queen Anne, who was wiser and stronger than most historians give her credit for. A woman could therefore act as God's representative on Earth, command armies, and appoint ministers and bishops.

During the same century, women wrote plays, poetry and romances and were now able to perform them on the stage. They started up their own enterprises and become successful businesswomen in their own right. They migrated to the city to find work, and lived and thrived the best they could. They had managed estates, and plotted new developments that transformed cities. They preached the Word of the Lord to vast crowds gathered in fields and city streets. They were at the forefront of protests and insurrections. They did men's work – there is plenty of evidence, for example, of female masons working on the rebuilding of St Paul's Cathedral. Notorious piratesses piloted their own ships. Margaret Cavendish was content to argue natural philosophy with the illustrious thinkers of the Royal Society in 1667 and write her own explanations of the physical world. Aphra Behn was a playwright, who spied for the king in Antwerp, travelled to Suriname, and translated an astronomical treatise into English.

When considering Mary's life, it is too convenient to accept History's silence as proof of women's passivity. Despite what the story of female social subjection tells us, regardless of the timid images of ideal femininity sketched by etiquette books and devotional primers, beyond the court records of how the husband stood above his wife, women throughout the seventeenth century were engaged in intense, individual struggles of self-realisation. She was finding agency in what she did, making sense of the world, placing herself into the vibrant, human flow of everyday life. If the record does not acknowledge these lives, it is incomplete and needs to be redrafted and evaluated anew.

And this is how we should see Mary, despite the paucity of the written record of her life. We see her most often through the gaze of others, and this offers an added complication in our attempt to reach her, to hear her, to understand the choices she faced and the decisions she made. We glimpse her through a bishop's diary. The account books of Eaton Hall. A brace of letters to her mother that hint at her interest in the running of her estate. A note of tender affection to her husband, and his response on the reverse page. The marking of children born, and soon in the grave in the family crypt, and the children that thrived.

There were also reports of a growing fragility of mind. Many of these were written after this time but dated back to this period. These retrospective testimonies also overlay the account of the most profound decision Mary made for herself during her marriage. For while still a teenager, she made the momentous choice to convert to Roman Catholicism. It is from these scraps that we must patch together an inhabited life.

As Mary travelled to Eaton Hall for the first time, the change in the landscape also marked her own journey from daughter to wife. She was the property legally handed from one man to the next, the particulars of the transaction set out in the contracts of October 1677. Yet a wife's obligation was different from that of a bride. According to *The Lawe's Resolutions of Women's Rights* (1632), both the husband and wife were 'but one person, and by this a married woman perhaps may ... doubt whether she be either none or no more than half a person.'[6] Certainly, in the eyes of the law, she was none despite the 'wise fiction' of an equal share, and the author knew no remedy to this negation. Within the actual partnership of the marriage, the daily management of things, however, there was something more than nothing, albeit far from equal.

The ideal wife was a model of 'modesty and temperance', nonetheless with the organisational skills of a quartermaster. Despite being spoken of in religious terms – the wife devoted to her husband as a supplicant before the Lord – the marriage expected a division of responsibilities across the complicated corporation of the estate. While her husband looked after the land, its tenants, investments, alongside a bailiff or steward, his lady oversaw the house and its personnel, the running of the family, hospitality; as well as acting as hostess to her husband's political aspirations. When the husband was away, the wife took on his tasks in his place. During the Civil Wars, many wives were left by their warring husbands and had to defend their own estates against attack. Many bravely scaled the battlements too.

This is what faced Mary as her coach drove through the ornate wrought iron gates, and past the new gatehouse, at Eaton Hall. Sir Thomas may have met his new wife at Chester in order to accompany her for the final miles as the coach crossed the fields to Eccleston and then turned towards Eaton Hall. The house itself was now near completion as she stepped down from the coach after the long journey. One imagines a throng of estate staff and domestic servants waiting to meet their new lady on the gravel courtyard in front of the house. Maybe she was still accompanied by her aunt, Mrs Mason.

But from now on Dame Mary, as she came to be known, was on her own, far away from the comforts of Millbank and London life, on the cusp of a new life. Elizabeth Livingston, who grew up in London and in 1670 married the Northumbrian Robert Delaval, offers insight into how Mary may have felt at this moment: 'it can not be denied but that it was very natural for a person of my age to have liked better staying in a place where I was every day much courted by people of the best quality ... than to retire to a country house, where notwithstanding the prospect of a happy, peaceful dwelling for a time ... I did not escape having many uneasy hours.'[7] Or, once she had settled in, found that she was always on display and yearned to be left alone, like Katherine Packer who wrote: 'many a time I go about my house and amongst my servants ... I had rather lock myself up in a room alone amongst my books for meditation.'[8]

Entering the house through the sturdy, stone portico, she made her way into the Grand Hall. This was the main public room of the house, where the family, the staff and the outside world inter-mingled. As she moved through the house, she learned that the nobleman's house was not just a home but also a sequence of spaces managing a hierarchy of encounters. There were places of display and social intercourse, servant spaces, as well as private, intimate

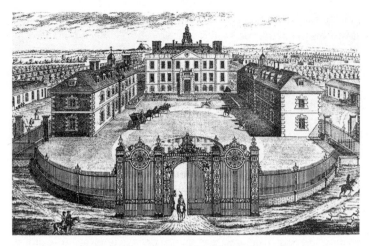

Eaton Hall, as designed by William Samwell,
showing the gates from the north west

enclaves that were accessed by invitation only. The divisions
between upstairs and downstairs was far more complicated than
often imagined, the balance between private and public in constant
tension. And these frictions were often given a symbolic geography
through the rooms of the house.

There are few records of the interior of Eaton Hall, and we can
only guess at the ways the rooms were divided by looking at similar
designs by the architect William Samwell. His work at the Grange,
in Dorset, is considered to be a sister building, and a sketch exists
at All Souls, Oxford, that appears to be close to the final realisation
at Eaton Hall.[9] The Grand Hall at the Grange was a space in which
Samwell was able to flex his architectural muscles with effect. It
was a cube, as tall as it was deep, and as wide. There was a mathematical satisfaction in such a conceit that appealed to Sir Thomas's
own interests in recent innovations in Natural Philosophy. It was
also an acknowledgement of Samwell's debt to architect Inigo Jones.
At the Queen's House at Greenwich, there is a main hall that shares
the same dimensions. This had been Jones's first commission for
Charles I and his wife, Henrietta Maria. In addition, a balcony

gallery ran along the first floor, allowing those upstairs to look down on the action below.

The decoration was simple but emphatic. The dynastic power of the family was on display here, with busts of ancestors embedded in scooped niches and painted portraits across the walls. There was often a big table across the back wall, and this was where festivals or celebrations were marked, where the classes mingled under the watchful eyes of the ancestors. Sir Thomas surely put his own, recent portrait by Lely here amongst the elders. This mixture of ancient and modern perfectly matched Sir Thomas's aspirations to establish his birthright, but also to project his ability to exceed the past with an embrace of the thrilling sense of the new. But it was also Mary's home, and there is a note from Francis Cholmondeley that, 'in the building and furnishing of this house, the lady had the satisfaction of her own fancy and contrivance.'[10]

The rest of the ground floor followed a symmetrical, geometric scheme. Across the floor plan, rooms doubled, mirrored and reflected each other. From the Grand Hall, one moved into a corridor, then through corresponding doors that opened out into another square room, the parlour, only one storey high. In contrast to the public state room, this was a private space for the family and associates to congregate. This was also where the family might take their meals. Retracing one's steps to the central corridor, to the west wing was the withdrawing room, where the family moved following their meals. This contained a large silver pendulum clock, silk chairs patterned with green and gold flowers and a card table for after-dinner entertainments. The library was stacked with almost 1,800 volumes.

To the east, was the Reception Hall. Here was a space for an impressive, elegant staircase, rising to the first floor. This room also contained two large marble tables and two marble stands. The staircase itself was usually an impressive work of ornamentation and engineering. Upstairs, both Sir Thomas and Mary had their own bedchambers, closets and dressing rooms, 'each equipped with tapestry hangings, silk bed curtains, tea tables, pictures, screens, cabinets and bed cages.'[11] In the corners of the building were smaller closets, private spaces for the family, containing chamber pots or close stools. The water closet was still very rare even in the best houses. Washing was often done with a pewter bowl and a water ewer in the bedchamber, rather than a separate room containing a bath. Because the house was also a place for rolling hordes of guests, who often stayed for long visits, there were a number of bedchambers on the ground floor as well as across the upper floors, including spaces for their servants.

On either side of the courtyard were two other buildings extending out from the main house. Sturdily elegant but unadorned, in brick, these were both the stables and the 'house of office', which included the kitchen, pantry, buttery and larder; maybe also a bakehouse, brewery, wash house and laundry. Here was the engine room of the household, which kept the gears and mechanisms of the country house turning over. The constant churn of linen – napkins, bedsheets, clothes – was a military operation. The kitchens had to feed not just the family and the diurnal flow of guests and visitors, but also the household itself. There was also often a slaughterhouse within the house of office, to supply the formidable demands of the family table. Much of the gardens beyond – orchards, walled gardens, orangery, pastures – was dedicated to the provisioning of the household.

Mary would have encountered plenty of advice on how to behave like a lady, both as a wife and as the lady of the house. But once again the distance between the ideal and the reality are noticeable.

How did the teenaged Mary adapt to this role? Did she have time for charitable works in the community? Many wives also learned how to heal the sick and make medicines; Sir Thomas's mother kept a recipe book of potions and cures. Or did the young mistress, in rare moments of quiet, take time to read some of Sir Thomas's volumes in the library? Although only a few letters remain, and her writing is basic, Mary kept in contact with her mother and with the management of her inheritance in London.

For lesser estates, often the wife managed the provisions, domestic chores, servants and rearing of children. But with an estate the size of Eaton Hall, it was likely that there was an estate manager. The accounts for the house were in the hands of a factotum, Thomas Burton, and were signed off by Sir Thomas, although at least some of the planning, ordering and distribution of the expenses was probably under Mary's purview. The role of estate manager was becoming increasingly professionalised, and Burton combined the skills of accountant, agronomist and surveyor. The account books record the purchase of copious amounts of foodstuffs, from baskets of fruit, which were clearly luxurious enough to be listed as a noteworthy expense, to lobsters (1s 6d) and a barrel of herring (17s 6d), as well as a constant flow of beer and wine, some of which needed to be carried up from London.

The running costs of the house were also meticulously itemised. Fabric for dressing and upholstery, stitched by the women in the household. Four hundred and thirty boards of wainscoting were ordered from the capital and delivered by a master craftsman, for a sizeable fee of £10. New pewter was always in demand to replace the old dishes and pots. The books also contained more substantial purchases and repairs. Sizeable work was done in 1683, as Mary was settling in, in 'removing of the Banketting house from ye old orchard to the new and framing a new roof to it' with slates.[12]

Livestock for the farm was a big investment: 'nine Irish bullocks and sixty weather sheep' in 1679, as well as a 'Woolfe Dogg' from London. Sir Thomas also had a passion for racing and there was a steady flow of expenses on 'running horses'. At other times, scorpion oil was bought from 'Mstr Gouldburn' to dress an ox who had been bitten by an adder, while 'verdigris and quicksilver and allum' was used to cure the dogs of mange.

As with the house, Sir Thomas wished to modernise the surrounding landscape. There is in the archives a map of the farmland before 1682, before the transformation. The surrounding land was agricultural rather than horticultural: four large fields encircled the new house, and were divided by drainage channels that ensured the land was always irrigated. There were enclosures for cattle and horses, and an orchard near the house. If there were formal gardens, they did not appear on this surveyor's chart, which was more concerned with measurements.[13]

As Dame Mary arrived, Sir Thomas was turning the farmland into a grand garden, one planted for delights rather than crop yields. Furthest from the house, the drained fields had been turned into flood meadows and a deer park. Closer to the house, the gardens expressed man's conquest and improvement of Nature as an object of contemplation and profit. The land closest to the house was formalised into geometric forms. Two parterres, in the French fashion, twisted hedges and flowers in orderly patterns. The account books included sums for roses for the formal garden at the back of the house; they also record the gardener John Scalping going to nearby Chirk for strawberries and other plants.

From the parlour windows, one viewed a formal English lawn, around a central pond. And beyond, orchards, and a walled garden for flowers, herbs and foodstuffs. A dovecot sat within a pasture field, and somewhere there was a private family chapel. Although John Evelyn never visited Eaton Hall, he might have approved of the tree planting, in the creation of an 'elysium of delight' that combined the latest styles from Italy and France, in order to make something thoroughly native. The organisation of the gardens led 'from a terrace with semicircular summer houses through a parterre to a wilderness and then via a rectangular canal lined with trees, to the distant prospect of Beeston Castle on the horizon'.[14]

This was the theatre for the dramas of Dame Mary and Sir Thomas's intertwined lives.

The marriage was a transaction, but one hopes that after initial hesitations the couple found an accommodation. In courtly circles the forming of affection between husband and wife was discouraged. Elsewhere, there was a distrust of passions that could rise or be extinguished. As Lady Anne Blount wrote to a would-be wooer: 'Ah, if you love yourself or me, you must confess that I have reason to condemn this senseless passion; that whereso'er it comes destroys all that entertain it; nothing of judgement or discretion can live with it.'[15]

Nonetheless, some affection was needed to make a marriage work. A letter, dated 30 August 1683, marks one of those celestial pinpricks that make out the constellation of Mary's life and reveal so much. Written when she was still only eighteen years old, Mary addresses her husband as 'Dear Pogg'. She updates him on what she has been up to on a visit to Alstrop and how she planned to go to a fair with Sir Thomas's close family friend, Charles

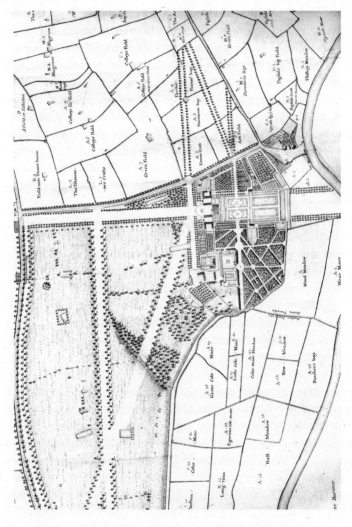

Map of Eaton Hall gardens, showing the transformation
from farmland to ornate park

Cholmondeley, 'for I would not do anything that did not look well in the eye of the world, and what I thought you liked'. After some other news she signs off: 'My Dear, pray take care of yourself for in your eyes lies all my happiness, and though I am not so good at expressing myself yet there is none can have a greater love for a husband than I have for you …Your ever constant wife and humble servant.'[16]

Was this the language of obedience or true sentiment? And was this feeling mutual? On the reverse of Dame Mary's note, Sir Thomas scratches his reply, as he fumbles towards the poetic mode, asking her to come home as soon as she could:

> Your kindness to me sometimes strikes me to the heart, and you do not know the hurt it does me, the which if you would strive to leave [Alstrop and come home] I should be the happiest man living, for I love you so well that I am not able to bear the least unkindness, the which, if you will leave, I should think all the trouble in the world too little to deserve you, and you shall command my life, Estate, and all things else that I am capable of. If you will not, you shall never find an alteration in my kindness and respects … This I tell you out of my great kindness I have for you, and all my belief that you have the same for me.[17]

For a man of studied reason and status, this is a lot of emotion. It discards the fashionable notion of being dispassionate or that the relationship between the lord and his lady was one solely of obligations and duty. Despite the nature of their bonding, this union appears to have found a sentimental proving ground. One can only hope that as the teenaged Dame Mary settled, she found a home amongst the rooms, objects and perpetual churn of people at Eaton.

* * *

Unlike Mary, whose world now encompassed the domestic politics of the Hall, Sir Thomas was destined to be a public man, making his way in the world of national politics. When Mary married, her husband was already an alderman in the city, and, by the time she travelled northward, the local MP, his election uncontested. For the next two years he travelled seasonally to London to sit in Parliament. Here, he claimed, he 'would also favour the good of the city before his own interests'.[18] He campaigned on the trade of Irish cattle that came though the city's port and sat on a committee concerned with the speedier convictions of Catholics who refused to comply with the new Recusant laws. But beyond that, he did not seem to have made much impact on the political stage at Westminster. Certainly, on the major debates of the day, he had little to contribute. Yet in Chester, the Grosvenor name continued to have clout.

Travelling to the city today, the imprint of the family can be found almost everywhere. Coming out of the railway station, you start to see names that seem eerily familiar, a palimpsest of some of the most exclusive parts of London. Moving into the city centre, you come to Grosvenor Park, the Chester Grosvenor Hotel, the less ritzy Grosvenor Shopping Centre, the Grosvenor Museum that tells the history of the ancient city.

Walking from the city to Eccleston, a village within the Eaton Estate, where the family vault sits within the neatly landscaped St Mary's churchyard, I crossed the Old Dee Bridge and headed out on the Eaton Road. I approached the Grosvenor Arms, and then, yards later, I came across a cluster of houses on Ebury Place. After a few minutes' walk, the suburban Victorian villas gave way to more modern twentieth-century housing by Eccleston Avenue, and then there are the modern detached homes of Belgrave Park. Finally, countryside, until I entered Eccleston, an enclave of neat, brick houses owned by the estate, many of them built by the Victorian architects Douglas and Fordham. Wherever one looks, the family's history is etched into the landscape.

As the son and grandson of Royalists during the Civil Wars and the bitter aftermath of the Interregnum, Sir Thomas continued the family's tradition of representing the king's interests in Chester. During the 1640s, the city had been in the thick of the tumults. As one of the key strategic cities in the north-west, it could hardly avoid the division and violence that swept through the four nations.

It was an ancient city that in 1660 had a population of about 7,500 and over 1,700 dwellings, enclosed by fortified walls and clustered between the cathedral, the marketplace and the castle.

Its wealth came from trade with Ireland as well as dairy farming across the surrounding flat Cheshire plains. It was the social, religious, legal and trading centre for the region, long before the village of Liverpool grew into an industrial trading metropolis. Large enough to have its own guilds, after the grant of a charter in 1506 the city had an administration consisting of a mayor, sheriffs, aldermen and councillors. Needless to say, these positions were often dominated by the large gentry families that lived outside the walls – the Grosvenors of Eaton, the Cholmondeleys at Vale Royal, as well as the Delamers, Breretons, Needhams and Willabrahams. The county was noted as 'the most surpassing nursery of ancient gentry above any county in England'.[19]

Many of these families suffered during the wars, and support for the king resulted in heavy fines. Robert Cholmondeley, captured by the Parliamentarians at Oxford, was compelled to give up his mansion, which was turned into a 'pigsty' and 'unfit for a place of residence for a person of such quality'.[20] Sir Thomas's grandfather was struck down with terrible debts, a tenth of his annual income, which would bleed down the generations.

Nearing the end of this era of uncertainty, as Cromwell's powers were waning, the gentry of Chester rose up in 1659, when George Booth, first Baron Delamer, attempted to muster a revolt from Chester and march towards York. Sir Thomas's great aunt was married to one of the uprising's leaders, Edward Massey. Easily defeated, Massey escaped and made his way to London where he inspired an anti-Parliament riot amongst the soldiers over their arrears. The conspirators were saved when Charles II was restored to the throne.

Twenty years later, as Sir Thomas entered national politics, many of the same local families continued to hold power in the region. At the same time, Grosvenor found himself drawn into a political rupture that began in Westminster, but reverberated in Chester, and eventually came to strike at the heart of his marriage with Dame Mary.

The Exclusion Crisis began to emerge in 1678 and, while couched in religious language, raised the question of where power lay in the nation. Since the Restoration, there had been restrictions on Catholic activity, enshrined in the Test Act that demanded that anyone who wanted to hold office was obliged to make a declaration of allegiance to the Crown and the established Church. These strictures had been put in place by Parliament, which remained suspicious of Charles II. As Charles's health started to fail in the later 1670s, he remained without an heir, and it was increasingly obvious that the next in line was his brother, the openly Catholic James, Duke of York. To most straight-backed Protestant Englishmen, the idea of handing their nation to the Pope or worse, the French, became a very present danger.

This may have remained a Westminster problem, until events spilled out beyond the debating chamber. In 1678, a supposed Jesuit priest, Titus Oates, came forward with notes on a conspiracy to assassinate the king. The conspiracy was a tissue of lies, but that did not seem to matter: it gave ammunition to every party that wanted to take advantage of the situation. Furthermore, the magistrate who took Oates's testimony, Sir Edmund Berry Godfrey, was later found dead. Was this connected to Oates's plot? Could the queen, the Portuguese Catherine of Braganza, be involved? Or did the magistrate commit suicide? The mystery has never been solved, but it added fuel to the flames of panic that had begun to burn up the nation.

Political factions took advantage of the hiatus to attempt to bar James's route to the throne. A faction around the Earl of Shaftesbury, the Whigs, started to put together legislation to exclude Catholics from ever becoming king. Shaftesbury proceeded cautiously, undermining the Duke's support before attacking him directly. That year, Parliament expanded the Test Act so that every MP and member of the House of Lords had to swear fidelity to the Anglican Church.

Sir Thomas was considered 'worthy' by Shaftesbury's faction, which suggests that he was sympathetic, but like many MPs he was conflicted between his duty to his king, and his religion.[21] As a result, when the first Exclusion Bill was debated in Parliament on 21 May 1679, he was absent from the vote, and the Bill was not passed. A second Bill was brought to the House in November 1680; however, by this time, Sir Thomas was no longer an MP, but back in Chester, acting as county Justice of the Peace. Yet even here, far from the capital, he could not avoid this storm. And now he had his new wife with him at Eaton Hall, even she was also drawn into the gyre.

In London, the anti-Catholic hysteria was stoked on all sides. In November 1680, there was a 'Mock Procession Against the Pope' that snaked through the city. History was rewritten and a plaque was attached by the Common Council of the City to the pediment of the Monument, created by Sir Christopher Wren and Robert Hooke, to mark the 1666 Great Fire: 'the City of London was burnt and consumed with fire by the treachery and malice of the Papists in September in the year of Our Lord 1666.' Known Papists were rounded up, their houses raided. Across the country, about a hundred Catholic preachers and missioners were arrested. Seventeen were executed 'with a butcher's cleaver and apron, halter, quartering block, fire and tar', and another twenty-three died as a result of torture and the harsh conditions in prison.[22]

The Catholic community in Chester was small. There were probably no more than fifteen inside the city according to a list taken after the Oates scandal erupted.[23] Beyond the walls, a handful of gentry families had held on to their faith for decades, including the Pooles, the Stanleys of Hooton Hall, and the Masseys of Puddington Hall. The role of the city as the main port to Ireland had always meant that it was watched for fear of invasion, but – crisis aside – the communities tended to leave each other alone. The laws, if they had been enforced, may have made Catholic observance difficult, but what was out of sight usually remained out of mind.

There was a certain amount of theatre about this. Most Catholics had been supportive of the king during the Civil Wars, seeing the Parliamentarians as the greater threat to social order, and remained committed to political stability after the Restoration. Many Catholics performed their obedience to the rules by attending an Anglican service once a year. Lancastrian Sir Richard Shireburn dramatically 'stopped his ears with wool' during the sermon. John Earle pulled 'his hat over his eyes and frowns out the hour'.[24] Their presence, however truculent, was enough to satisfy the legal requirements of the Act. And, outside of sporadic moments of hysteria, such actions were enough.

Instead, believers were compelled to practise their faith in private. Services were conducted at home, or in private chapels, sometimes hidden in the attic. And often prominent families had their own lay missioner who acted as schoolteacher and confessor. Ordained priests were few and far between; zealous Jesuits rarer still. The number of churchmen was so small that most believers expected to live out their faith without regular access to the sacraments, but instead followed a regime of fasting and festivals. At least a third of days in any given year were fast days. This included every Friday, the forty days of Lent, the ember days, as well as the vigils of local festivals. This could be very strict, although there were official complaints in 1676 that many Catholics in the north were eating egg on Friday in Lent. This was contrasted with feasts, that could be Saints' days, Christmas or Easter. Often, the larger houses that had a chapel hosted a breakfast after Mass on Sunday.

The Exclusion Crisis threatened to wreck this quiet accommodation. A priest, John Plessington, had been part of the Massey household since the 1660s. Records show that there was 'a schoolmaster ... who comes not to church',[25] who acted as tutor to the young William, son of Edward Massey, a relation by marriage to the Grosvenors. They lived at Puddington Hall in the Wirral, where the River Dee flows into the Irish Sea. The house had long been a refuge for priests and had a hiding place built into the chimney stack for safety. At some point in December 1678, the now eighteen-year-old William Massey was arrested, alongside the other Catholic gentry of the region: Rowland Stanley, James Poole, Michael Fitzwilliams. On 28 December, the infamous priest catcher Thomas Dutton raided Poole Hall, and after that Puddington Hall, where he found John Plessington, who was then taken to Chester Castle.

In May, Plessington pleaded not guilty before the court, yet three witnesses spoke against him. One was mentally ill, the second pretended to be a member of the Massey family but the priest swore that they had never met before, leaving a single witness to persuade the jury. The case had been decided long before, however, and Plessington was condemned to be hanged, drawn and quartered. The judge demanded that the quarters of his body be hung from the corners of Puddington Hall. On 19 July, Plessington made his way to Gallows Hill in Boughton and, after a public prayer, was executed. When the soldiers delivered his body to the Massey family for the final humiliation, they were stoned by locals and had to retreat. The body was then quietly buried in the local Burton churchyard.

These events could not have been closer to home for Sir Thomas Grosvenor. He would have known Plessington through his regular contact with the Masseys. In addition, the priest had been a resident for some time in Holywell in North Wales, which was part of the Grosvenor estate. The settlement was home to St Winefride's Well, which remained a shrine to the Catholic community throughout the period. None of this could possibly have gone on, or have been permitted to continue, without Sir Thomas at least turning a blind eye to the activities.

For a landlord, it was possible to let such things pass, but for a government official such an attitude was becoming increasingly unsustainable. This came to the fore in 1682, when the spectre of the Exclusion Crisis once again arrived in Chester. The Third Exclusion Bill had failed in Parliament and the opposition was ready to take desperate measures. Charles II was becoming increasingly frail and the prospect of a Catholic king more assured. The king's illegitimate son, the Protestant Duke of Monmouth, put himself forward as a possible alternative monarch and started to march across the country with a growing band of supporters.

On Saturday 9 September, this troop entered Chester. Here, they found a mob, well greased with ale paid for by a local alderman, and a cluster of mounted butchers ready to join the cavalry. Monmouth stayed the night in an inn and the next day went to meet the local gentry under the guise of a horse racing meeting. That night, there was more celebration ending with the rabble rioting in the streets, setting bonfires and calling for the reign of 'A Monmouth'. Over the following days, Monmouth stirred up the crowds. He rode to Liverpool, and then on to Knutsford, where he was met by the Earl of Macclesfield. At all these events, there were royal spies who later acted as witnesses to the seditious and dangerous speeches and threats that were stirred up by these events. Monmouth supposedly called a 'junto' of the leading men to plan 'that insurrection which was afterwards attended to with such fatal consequences'.[26] On his way back to London, Monmouth was arrested, and he and Macclesfield were accused of inciting rebellion, and then quietly released. Monmouth was forced into exile in Holland.

The following year, in September 1683, Sir Thomas was drawn into the controversy when he was called to be part of a case held at the Hall of Common Pleas in Chester. He named some of the local gentry who had attempted to 'alter the succession of the Crown … [and] assembled with schismatics and disaffected people in the public reception of James Duke of Monmouth (who hath appeared a prime confederate in the late treasonable conspiracy).'[27] In retaliation, Sir Thomas was accused of libel and had to take precautions against attacks from local Whigs.

* * *

Back in London, Charles II's reign was coming to a close, and the nation waited to see what might happen. Drama was closer at hand at Eaton Hall for, according to a family record, Dame Mary 'was reconciled to the Church of Rome, about the latter end of King Charles's reign or the beginning of King James's'.[28]

Why? There is little evidence available to predict such a decision before it happened. And there is even less source material on how she made this momentous change. We can do little more than guess at how it affected Mary's relationship with Sir Thomas or her family. With this lack of material such an act might appear random, a flash of impetuous madness. But we must resist such hasty judgements. Consider the psychological rupture of a young girl leaving everything she held dear in order to give her life to another, a man she barely even knew. In doing so she was no longer a daughter or heiress, but entered into a new life of duties as wife and lady of the household. She was expected to be modest and obedient towards her lord. He, in turn, became responsible for her property, her representative in law, and her spiritual guide. In a life of such obligations, a decision such as this – to determine the future direction of one's soul against husband, family and even the nation – was an extraordinary statement of self-definition. Still a teenage girl, this was Dame Mary's moment of saying *this is who I am. In defiance of everything around me, this is what I believe.* This is surely the brightest star in the constellation of her life so far, and the bearing that came to determine her future course.

Why did she convert to Catholicism? We will never truly know. Who can read the human heart at such a distance? It is unlikely that she was tutored in the catechism by a secretive Jesuit priest. There is no indication that her library was crammed with devotional texts. This was a divided time, and these fissures expressed themselves in religious language; but there is no indication that Dame Mary was making a political statement. Rather, it seems that she made this essential act in the hope of finding out who she was.

Her first, deep encounters with Catholicism are likely to have come about only once she arrived in Cheshire. Back in London, she was the granddaughter of a noted Anglican cleric. Neither her mother nor John Tregonwell showed any sign of being anything more than staunch members of the established Church. Tregonwell had even voted for the Exclusion Bill in Parliament in 1679. So the impetus could not have come from her immediate family. One potential source of inspiration may have been her growing friendships with leading Catholic families in Chester, whom she encountered as she entered local society. In particular, it appears she had a strong friendship with her husband's relation William Massey and the household at Puddington Hall. The story of John Plessington's bravery at the moment of his death may have been a common and inspiring topic of conversation.

Yet this does not fully explain the solitary, spiritual journey that Dame Mary might have had to make in order to arrive at her new faith. The rituals for fasting and feast days may have appealed to a young woman who wished to take control of her life. Historian John Bossy asks why a woman in the early modern period might challenge the turn of ecclesiastical history, concluding 'to a considerable degree, the Catholic community owed its existence to gentlewomen's dissatisfaction at the Reformation settlement of religion, and that they played an abnormally important part in its early history'. He argues that the Reformation had not been designed with women in mind. As a wife and head of a household, 'a whole sequence of ritual functions had been removed from her jurisdiction by the decline of fasting and abstinence and the desacralisation of holidays.' Secondly, Protestantism was a religion based upon education, which made for 'genuine differences of feeling between a man and his wife'.[29]

And what about Sir Thomas? What happened now that he found his authority questioned, and his family put into jeopardy? There was no question of his faith; he was an Anglican born and bred. The couple now had to accept that 'they lie in the same bed and in the eyes both of God's Law and Man's are both one … yet be of two churches.'[30] The house was divided.

There is some indication of the conflict when the new Bishop of Chester, Dr Thomas Cartwright, recorded in his diary his many interactions with Sir Thomas during this time. In between the lines of the journal, one can read the ongoing dispute between Dame Mary and her husband. On 7 December 1686, Cartwright notes: 'after supper Mr Massey came to me again, and discoursed with me concerning Sir Thomas Grosvenor's carriage to his wife, and her resolution to enter into a monastery if he did not alter speedily, and consult her reputation and his own better than he did.'[31] The next day, Cartwright records that he had acted as peacemaker between the married couple on the question of how Dame Mary was able to worship. It was agreed that Massey was to be permitted to visit Eaton Hall 'at any time, when he was in the country, and be entertained as others'.

The bishop as marriage counsellor found a compromise. Dame Mary was to be allowed to follow her faith 'in private', while at the same time 'no public discourse of religion should be suffered in this house.' However, in order to protect the family, 'if any servant carried any tales between them on either side, they should be turned out.'[32] Dame Mary was so pleased with the negotiation that later that night, dining with the bishop and his family, she gave them a cheese in thanks.

This was a significant, and potentially dangerous, accommodation between Sir Thomas and his lady. Dame Mary was now free – in moderation – to practise her new-found faith. Was this the behaviour of a devout believer who wished only to approach her God in her own way in private, or the demand of a stubborn wife? Did Sir Thomas acquiesce out of affection, duty or patient understanding? Either way, Sir Thomas was to face the consequences in Chester society, Parliament and even in the afterlife. Such a bargain undoubtedly placed Sir Thomas in a complicated matrix of balances.

Soon, political events came to test that alliance. On 6 February 1685, Charles II died, leaving the throne to his brother. There were even rumours that Charles had converted to Rome on his deathbed. He bequeathed a divided nation, reflected in the complicated marriage between Dame Mary and Sir Thomas. Matters became more dangerous when in June the Duke of Monmouth returned to Britain at the head of a band of mercenaries and called his supporters across the nation to him. Grosvenor undoubtedly looked on in horror as many of those figures who had stirred up trouble in 1682 rushed to his flag in Dorset. Back in the city, the annual fair was cancelled and the Lord Lieutenant was ordered to arrest 'all disaffected and suspicious persons'.[33]

The new king immediately raised his own troops led by the Earl of Faversham and John Churchill, later the Duke of Marlborough. Monmouth's troops were never a match for the better-trained militia. They attempted to besiege the city of Bristol, but were easily repelled. The Duke finally was backed into a corner and was quickly defeated on 6 July at the Battle of Sedgemoor. The Duke was executed for treason nine days later at Tower Hill. The executioner's axe swung seven times before the head was severed. And many of his supporters were brutally punished, James noting that he desired to have his enemies 'destroyed'. Following the Bloody Assizes conducted by the ruthless Judge Jeffreys, at least 150 were executed and 800 sent as slaves to the West Indies.

As the rebellion was fomenting, Sir Thomas was named as a 'captain of a Troope of horse' and commanded to raise soldiers to combat a possible rising in the north. He gathered together between thirty and forty men and quartered them at Nuneaton. They did not see action but they cost a lot of money, and Sir Thomas was expected to bear the expense. An account book holds a thorough audit of the proceedings, including a pair of engraved silver trumpets, saddles, ribbons as well as food and charcoal for the daily provisioning of the muster.

Once Monmouth had been defeated, James II refused to stand the militia down, as there were, he claimed, legitimate fears of another uprising brewing at any moment. At the same time, James II wanted to offer a show of strength to anyone – in particular the recalcitrant Parliament – who might consider blocking his way. Such posturing was perceived by Parliament as a snarling glimpse of absolutism. What was Sir Thomas to do? On the one hand he was loyal to the throne, whoever sat on it; on the other, as a Parliamentarian, James II represented so much of what he feared. If that was not perplexing enough, at the same time Dame Mary was cajoling him to take the king's side.

This conundrum came to a head sooner than expected, in April 1687. James II had not disbanded his troops following the victory over Monmouth, but had gathered the forces at Hounslow Heath, to the west of London. This was an act of overt belligerence, challenging the opposition to make their move. Parliament had been suspended, but plots and factions were stirring. Over the previous weeks, James had attacked some of the established pillars of Anglican power and, on 4 April, the king decided to double down by announcing a Declaration of Indulgence to all Catholic and Nonconformist believers. This suspended all penal laws against non Anglicans. James hoped that by offering succour to the Puritans at the same time as the Papists, they might swing their support behind him against the Parliamentarians. They were not to be so hoodwinked.

Such a triangulation also put men like Sir Thomas into a quandary. Should he continue to support the king's effort, putting his faith in the sanctity of the social order come what may? As the head of the troop he was actively part of the threat against his own co-religionists. He may not have been a supporter of the Earl of

Shaftesbury's Whig faction, but could he stand by and watch the constitutional rights of Parliament being trashed in this way? And then there was Dame Mary. The Declaration allowed her to worship as she wished without fear of persecution. What other gift might a husband desire to give his wife except the safety to follow her conscience?

As a result, on the night of 7 April, Sir Thomas visited Bishop Cartwright in his Palace in London to ask his advice. What was the right thing to do? 'Whether in conscience he could submit to the taking of the penal laws'.[34] Cartwright read through the Declaration with his friend and seemed to think that it meant 'the taking off of all penal laws'. Did this give him the satisfaction he sought? It seemed as if Sir Thomas remained confused as he rode back to his regiment at Hounslow. But there he made a dramatic decision. He went to see the king to share his troubles. In response the king offered him preferment: his own regiment, a peerage even. But Sir Thomas's mind was made up. And according to a later record: 'he refused, preferring the religion and liberty of his country, to all honours and power, so likely at that time to be attended with popery and slavery; and thereupon he quit his commission.'[35]

What was more dangerous: to silence one's own conscience or both to defy one's king and to go against the wishes of one's wife? It appears that Sir Thomas was willing to take action, and follow his own purpose. Such a dangerous decision was tested that summer when in August James II visited Chester. On the first day, Bishop Cartwright took the king to the cathedral, where he touched 350 people, a ritual laying-on of hands intended to heal the sick. The next day, the royal band rode to the pilgrimage site St Winefride's Well, at Holywell, on Sir Thomas's estate. Here, the pregnant queen was blessed with the hopes of producing a male, Catholic heir. Although there is no record, Sir Thomas and his lady, especially, were undoubtedly in attendance. What must they have said to His Majesty?

Sir Thomas lasted another year in his role as alderman in Chester, but was expelled in a widespread purge of the City Corporation. But by that time the reign of James II was increasingly precarious. There was talk of an invasion from Europe led by the Dutch

Stadtholder, and the king's son-in-law, William of Orange, married to Princess Mary. The Dutch fleet arrived at Brixham in Devon on 5 November 1688, and William made his way to Exeter, where he declared his intention 'to have a free and lawful Parliament assembled as soon as possible'. As he marched east towards the capital, William continued to attract supporters, until he faced the royal army at Salisbury. Instead of engaging, James commanded that his forces retreat to Reading. And then things fell apart as the royal faction began to fracture and fly. James attempted to escape in disguise, but was arrested upon a sinking boat in the Thames, and, after a short imprisonment in Rochester, found his cell door open and was allowed to escape to France. In contrast, William was given an open road into London where he was greeted by jubilant crowds.

The Glorious Revolution was not as bloodless as the historians have painted it, but it was quick. It saw the establishment of the constitutional monarchy, defined and guided by common law. This placed power into the hands of Parliament to a degree unseen before. In some sense, the revolution started in the 1640s saw its summation nearly fifty years later. The nation was still ruled by the Crown, but it was now controlled by MPs. This was the victory of the landowners over the arbitrary rule of the throne. The interests of property were now firmly established as the compass of the nation above the Divine Right of Kings. Put another way, while these events may have thrown Dame Mary's rights of conscience into jeopardy, it was a revolution that further consolidated the power of her inheritance.

'To Such a Mad Intemperance
Was the Age Come'

IT WAS A time of reason, and therefore its opposite, unreason. A new faith in rationality turned its experimenter's eye onto every matter as the rightful subject for what came to be seen as the scientific revolution. It sought to observe the laws that underpinned the universe, the causes of gravity, the varieties of species, as well as the secrets of human behaviour. Therefore, the Enlightenment emerged not only with a heightened fascination with the order of the world but also madness. These pursuits combined seamlessly with the rising tide of speculation, the development of markets and the exchange. The 1690s could be said to be the decade, after the upheavals of war, plague, fire and revolution, when the seedlings of modern capitalism started to germinate in London soil. The city was rich loam for finance, trade and empire-building. During this time as well, new banks – Child's, Hoare's, the Bank of England – were establishing the mechanisms of finance: mortgages, debates on the correct rates of interest, and the nature of money itself. Yet land remained the most valued commodity. The madness of speculation and the speculation on the nature of madness also intersected in the lives of Sir Thomas and Dame Mary during this period, with tragic consequences.

The Grosvenors continued to come down from Chester to London, especially when Sir Thomas was sitting in Parliament. Mary's lands were now in her husband's hands, and the signature on the various contracts during the period was his. In January

1679, he signed fourteen new leases with already sitting tenants, marking the change of landlord from the Tregonwells to the Grosvenors. Two years later, in 1681, Goring House was finally sold to the then tenant, Lord Arlington, and was renamed after the new owner. Beyond that, there seem to have been few changes to the estate. Sir Thomas was likely to have been more focused on managing his mining interests and farms in the north, rather than transforming his new acres on the outskirts of London. Nonetheless, the land was now producing a healthy income of at least £3,000 a year.

But elsewhere the city was on the move. The capital was being passed from courtly grandees like Clarendon and Berkeley, who wished to display their new power through architecture, to speculators, who wished to profit from ambitious projects, turning the city from aristocratic *hôtels* to bourgeois squares and streets. In the decades following the fire of 1666, London had emerged an altered city from the debris and chaos. By 1700, it had expanded beyond imagination: a throng of over 57,000 dwellings, home for more than 500,000 citizens. It was the largest city in Europe, maybe the world. The capital had become a beacon to many throughout the nation with the hope of fortune and advancement; it was also an international trading centre. In 1702, Thomas Browne observed: 'London is a world by itself. We daily discover in it more new countries, and surprising singularities, than in all the universe beside. There are among the Londoners so many nations differing in manners, customs and religion, that the inhabitants themselves don't know a quarter of them.'[1] Such transformations were a boon to landowners and property developers alike.

The city started to grow outwards, into the pastureland and meadows that ringed the huddled metropolis. But such expansion was not evenly distributed. The best land was close to the current centres of business: the City and Docks, the markets, the Inns of Court, the royal court. Good quality land, that did not need drainage (unlike Millbank), was sought, where sewerage and road building could be easily managed. High ground was considered healthy, offering fresh air away from the noxious fug of the busy streets. This meant that the western parts of the city, between the financial centre and Westminster, were most highly prized: Covent Garden, Bloomsbury, Soho. There were also developments south of the river, around Southwark and the Borough, as well as to the east where the Docks linked with the City, popular with merchants and immigrant communities who had just arrived, and wished to be close to their places of business.

By the end of the century, the farmland that had once been on the fringes of the city, home to the great houses of the newly returned grandees, had been turned into streets and developments. Here, on this western frontier, in an area called Brooke-Field (today, Curzon Street and parts of Shepherd Market), was staged the annual Hay Fair, in May, that had been moved from the now built-up neighbourhood of St James's – called Haymarket. This was a traditional fair that had become an institution in its new location, offering more than spring horse feed. This was an excuse for a full-on, bucolic carnival, that was starting to gain the disapproving attentions of its new metropolitan neighbours. According to the *Tatler* in 1701, visitors to the spring festival could see 'the city of Amsterdam carved in wood, the calf with five legs, the elephant, the tiger and the excellent droll named "Crispin and Crispianus". On a stage the mountebanks of Mr Penkethman's company performed their amusing tragedies.' And if that did not take your fancy, then there was also a rope dancer, said to be the daughter of a Florentine nobleman, who had run away with a showman called Finley.[2]

The following year, there was more scandal when, after a call from Queen Anne for public morality, the constables came to arrest a group of prostitutes. Their task was thwarted, and in a scuffle, a constable was murdered and a bystander, John Cooper, stabbed. The authorities later traced the perpetrator, a Gloucestershire butcher called Cook, to Dublin. In court he was found guilty and when he was hanged at Tyburn, it caused a riot. His body was taken by the crowd and laid in state in Clerkenwell.

By 1708, it was officially noted that the May Fair no longer pretended to be a meeting for trade and merchandise, but a place where 'many loose, idle and disorderly persons do rendezvous and draw and allure young people and servants to meet to game and

The May Fair at the beginning of the eighteenth century,
soon to be abolished

commit lewd and disorderly practices.'[3] Despite this, the festival
was coming to its natural end. It was development, not the law,
that tolled the death knell for the festival. By 1721, Brooke-Field
was turned into housing, now forming the western edge of the city.

This was the beginning of the West End. The aristocrats who
had been given land or bought a plot since the Dissolution were
now able to turn their gift into profit. An intricate system of leases,
ground rent and speculation allowed the Lords to make their land
work for them without unnecessary risk. They leased out the land
to speculators, who did all the work of planning, construction and
selling, and still they earned a regular income from the rents.

In some of these schemes the courtiers themselves were willing
to take the role of lead speculator; such as we have seen with Lord
St Albans, Henry Jermyn, at St James's Square. Another example
of an aristocratic speculator, whose life runs in parallel but counter
to Dame Mary's, can be found in Bloomsbury. In July 1683, the

heiress Lady Rachel Russell was left bereft when her husband, Lord Russell, was convicted and executed for his role in the Rye House Plot during the Exclusion Crisis. Political machinations through Parliament to stop the accession of James to the throne had been defeated and a desperate plot was devised to do away with the threat once and for all on the road to Newmarket, as the king and his brother made their way to the races. The conspiracy was foiled and Russell was executed after a summary trial.

The supposed traitor left his widow drowned in grief, but in possession of a tranche of London land that stretched from Covent Garden to St Pancras, including the pastoral manors of Bloomsbury and St Giles. Following the execution, Lady Russell decided not to remarry; her wedding to Lord William had been her second, and a rare thing, a love match. She lamented: 'I want him to talk with, to walk with, to eat and sleep with. All these things are irksome to me. The day unwelcome, and the night so too.'[4] She was determined to become mistress of her own fate. She put her energies into developing the property and to increasing the family estate. She turned her back on court society and vowed to 'converse with none but lawyers and accountants'.[5]

Her father had built Southampton House in the 1660s in the fields to the north of Holborn, in what was considered to be the highly desirable quarter of cherry orchards, flower fields, and the famed 'Liquorice Garden' of medicinal herbs. The area was known for its 'country air, pleasure and city conveniences'. During the 1670s, Russell and Lady Rachel had continued her father's work by leasing out forty plots around what became Bloomsbury Square.[6] It soon became, in the words of Macaulay, 'one of the wonders of England'; Evelyn named it 'a noble square or piazza, a little towne'[7] and it was hugely fashionable amongst the well-to-do. Even as she divided up, leased and sold off bits of her estate, Lady Rachel continued to refer to it as 'Our Square' rather than using its common name.

During the 1680s, she continued the expansion programme as work started on Great Russell Street, which ran from the square westwards to Tottenham Court Road. Twenty-six houses started to emerge, including Montagu House, designed by Robert Hooke (later the site of the British Museum). According to John Strype in the 1720s, the thoroughfare was 'handsome, large and well-built', and attracted a dazzling roster of tenants.[8] The houses on the north side were the most desirable as they had gardens that looked out across countryside towards the rise of Hampstead Hill. Developments had also started on King Street and Southampton Street that ran northwards, on the eastern edge of the estate, and these too became hugely popular amongst the fashionable.

Business continued when Lady Russell negotiated the marriages of her children. Her eldest daughter was married at fourteen to the future Duke of Devonshire. The younger daughter was allowed to wait until she was sixteen before becoming betrothed to Lord Roos. The future of her most important prize, her son, the Marquis of Tavistock, was sealed in an agreement with another widow, Mrs Howland of Streatham and Tooting Bec, who owned significant lands south of the river and had a twelve-year-old daughter. In this way the estate was increased and made secure for the next generation. In the long run, the power of land proved to be more persistent, and profitable, than the ups and downs of politics.

Yet such fortunes were dependent on the evolution of a new generation of professional builder-speculators, who found a means to profit from turning land leases into small towns. Men like Nicholas Barbon, for example, who is often referred to as the first modern property developer: an innovator, manipulative genius, beguiling villain, and (occasionally) out-and-out crook. No thumbnail portrait can do him full justice. Born the son of the firebrand Puritan preacher Praise-God Barbon (nicknamed Barebones), he was baptised 'If Jesus Had Not Died For Thee Thou Wouldst Be Damn'd' Barbon; but even with such a name he was rarely saintly. He first tried his hand at doctoring and worked in one of the pest houses during the plague of 1665, yet he found his true calling after the Great Fire. He began as a builder restoring houses damaged during the conflagration, until his ambitions grew and he started to plot not just individual houses, but whole suburban schemes beyond the city limits. He also developed the first example of fire insurance, including the formation of a small troop of firefighters, who only came to the rescue of a property that had a fully paid-up policy.

By the time he met the lawyer Roger North in the 1680s, Barbon was living the life of a hugely successful property magnate. North recalls coming to his home on Crane Court, near Fetter Lane, where the speculator kept his visitors waiting in the drawing room until he descended from his room, dressed in a silk coat. He presented the image of the mogul, claiming 'it was not worth his while to deal little; that a bricklayer would do.'[9] His great skill was to take on grand developments, move fast and turn a profit as quickly as possible. He mastered the skills of keeping his cash in hand, and his dealings one step ahead of the banks, and the law. To help him maintain his edge, he employed a 'gang of clerks, attorneys, scriveners and lawyers'. To his enemies, he played divide and rule: 'lure them singly by some advantage above the rest, and if he could not gain all, divide them, for which purpose he had a ready wit'.

During the late 1670s and '80s he took on projects across the city: on St James's Square, in Soho, Gerrard Street (now the main thoroughfare in Chinatown), as well as in Bishopsgate, Holborn and Bloomsbury. His first major project, Essex House, typified his modus operandi. Here, he bought an old aristocratic house on the Strand, against the wishes of the Crown. He knocked it down despite the protestations of the residents, who took him to court. By the time the judge had made his ruling and fixed a fine, he had replaced the Tudor palace with a small enclave of 'houses and tenements for taverns, alehouses, cookshops and vaulting schools', and sold it off. He passed the fine over to the new owner. His next grand scheme was Red Lion Square, near Bloomsbury Square, next to the lawyers at Gray's Inn, who complained bitterly of the nuisance and noise. When they tried to intervene in the works, Barbon's workmen 'assaulted the gentlemen and threw bricks at them'.[10]

In 1685, Barbon wrote the pamphlet *An Apology for the Builder* as a justification for the new era of development. In the process of completing the work of restoring the neighbourhoods destroyed in the fire, the speculators had road-tested and improved techniques of construction, project management and financial chicanery that underpinned their new industry. Now, they wished to profit from new projects beyond the circumscribed boundaries of the capital. In his broadside, Barbon argued that any restriction on building was a halt on economic growth. The rise of the city was natural and should be encouraged by the king, court and Parliament for the benefit of all: 'the citizens are afraid that the Building of new Houses will lessen the rent and trade of old ones, and fancy the inhabitants will remove on a sudden like rats that are said to run away from old houses before they tumble ... But this is certain, there are no more houses built every year than are occasion for.'[11] And despite the concerns of the authorities, the bizarrely nicknamed 'police architectonic' and the city elders, who had until recently attempted to halt the growth of the city's boundaries, developers like Barbon were starting to construct new suburbs, like rings on the metropolitan tree.

Yet Barbon's sharp practices had a profound impact on the shape of the modern city. For not only did it herald new suburbs, it determined the shape of the London terraced house. The typical Georgian terrace is often seen as an eighteenth-century innovation but had its origins in these post-fire developments. This was determined as much by financial considerations as architectural tastes. Barbon's profit-seeking, and the way that speculators like him leased plots from aristocratic landlords, dictated the proportions of the standard house: tall, thin along the street, and deep. This shape resulted from the peculiarities of how the landowner collected ground rent. Each house was rated by its dimensions on the street front, and so the developer was encouraged to pack as many dwellings on the plot as possible. Noticeably, it was often the landowner themselves who commissioned the widest property on a square, often taking up one whole side.

Furthermore, the way the houses were constructed influenced their form. Barbon was one of the first developers to standardise their work: so that items like staircases and fireplaces were created in workshops off-site and only brought to the property when necessary, ready to install. The speculator also desired to make the house as plain and unadorned as possible, as they tended to sell the property as a 'carcase', and the first owner then selected their own decoration schema. Hence, the new early modern home was a blank canvas on which the new homeowner could choose how to adorn each room, in order to represent their own taste and personality.

Luxuries such as tapestry, clocks, scientific instruments, glass and portraiture were to be found in an emerging consumer market. This revolution in acquisition also reflected a social transformation: the new bourgeoisie articulated their taste – and their selves – through what they bought and displayed. Despite his baser intentions, Barbon provided something that people wanted, as a description of one of his houses on Gerrard Street reveals. This was a show home marketed at what he called the 'emulators'; that is, those who 'by their perpetual industry are struggling to mend their former condition'.[12] These were the first Joneses who were to inspire the jealousy of their neighbours. The interiors were 'wainscotted and painted ... All the fireplaces had painted chimney pieces, firestones and marble hearths, and were set with "galley" tiles. At the rear of the house was the kitchen and a "lardery", the former fitted with a buttery and supplied by a pump from the New River Water.'[13]

While many grandees worked with speculators for their mutual benefit, other aristocrats in the city found themselves dealing with such types in less fortunate circumstances. Such as when the money men started to encircle aristocrats like the Berkeleys and the Earl of Clarendon who had built their powerhouses along Piccadilly, and then fallen on rocky times.

This process had started in the 1680s, when both the Berkeley and Clarendon families found that their initial ambitions for aristocratic palaces had turned out to be hubris. For both, politics was fickle and fate a trickster. Clarendon's fall from grace came first. When Charles II turned his back on his Lord Chancellor in 1667, Clarendon found he had few friends left, and one night a crowd broke in and cut down his trees and broke every window in his new home. He left for France, where he lived out his exile, regretting his architectural pretension as a 'rash enterprise that proved so fatal and mischievous'.[14] He had spent over £40,000 and was now a broken man. The house was rented by the Duke of Ormonde, and then, in 1674, sold by Clarendon's heir to the second Duke of Albemarle.

From the outset, the new owners wished to develop the plot, and John Evelyn recalls passing the site in June 1683, alongside the second Duke of Clarendon, as they demolished the aristocrat's exquisite palace: 'I turn'd my head the contrary way till the coach was gone past it, lest I might minister occasion of speaking of it, which must needs have grieved him, that in so short a time their pomp was fallen.'[15] However, the project was too much for one aristocrat, and so that year, Albemarle sold the plot to a consortium of speculators fronted by the baronet Sir Thomas Bond, a relation of Henry Jermyn. As Evelyn continued: 'He sold it to the highest bidder, and it fell to certain rich bankers and mechanics ... They design a new town, as it were, and a magnificent piazza ... I was astonished by this demolition, nor less at the little army of labourers and artificers levelling the ground, laying foundations and contriving great buildings.'[16]

Next door, that very same year, the Berkeleys also faced hard times. Once again, Evelyn acts as our narrator when he went to visit his friend, Lady Berkeley, who had now lost both her husband and her first son, Charles. It was decided then that some of the family land, once elegant gardens, was to be dug up and developed. Evelyn notes on 12 June 1684:

> I went to advise and give directions about the building two streets in Berkeley Gardens, reserving the house and as much of the garden as the breadth of the house. I could not but deplore that sweet place ... should be so much straitened and turned into tenements ... [it] was some excuse for my Lady Berkeley's resolution of letting out her ground also for so excessive a price as was offer'd, advancing near £1000 per ann. in mere ground rents.

He was entirely in shock at how London was growing: 'to such a mad intemperance was the age come of building about a city, by far too disproportionate already to the nation.'[17]

Lady Berkeley had done a deal with another syndicate, led by the merchant John Hinde, who set about accumulating a small estate from the neighbouring landowners. Hinde himself was a man of many parts; born the son of a baker, he trained as a goldsmith, but quickly turned his skills towards banking, listed in a register of 'goldsmiths that keeps Running Cashes'. He was an early investor in Nicholas Barbon's fire insurance enterprise, and by the 1680s was a rich man. It was soon revealed that Hinde too was the money behind Sir Thomas Bond's endeavours at Clarendon House.

The syndicate included members of his extended family, whose names Hinde used on a number of leases, as well as schemers such as Richard Frith and Cadogan Thomas. Builder-speculator Frith was also investing at that time in the fields of Soho, where a street was eventually named after him, and on Leicester Square. Thomas was a timber merchant from Southwark who sought to turn a profit in buying up 'void ground and decayed buildings' at low prices and long leases. Barbon also got a look in on a number of properties across the development. The whole scheme stretched along Piccadilly from what is today Stratton Street to Old Bond Street, centring on the proposed Albemarle Square.[18]

Despite the increased political uncertainty in the city, it appears that ambition rewarded the brave. Plots were marked out and sold to create Stafford Street, Albemarle Street, Dover Street and Old Bond Street. The buyers were various; from builders who bought up one or two sites, to large scheme developers, as well as other members of the syndicate who wanted to be landlords and speculators to maximise their profits. The syndicate also had to look to the development of an infrastructure that could cope with the rapid growth of the neighbourhood. There were fears that the River Tyburn might not be able to cope with the raw sewerage and run-off when it rained. Inhabitants might 'be drowned in their Houses upon any great Rain'.[19]

Yet ambitions and cash flow are rarely friends, and by the end of 1684, Hinde and his partners were forced to start mortgaging the unsold plots, and to sell freeholds rather than providing lease-holds. The syndicate had overstretched itself and as soon as the economic climate began to turn, these bad decisions started to be seen as terminal. Just as the post-fire developments of the 1670s inspired the first Boom, the over-speculation of the 1680s saw the first Bust. Supply outstripped demand. Developers found them-selves without cash, and their investments losing value.

On 14 September 1685, Hinde was imprisoned in the Fleet for his debts, and within weeks he declared himself bankrupt and his property was seized. A meeting was called for all his creditors to congregate at the Sun Tavern, by the Royal Exchange, to negotiate a return on their money. Hinde died four months later, hoping that the sale of his goods might pay off everyone and leave something over for his wife and children. Frith and Cadogan Thomas both fell into trouble at the same time, and spent the rest of their lives in and out of the debtors' courts. Even by 1720, it was reported that the works were 'not to this day finished, and God knows when it will.'[20]

The 1690s saw a continued slowdown in development throughout the city that, of course, had an impact on the value of land. Nonetheless, the speculators were now deeply involved in the debates on the future of the nation's economy. Debates raged on the nature of money and the correct level of interest. Across the bourse, an overambitious stock price was jokingly dismissed as 'bare-bon'd'.[21] The relationship between land and finance was now firmly established. Land represented not just a place to stash value but also an abstracted, futures market. This was seen in the proliferation of land-based financial instruments, the land bank and the mortgage, to finance and secure deals.

* * *

These machinations and financial instruments were as important to the goings-on at Millbank as within the City walls. While the Manor of Ebury was now Sir Thomas's property, Dame Mary kept an interest in her inheritance. The couple had to continue to work with the Tregonwells, who still had interests in the widow's third of the estate. While development was creeping ever closer to the estate, there were no plans to build beyond the small enclave near Millbank. According to Strype, in 1707, this still marked the western edge of the city:

> that part beyond the Horseferry hath a very good row of houses, much inhabited by gentry, by reason of the pleasant situation

and prospect of the Thames. The Earl of Peterborough's house hath a large court-yard before it, and a fine garden behind it, but its situation is but bleak in the winter, and not overhealthful, as being so near the low meadows on the south and west parts.[22]

A couple of documents remain in the archive in Mary's hand showing her interest in the estate. The first one, dated November 1691, is to her mother. It relates to a lease on land that was part of Mrs Tregonwell's widow's portion. She writes: 'If for the improvement of the Estate I am very willing.' But she slyly hints that her mother should be thinking not just of her profit but what she hands over in the future: 'I won't be so tied up that I cannot give a relation a farthing or leave a legacy where I please.'[23] In the second letter, from 1693, to a certain Moysar, it is clear that she keeps a close eye on dealings with the estate, and is not above wondering how to get more from her tenants: 'I have already signed Crosse's [lease] because Sir Thomas desired it, but I fancy I might have had more rent ... I desire you to let me know the truth' before she signed any other agreement.[24]

Back at Eaton Hall, life within the Grosvenor family continued apace. The new political settlement following the Glorious Revolution of 1688 seems to have had little impact on the domestic politics of the estate. Sir Thomas's political career stumbled when he did not stand in the 1689 election. He was a Tory during a period of Whig preponderance, the first years of the 'double bottom'd' reign of William and Mary. At the same time there were complaints about Mary's open worship; as MP Charles Trelawney noted that September: 'the frequent and great meetings of Roman Catholics every week at Sir Thomas Grosvenor's have occasioned his neighbours to complain of him.'[25] The Earl of Shrewsbury responded that if there were any definitive reports of Jesuits, then the magistrates were to be informed and all participants to be arrested; but such a dramatic intervention was never called for.

In spite of this, Sir Thomas won in the 1690 election and took his seat at Westminster again. Fair to say, however, that he rarely distinguished himself, nor was noted, in Parliament from then on. He was put on a committee to consider 'A Bill of Relief for Poor

Prisoners' as well as an inspection of the Fleet prison, where his grandfather had spent a decade in the 1630s. Closer to home, he campaigned for work to be done to make navigable the River Dee that curled from Eaton to Chester towards the Wirral.

At the same time, for Dame Mary, the life of the politician's wife became dominated by the burdens and joys of motherhood. In 1690, she was twenty-five years old. By this time, she had probably given birth to three boys – for the first two, Thomas and Roger, we do not have their birth dates. However, we can calculate that Mary was probably pregnant for the first time while still a teenager. One might speculate that when she wrote her affectionate letter to Sir Thomas in 1683 from Alstrop, she may have been visiting St Rumbold's Well, a shrine dedicated to the British saint who only lived three days, and was said to intercede on matters of fertility and the blessing of children.

Mary continued the cycle of pregnancy, birth and motherhood for at least fourteen years. Three more boys arrived – Richard came into the world in 1689, Thomas in 1693 and Robert in 1695 – who all survived. And there was also a daughter born in 1700.

The first two boys died at some point in the 1690s, but we cannot be certain exactly when. There was a convention that the first child took on the name of the father, so Thomas probably came first. And after his death, the name was passed on to the next son; so he probably died after 1689 and before 1693. We do not have a date of death for Roger. Neither name appears on the family memorial plaque in St Mary's parish church, Eccleston.

Inheritance absorbs new significance when it takes into account the creation of heirs. A daughter becomes a wife, and then a mother. These are the gradations of female power, especially when it comes to the management of property: Mary's status within the family and household was transformed with each stage. Mary's inheritance was passed from her to her husband at the altar rail at St Clement's, and in the terms of the agreement between Sir Thomas and Tregonwell. Now, Dame Mary's body was the forcing ground from which the future of the Manor of Ebury germinated.

Pregnancy and childbirth are periods of immense risk for both child and mother. In the early modern era it was also a period of contestation that pushed against the rigid patriarchy of the family. While the devotional texts and medical manuals may have preached one thing, what actually occurred through the pregnancy, and then across the precarious hours of childbirth, and the first weeks and months of motherhood, were often in contrast. Pregnancy was not a private matter. As soon as a woman found that she was pregnant, her body was not just her own, but shared with the unborn child, the family and wider society. For Dame Mary, this was even more so.

During this period there were conflicting views about what was happening in the mother's body. Without modern imaging technology, pregnancy was a mystery that mixed medical judgement, religious divinations, and political designations of gender and power. A woman rarely knew she was pregnant until she had missed her period; it would also be diagnosed by how she felt, as one soon-to-be mother told her doctor: she felt 'somewhat roving in her body as if she were quick with child'.[26] Other women noted that they felt their blood congeal or ferment within their bellies.

The traditional view was that the man's seed had entered the woman's womb, where it grew as if in an oven. In this view, 'the wombs were hired by men, as merchant ships'.[27] But there were others who suggested that the mother played an active part in the pregnancy. Nicholas Culpeper wrote: 'your child is nourished by your own blood, your blood is bred out of your diet, rectified or marred by your exercise, idleness, sleep or watching.'[28] In time, it was acknowledged that the mother was at least an essential partner in the nurturing of new life, and therefore had to be looked after during the pregnancy. Rituals and superstitions surrounding the diet, exercise, temperature and mental exertion of the mother during these months were hotly debated and medicalised.

Thus, the welfare of Dame Mary become the public concern of the whole household at Eaton Hall, and probably stretching to Mrs Tregonwell's home at Millbank. There were to be no arduous journeys. A diet was promoted that sought a balance of the humours within the increasingly heated body. There was also recourse to amulets, charms and prayers to protect the unborn baby and the mother. There was a constant fear of miscarriage, which could occur unexpectedly at any stage. There were copious words of advice, manuals and books produced during this period. Sir Thomas's grandmother had kept a recipe book during the 1640s that noted preparations for significant events as well as medicines and potions.

For such a prominent family, a male physician might regularly visit the expectant mother, but as her pregnancy progressed Mary was increasingly surrounded by the women. Female members of staff – maids, cooks and servants – encircled her. As the moment of the birth came closer, a midwife was engaged. By this time, this role had been regulated and licensed. The professionalisation of midwifery also defined the right and wrong ways of giving birth, as well as preventing the worst outcome. Furthermore, local ladies and family friends were probably also involved and, one imagines, Mrs Tregonwell may have made the trip from London as well as one of Dame Mary's three stepsisters. For example, at the moment of the birth, the Yorkshire woman Alice Thornton had six women with her: a midwife, her maid, an aunt, two sisters and a local friend.

When labour began, this exclusively female community swung into action. The role of the man of the house was to keep out of the way, or to fetch and carry. However, he remained close by so that he could come in at the moment of emergency or joy. The room where the birth was going to happen was sealed. Heavy curtains were drawn across the windows. Even the keyholes were stuffed up. The room was dark apart from the fire and the flicker of candles. A womb or a tomb? And within this purposeful murk the women got on with their business: 'the sweat did run down their faces, in performing their work.'[29] According to Genesis the pains of childbirth were Eve's punishment for her transgressions. In addition, birth pains were in proportion to the sins of the mother. So she was expected to suffer in grace. The only salve for the trauma was cups of caudle – warm, sweet and spiced ale or wine, sometimes fortified with an egg yolk to give strength.

The labour could endure for days; mother and child caught between life and death. During the birth of Alice Thornton's fifth child, complications occurred: 'I fell into exceeding sharp travail in great extremity.' But, she continues:

the child stayed in the birth, and came crosse with this feet first, and in this condition continued until Thursday morning … At which time I was upon the race in bearing my child with such exquisite torment, as if each lim[b] were divided from [the other], for the space of two hours; when at length, being speechless and breathless I was, by the infinite providence of God, in great mercy delivered.[30]

Elizabeth Egerton described the 'great torture' of childbirth, and prayed for divine mercy.[31] The event combined to create a diptych of martyrdom and holy deliverance. The darkened room was filled with busying bodies, tending to her needs and witnessing the test with kind words and encouragements.

Once the baby was delivered, the threats were not yet over; there was still plenty of work to do. According to the words of midwife Jane Sharp in 1671, 'Women are in as great danger if not more after the young is born.'[32] The new mother had to expel the placenta, and the lochia, which was considered to be the toxic blood, sweat and waste that had been stored up during the pregnancy. This bleeding could last for up to a month. To retain this blood was considered to be very dangerous and a cause of great illness. Culpeper recommended 'friction of the legs, ligatures and cupping with scarification' to expel the bad humours.[33]

During this time, the mother remained apart from the rest of the house, as in social isolation. For the first few weeks, she accepted only female visitors, apart from close family members. There was an 'up-setting' ceremony when the new mother sat up in bed and was greeted with a fortifying meal with the midwife and others, and plenty of 'gossiping'. This meant that Dame Mary may have missed the baptism of the child in the first week of the birth. Most likely the child was in the hands of a 'monthly nurse' who oversaw the first weeks of the lying-in as Dame Mary recovered. This period ended after about a month when the mother was 'churched', a ritual involving prayers and blessings and symbolic purification. It also marked the taking up, once more, of household duties.

Did Dame Mary breastfeed her sons? It is unlikely. At that time there was a strong turn towards mothers taking on the feeding of their own babies, yet most elite women still tended to use wet nurses. Opinions were changing during this period on whether this was wise or not. The usual period of feeding was between a year and eighteen months, so was a burden on the mother. There were concerns with some mothers finding it difficult to produce milk, or to suckle the baby. There was the problem of sore breasts, which caused pain although not considered life-threatening. Some prided themselves on providing for their own children, while for others it was seen as a social inconvenience. Contemporary writers suggested that it was the husband who demanded the outsourcing of the task, as having sex 'troubleth the blood, and so in consequence the milk'.[34] Maybe Sir Thomas did not want to share his wife with his child; or Dame Mary was happy to hand her sons over to others, just as Mrs Tregonwell had done with her.

In time, Dame Mary returned to being a wife and mother within the machinery of Eaton Hall. There was always some work to oversee, a journey to prepare, guests to receive or visits to make. Whether in London or in Chester, life was on the move. If the diary of Bishop Cartwright, who was in Chester between 1686 and 1689, is a fair witness, the Grosvenors were at the heart of local society. The bishop regularly dined with Sir Thomas 'and his lady', stayed at Eaton Hall, or supped with one or other of them at someone else's house. In November 1686, they ate together six times! There seemed little time for privacy, or quiet moments with the family.

Nonetheless, despite the assistance of maids, cooks and servants, Mary's life was dominated by this constant churn of pregnancy and motherhood, and at times she surely mourned the reduction of her horizons that this imposed. She was still a young woman, who may have felt a terrible sense of missing out while remaining stuck away at Eaton Hall. In a letter to a Mrs Turnour, a visitor to the estate in 1696, whom we will meet properly later, Mary revealed her frustrations: 'Though Chester is so near I scarce ever see it … The players are gone to Shrewsbury from thence. I saw none of their plays.' She goes on, like one of the young characters in an Austen novel, to discuss the recent balls in the city. At one, there was gossip about 'Mrs Booth's daughter, who they say dances the finest in the world. She's a good pretty young widow.' As a dutiful wife she had missed all the fun as Sir Thomas was ill, and she had to stay behind and look after him. Apart from that, she reported on the usual social rounds: 'the ladies play at cards every week at one another's houses, and raffle at the Indian house is all I can tell you.'

The letter signs off: 'My three boys are well, and the eldest much your servant.'[35] This brief adieu is a keen reminder of a terrible absence. By the time Dame Mary was sharing her disappointments with Mrs Turnour, she was also lamenting the departure of two sons, Thomas and Roger. However long they had stayed on Earth, they would have been mourned by all in the family. There are no records of the deaths. We can search for the shadows of their loss in other ways.

Because of the high rate of child mortality, estimated at one in five for one-year-olds, it is assumed by some historians that parents in the early modern era remained emotionally detached from their children, fearing that getting too close might make the loss more unbearable. The employment of wet nurses, maids and tutors freed the adults from obligations of care, and therefore attachment. A child of the very well-off might spend only sporadic times of the year under the same roof as his parents, shuffling between school, universities, uncles and Grand Tours. Nonetheless, within this period there was an increase in parental affections and the first signs of 'the child-oriented society we know today'.[36] That is to say, they showed their affection in different ways, rather than not at all. And this was particularly true of how they mourned the passing of a beloved child.

The letter to Mrs Turnour suggests that Dame Mary had already, or was about to, take her correspondent's brother into the household at Eaton Hall. Lodowick Fenwick, the same man as we saw in Paris, was a Benedictine monk who, at considerable risk to himself, was a missionary about the country. At some point in the late 1690s, he became Dame Mary's confessor. We know little else about how he fitted into the daily workings of the family. He was not involved with the education of the children, as Sir Thomas was adamant that they be raised within the established Church. However, it was clear that Fenwick grew close as a confidant to Dame Mary. He was a comfort to her at the times of her loss, as well as a spiritual guide to the neophyte.

Fenwick came from a respectable Catholic family in Northumberland, yet in recent years they had come unstuck. The head of the family, an uncle, Sir John, had been a general in James II's standing army, and on the accession of William III continued his defiance, plotting against the new Crown. In 1691, he was charged with insulting Queen Mary, and three years later involved in an assassination plot against the king. He was beheaded in 1697. (Sir Thomas Grosvenor was one of the MPs to vote against the Act of Attainder that warranted the execution.) However, the dead rebel did have his revenge, according to Macaulay, when William confiscated one of Fenwick's horses, White Sorrell. Riding out one day on this horse, the king stumbled on a mole hill, and later died from his injuries.

The outer relations of the once prominent Fenwick family were now on their uppers, and were forced to be content to join the army or attend to the religious tuition of the Cheshire elite. As a monk, Lodowick did not have the right to give the sacraments. Nonetheless, on feast days and Sundays, he led the small congregation in prayer. Certainly, the presence of the monk delivered the religious succour that Mary needed as she came to terms with her grief. As a chaplain, he became part of the lady's household, rather than a servant. His presence was noted but he surely maintained a discreet distance from the rest of the family.

Whether Fenwick was on hand to offer consolation during the summer of 1696 is unclear, but at that time Mary fell gravely unwell. Her symptoms were to be examined and probed in intense detail later in the trial of 1703 and all the descriptions of her illness here are taken from those later court papers. Therefore, we must be very sensitive to their intent, as well as explore the language of whoever is in the witness box. First of all, Dame Mary's own views on her mental state were never recorded, and so these prognostications are always through the eyes of others. The outwards signs of her inner turmoil are parsed by doctors, lawyers and priests, as well as friends with Mary's best interests at heart, but they do not necessarily amount to a clinical diagnosis.

Madness has always been a thing observed. There were those who wanted Mary to be mad, and those who did not. Those who cared for her welfare and wanted to see her get the best care, but did not have the language to distinguish one disturbance from another. The language of the age itself was limited and a poor tool to describe the many different states of Dame Mary's mind. Furthermore, the fate of the Manor of Ebury itself depended on the proof, or not, of Mary's mental health. And thus, there were no neutral bystanders.

Reading these eyewitness accounts, Mary was as likely a 'lunatick' as she was fragile, depressed, or broken by grief. It is still heart-breaking to transcribe these events from the original documents that have sat in the archives for over three hundred years and make sense of them from their multiple perspectives, or even to attempt to find the truth. The distance of time does not make the reader any more objective to Dame Mary's plight. She appears as a young woman bound up in confusions, so much so that this anxiety becomes her identity. She needs to escape something, but what? Her home? Her family? The loss of two babies who haunt the corridors at Eaton Hall?

What was madness anyway? In many of the accounts, the expert witnesses cannot agree. Dame Mary herself spoke of the burden of grief, which seems perfectly rational.[37] Others discuss her unbalanced humours, her disposition to melancholia, her muddled brain, her nerves or spleen. For some, that she was a woman was reason enough to think that she was vulnerable. To many, her conversion to Catholicism was a sufficient sign of mental disorder.

The episodes of Mary's sickness also marked the birth of psychiatry, the scientific study of the mind. The mad were no longer blessed or holy fools but a subject for empirical observation. And just as the chemist measured the quantities of air, or the engineer constructed the arch, the emerging natural philosophers of mind were debating how symptoms expressed themselves: what these outward signatures indicated about the inner life of the patient. What mechanical explanation there could be for this aberration. And what medicine, or restrictions, might work to restore or calm the wretched soul.

The mad became a social category. But were the mad excluded as a result of a diagnosis of their behaviour, or was their exclusion enough to call them mad? For some contemporary historians, the social exclusion of the 'mad' came first, before the regimes of scientific measurement were refined to qualify the action. In the case of Dame Mary, what other behaviours were discounted – grief, anxiety, a profound sense of powerlessness – before she was labelled as a madwoman?

In the summer of 1696, according to William Rippon, a servant at Eaton Hall, Dame Mary fell into a deep melancholy. She had given birth to her youngest son, Robert, a year before, but a depression came over her. She started to have anxious fits, and locked herself in her closet. She ran around the room in a panic. She claimed to see 'fantoms' around the room, of 'witches and some persons of quality'.[38] He continued: 'She bid the spirits be gone, and ran to the other side of the room, and I did endeavour to tell them they ought to be gone, which she was pretty well reconciled.'[39] And then, following these moments of raving, she once again fell into deep silences of sadness. These episodes lasted for ten days at least.

The following summer, Dame Mary's condition worsened. There were incidents of uncontrolled rage, and the throwing of 'chyna'.[40] More dishearteningly, she once locked herself into her closet and attempted to throw herself out of the window. William Rippon was there alongside a number of other servants, and he had to take hold of her and prevent her fall. From then on, a servant sat up with her each night, and for a few days a servant was stationed below her window in case she attempted suicide again.

Later that summer, the disturbances continued. One early morning, Rippon found Dame Mary rushing through the Hall, and he called after her. She ignored him and went outside, across the courtyard to the stable, and commanded the groom to prepare a horse. She indicated the largest animal, but the groom suggested that it was too strong for her to ride. She then bolted from there and walked towards the ferry house that stood beyond the house, close by the River Dee. Here, a floating platform connected to a cable strung across the river allowed traffic to cross the waterway. Dame Mary attempted to pull on the cable in order to get across.

At this point, another servant, Rob Davis, rushed to get Sir Thomas who was in the house, and once he had hurriedly arrived he started to talk to his distraught wife. As Davis later recalled: 'all that while she gave him no answer but fell down upon the stones and cried, and Sir Thomas and all that were with him wept.'[41] He picked her up in his arms and carried her back to the house. According to Davis, she once again attempted to escape out of the window after this.

When Sir Thomas was away, sitting in Westminster, a family friend, Sir Thomas Cholmondeley from nearby Vale Royal, visited and oversaw Dame Mary's care. Davis recounts another episode when Mary was wandering through the formal garden around the house, and refused to move from her spot by the half-crescent pond. Cholmondeley went out to try to persuade her back into the house, but he was repelled. The chaplain, presumably Fenwick, also attempted to calm her spirits and bring her back to safety. Davis ended his testimony by noting that he never saw her well again.

How are we to read these moments in the history of madness? On one of her travels to London, Dame Mary, like most of fashionable society, might have visited Moorfields, to the north of the City walls, and have seen the recently completed Bethlem Hospital, designed by Robert Hooke. Here on the imposing façade she may have encountered Caius Gabriel Cibber's dreadful frieze of the two faces of madness that surmounted the portico. On one side stood melancholy, limply lying across a bed of straw, his face vacant; on the other, mania in chains, muscles tensed in anxiety, straining. These were the two poles upon the spectrum of unreason, and were both observed within Dame Mary's disturbed behaviour.

But beyond this, thinkers, anatomists and experimenters were attempting to create a new field of the science of the mind. The traditional image of the fool, blessed or punished by God, was no longer accepted wisdom, and was to be discarded alongside the image of the witch. King Lear's Fool, who spoke truth in nonsense, was seen as a fiction as much as Edgar's performance as Tom O'Bedlam, who spoke madness to hide the truth. These public images of madness were joined by the religious fanatic, the possessed unfortunate, the crushed lover, the boastful fantasist.

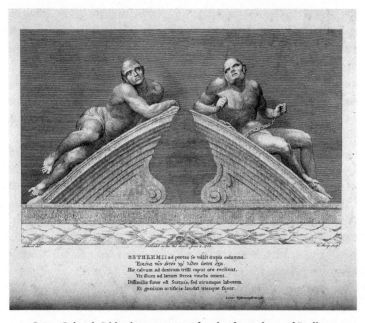

BETHLEMII ad portas se tollit dupla columna.
Ἐκείνα τῶν ἐντός κỵ Λόγι ἐντός ἔχι.
Hic calvum ad dextram tristi caput ore reclinat,
Vix illum ad lævam ferrea vincla tenent.
Dissimilis furor est Statuis, sed utrumque laborem.
Et genium artificis laudat uterque furor.

Caius Gabriel Cibber's two statues for the front door of Bedlam:
'Melancholy' and 'Mania'

Meanwhile, the ancient physicians' theories of the humoral balance of the body were slowly being replaced by the empirical method: diagnosis based upon observation rather than ancient authority. Nevertheless, melancholy remained the totem expression of the disorder. In his magisterial *The Anatomy of Melancholy* of 1621, Robert Burton proposed that madness was widespread, and natural. But the engine of this disorder was within the body, and an affliction that was displayed by degrees: explained by an imbalance of black bile. But how did this happen?

Burton's book is an exhaustive catalogue of symptoms, lore, ancient philosophising, surmising and dubious cures. It is also one of the great works of literature of its age; a more accurate portrait of the early modern *mentalité* than a dry, medical treatise. It is encyclopaedic in its taxonomy of melancholia's many faces. Everyone was melancholy at times, it 'comes and goes upon ever small occasion of sorrow, need, sickness, trouble, fear, grief, passion, or perturbation of the mind'; and the English more than others.[42] It could be caused by the wrong food, bad air, witches and curses, both too much exercise and idleness, God, over-eating, virginity, envy, a love of immoderate gaming, vanity and studying too much, amongst others. But nonetheless it created two divisions of madness: of the body and the mind; and two classes of people: the sane and the insane.

One particular diagnosis deserves closer attention. Subsection IV of the first part is on *Sorrow*. Burton writes: 'In this catalogue of passions, which so much torment the soul of man, and cause this malady, the first place in this irascible appetite may justly be challenged by sorrow … the mother and daughter of melancholy, her epitome, symptome and first cause.'[43] Burton's remedy was moderation in all things: a sensible message for a doctor writing on the cure of social ills in a turbulent age.

Burton was a fine judge of the signatures of the disease, but others wanted to look deeper in the body to fathom the causes of mental anguish. For some anatomists, proof that the womb did not wander around the body put paid to the long-held assumptions concerning hysteria. Instead, they explored the spleen as the seat of black bile. Dr William Stukeley, who was most famous as the first investigator of the ancient monuments at Stonehenge, also went in search of the anatomical proof of the humours. Others, such as Dr John Purcell, searched for a chemical diagnosis, using the latest notions of atoms, proposing that 'raving is produc'd by a Mixture of Heterogeneous Particles with the Spirits, which fermenting with them make their motions violent and irregular in the Emporium of the Brain.'[44]

Thomas Willis was part of the 'invisible college' of natural philosophers who congregated in Oxford in the 1650s, and later became a founder, alongside Christopher Wren, Robert Hooke and Robert Boyle, of the Royal Society. At that time, Willis was cutting into the brain as the location for consciousness. He was the first to identify the fibrous network of cerebral nerves that worked like a tree through the body 'like so many little branches, twigs and leaves', spreading 'animal spirits' throughout the body.[45] Depression was, therefore, 'a complicated distemper of the Brain and Heart; For as Melancholick people talk idly, it proceeds from the vice or fault of the Brain, and the inordination of the Animal Spirits dwelling in it.'

Does this explain Dame Mary's disorder? Her physician could not observe her brain or nervous system in action, but the signatures were noted and parsed. What did animal spirits look like exactly? This line of enquiry offered a stronger, more rational prognosis that did not depend on imps, devils or curses, but it did not necessarily deliver scientific proof on the level of Hooke's development of the microscope and drawing the common flea in dreadful detail. The same method – objective observation, deductive reason that was based on the evidence, a faith in repeatable experiments – was never possible with madness, which remained a socially constructed pathology.

As a result, while these pathologies were perceived as universal, madness was prejudiced, in particular on gender. Even if physicians no longer believed in the peripatetic origins of hysteria, women were still more likely than men to be victims of frenzy or melancholy. It was assumed truth that Eve, once susceptible to the Devil's temptation, now, in the age of reason, had a natural mental frailty. The literary scholar Elaine Showalter divines this in two ways: 'madness as one of the wrongs of women; madness as the essential feminine nature unveiling itself before scientific male rationality'.[46]

As the eighteenth century progressed, the supposed Age of the Enlightenment, the idea of reason itself became gendered. As a result, while more men were diagnosed as insane in the previous century, in the 1700s madness was feminised. And this was proved in the formation of 'the vapours', as a bodily expression of the mental imbalance. Therefore the problem was 'in the body' rather than 'of the mind'. As a consequence, George Cheyne, in his 1733 treatise *The English Malady*, concluded that being 'vapourish' was on the one hand a sign of refinement but, as every social convention has its shadow, women were the weaker sex, therefore were more susceptible to suffering and punished for their frailty.

Furthermore, as historian R. A. Houston points out, it was also possible that 'being classed as insane was an arbitrary act perpetrated on women who simply failed to conform.'[47] The mad woman was, therefore, locked up because she tried to escape (even when escape appeared the most rational action). Escape from what? Convention. The physical spaces that defined womanhood. The stifling rituals of marriage or motherhood. This was particularly true when land or property was under threat. The importance of property as the preponderant logic of society meant that any aberration from the norm was a threat that needed to be seen not just as a crime against ownership but beyond reason. Thus, every account of Dame Mary's trauma, even from the mouths of those who hoped to be her friend, can be interpreted as means of explaining her flight away from the overpowering burden that bedevilled her life, and an attempt to regain some kind of power, a modicum of autonomy. The signs of disturbance cannot be read without knowing of her inheritance. These are the intentions that we must read into the testimonies about Dame Mary as her mind unravelled.

The turmoil continued in 1698. That year, Sir Thomas and his wife came down to London and rented a house in Petty France, a fashionable neighbourhood south of St James's Park, and a short ride from Mrs Tregonwell's house at Millbank. Perhaps the couple came to the capital to consult the finest doctors. Dr John Nicholls later testified that he 'did take her to be mad at a very high degree'. On a series of visits to the house, he observed that the patient 'would be crying out murder, that Sir Thomas was murdered and the children murdered'. She also claimed that great men, 'this prince and the other Duke', were in love with her.[48] A nurse was hired, William Brerewood, who was tasked with looking after her welfare. He broke down the door when she locked herself in a closet, and alongside a clergyman, Charles Maddison, recalled that she sang for two days 'incessantly always in the same tone'.[49] The priest also confirmed that Mrs Tregonwell 'came down and saw her in that condition'.[50]

During that year, the couple also travelled to Bath, alongside Lady Cotton, who later claimed that she never saw Dame Mary disturbed. There is no explanation for this. However, according to other witnesses, taking the waters at Bath did not seem to change

Dame Mary's mental state. That winter, they returned again to London, this time taking a house at Pall Mall. Here, they also received Mr and Mrs Turnour again, who also later reported nothing out of the ordinary. It is possible that Lodowick Fenwick was also within the household at this stage, making the visits of his sister more of an intimate affair rather than a social duty. By the end of the year, there was further good news when it was revealed that Dame Mary was pregnant once more, at the age of thirty-five. It had now been five years since the birth of her last son, Robert.

* * *

However, as winter turned into spring 1700, Sir Thomas fell ill. And as the year progressed, his health did not improve. By the summer, the family were back at Eaton Hall and Sir Thomas was organising his affairs. On 21 June, he made his will, while 'weak of body' but still sound in mind. The house was full with guests and other stewards and servants preparing for the master's final days. Lodowick Fenwick was there, as well as the boys' tutor, Maddison, and Mr Brerewood.

Then, on 2 July, Luttrell's *Relation of State Affairs* reported that 'Sir Thomas Grosvenor member of parliament for Chester, is dead of a feavour.'

'A Woman of Great Estate'

GRIEF IS OVERPOWERING, and in the months following Sir Thomas's death Dame Mary's life must be read through this gauze of loss. Daughter, heiress, wife, and now – at the age of thirty-five – widow, Dame Mary was for the first time in her life in charge of her inheritance. And as a result, she was never more vulnerable and alone. She was, for once, in control of her destiny and, at the same time, at her most incapable of commanding it.

One day in July 1700, Sir Thomas's body was taken to St Mary's Church in Eccleston, and buried in the family vault. Today, the family graves are located beside the old wall of the fourteenth-century church, which was replaced in the nineteenth century and has been allowed to fall into a neatly curated ruin. Sir Thomas was laid to rest alongside his grandfather, the second Baronet, and was later joined by his three sons. In the coming centuries, these ancestors have been joined by later generations of Grosvenors up to the present day. Today, one can read the history of the family through the gravestones, like an ancestral conference.

The funeral itself was intended to manage the relationship between the social ritual surrounding the departure of a potent and wealthy man and an offering of religious comforts to those who mourned him. Sir Thomas was forty-five years old. Life expectancy in that era for a male was thirty-five, but that was because of the dangers faced at birth and in infancy. If an aristocratic man could make it to twenty-one, he was expected to live to at least sixty-four years old.[1] Sir Thomas's departure was therefore a shock to all, even those who had witnessed his recent fever. His decline had been rapid. While he had been able to sort out many of his affairs in his last weeks, there were still to be disruptions and disputes about the future of the estate.

The bells of St Mary's may have rung during Sir Thomas's last days and then again on the day of his funeral; as a mark of respect to the dead, to alert the community to the ceremony, a call to prayer, and a consolation to the grieving. The body was prepared soon after the death. It was washed and dressed. Some aristocratic bodies were embalmed to preserve them for longer. Most likely the body remained at Eaton Hall until the day of the funeral, which was soon after the death. It was common that someone – a family member, a servant, a group of mourners – sat up with the body. It was laid out in a public room and according to Francis Tate, 'covered in a sheet, and candles burning night and day'.[2] John Aubrey notes that such 'watching' could be accompanied by beer, tobacco and gossip, but this was increasingly looked down upon by polite society. In addition, Dame Mary was heavily pregnant and was unlikely to have been able to perform her widow's duties.

On the day of the funeral, the body was wrapped in a wool blanket in accordance with a law enacted by Charles II on behalf of the wool industry. By now, the body was likely to smell and there are plenty of accounts of bodies stinking out a house, especially during the summer months. It was common for local churches to have just one coffin that was reused for each ceremony, but for a figure of Sir Thomas's stature, it is probable that one was made and decorated according to his station. It may have even been lead lined, as well as with velvet, or 'quilted with silks'.

According to merchant Henri Misson, who observed English rituals like an early anthropologist, before one such ceremony, 'the relations and chief mourners are in a chamber apart, with their more intimate friends, and the rest of the guests are dispersed in several rooms about the house,'[3] until they were ready to go. Then, a procession wound its way the mile or so to the church, following the coffin that was probably carried in a carriage or on a hearse.

Once the cart had reached the church porch, there would have been pallbearers – estate workers, or more likely grandees of standing equal to the deceased – who carried the box for the final steps into the nave. A gathering of poor mourners may have clustered by the porch in the hope of receiving dole money from the congregation.

Mary wore her widow's weeds. It was the common practice that after a few days' retreat from society, the bereaved wife returned dressed from head to toe in black. In many wills of the period, provision was set aside for black cloth, and it was not unusual to remain in this mourning garb for a year. For others among the congregation, there were black gloves, black satin hatbands, scarves, black taffeta hoods and cloaks. This was reflected inside the church, where the pulpit was covered in mourning cloth for weeks and parts of the chancel swathed in black for a year.

The eulogy and the blessing were the focal points of the ceremony. Death made all equal before God, but the eulogy was a moment to praise the dead, and to commend his soul to the Lord. It was also a reminder to everyone that death was unavoidable and every mourner should prepare for a good end. Sometimes, these eulogies were printed and shared amongst the congregants as a memorial and a memento mori. And then the mourners gathered around the grave. As Misson continued: 'the guests were around the grave, and do not leave till the earth is thrown in upon it. Then they return home in the same order they came in, and each drinks two or three glasses more before he goes home.'4

Later, in the 1703 trial, it was noted that during Sir Thomas's funeral, the figure of Lodowick Fenwick was in close proximity to Dame Mary. As her chaplain, he might have acted as a raft following the shipwreck, steering her back towards the shore. It is possible that he was the only male that was allowed access to the widow in her moments of darkness, as well as in the weeks of lying-in after the arrival of baby Anne three weeks after the funeral. The mixed emotions of departure and new life surely caused a rupture that discombobulated Mary's fragile mind. Fenwick offered a glimmer of consolation, and Mary was certainly grateful for his steady companionship and counsel.

Sir Thomas's will, signed two weeks before his passing, made Dame Mary a very powerful and rich woman. Their first son, now Sir Richard, was eleven; the second, Thomas, six; Robert, five – and so were all in their minority. The document set out the supervision of the children's education and guardianship to three close relations: Sir Thomas Cholmondeley of the neighbouring estate Vale Royal, who was in his seventies and had been something of a father figure for Sir Thomas. Secondly, his younger brother, Francis Cholmondeley, who had been a fellow MP. In addition was Sir Thomas Cholmondeley's grandson Sir Richard Myddleton, a local land-owner across the border in Wales. These were all blood relatives and trusted friends. The estate, including all the mining interests, was to be passed to Sir Richard when he came to adulthood. Both Thomas and Robert were to get £500 when they reached fifteen and then another £1,000 at twenty-one.

Dame Mary was given her widow's third, and her jointure of £1,000 a year was guaranteed, to be managed by the trustees. She was allowed to keep 'her jewellery, my coach and five horses, all her rings'.[5] And she was also given use of Eaton Hall until the marriage of her eldest son. Most importantly of all, until her eldest son was old enough, Dame Mary was once again mistress of the Manor of Ebury.

On 29 October, a little less than three months after the funeral, Dame Mary signed a lease for ten acres of meadow in Mountfield, and fourteen acres of meadow in Netherfield to John Bowtell and Thomas Atkins, both brickmakers based in Soho.[6] This site was probably a rich source of clay that the craftsmen wanted to use to satisfy the city's almost insatiable appetite for construction. It was fortunate to have the source of supply so close to the building sites of Piccadilly and Bond Street, marking the transition of the land from pasture to the first intimations of the cityscape. More significantly, these were the first leases signed by Dame Mary. Widowhood had liberated the woman, married at twelve, from the legal death of couverture, and allowed her to be in possession of her inheritance. It was also the last lease that she was to sign.

* * *

For the month following Anne's birth, Dame Mary lay in until her churching ceremony some time at the end of August. It was a disconcerting ritual without Sir Thomas by her side, but Lodowick Fenwick was there to offer his support whenever necessary. In addition, long-standing servants such as William Brerewood had remained to attend their lady during the first months of mourning. The Cholmondeleys were always close by too, ready to offer assistance and consolation.

What went through Dame Mary's mind in her seclusion? As she moved about her rooms, shut away from the rest of the goings-on in the house, she thought about getting away. And these yearnings soon turned into a determination to leave Cheshire for London, as soon as possible. Sir Thomas Cholmondeley 'endeavoured what he could to stop her', but his exhortations fell on deaf ears.[7] What was to happen to Anne and the boys? Was it not too early to be rushing to the capital so soon after the funeral? In response to Mr Brerewood's cautions, Mary first demanded that he come with her, and then changed her mind and informed him that she had no use for him. In his later court statement, Brerewood observed that during this period Dame Mary was 'never composed, always disordered. I never saw her composed for 1/2 hour.'[8] He further informed the court that he was not able to restrain her, despite her disturbed mental state: 'I had not power over her … she was governed by the Priest.'[9]

And so it was only Dame Mary and Lodowick Fenwick and servants that travelled to Millbank that September, leaving everyone else behind. Mary moved into her mother's house, while she also made arrangements for her own house to be redecorated for the mourning. During that month, an inventory of all the house possessions was made, from the fabrics and tapestries, bed linen, plate and gold, and a complete list of titles in the library, to the more fashionable items all in the modish Indian styles.[10] However, it was soon clear to Mrs Tregonwell as well as Mary's three stepsisters that the new widow was not planning to stay in London. She had fixed her mind towards travelling to the continent; in particular, she wanted to go to Rome. Fenwick took charge of making the arrangements. This raised a question that never went away: was it his idea in the first place, which he then planted in Mary's mind?

In the later trial, William Dockwra, Alexander Davies's former solicitor and a family friend, revealed that he had known Mary since she was an infant and also admitted that, during this time, he and Mrs Tregonwell discussed whether to have Dame Mary certified as a lunatic. There is no other mention of this course of action anywhere else in the trial or family papers; it could easily have been imagined in hindsight as an opportunity missed and then optimistically inserted into the history. But it is a significant point of information. This was not a question of obtaining a medical diagnosis. The lawyer was discussing a legal procedure that gave a power of attorney over all of Mary's property. The estate finances would be taken away and looked after by trustees or the Chancery. There were no rulings concerning confinement, nor about what Mary needed to recover her state of mind.

However, Dockwra and Mrs Tregonwell decided against this course of action, for the sake of the children: 'we considered she was a woman of considerable estate, and her eldest son, Sir Richard, a Baronet of this kingdom, and ingenious hopeful young gentleman, who might suffer much in his fortune hereafter, if she his mother be proved a lunatic upon record, and therefore we did forebear it.'[11] Who would marry a young aristocrat with a mad mother and an estate bound up in complex legal chicanery? Once again, what was best for Mary was not the primary consideration for anybody who should have had her welfare in mind.

Perhaps only Fenwick cared. And through September he set about putting the arrangements together for the travels abroad. Firstly, who was to be part of the tour's party? At the end of the month, Mary and the priest travelled to Parndon in Essex to see her old friend, and Lodowick's sister, Mrs Turnour. It was suggested that she came with Mary, and brought her daughter, who was sickly and might benefit from the fresh continental air. There was some deliberation between Mr and Mrs Turnour, yet in the end the husband relented, with the reservation that his family go no further than Paris.

It seems like a very pleasant visit, seeing old friends, yet the absence of Sir Thomas would have been palpable. The last time they had been all together at Pall Mall the previous year, he had seemed healthy. Now he had gone, and the whirl of organising for the travels ahead did not hide the loss. However, there was a new guest to the party who might have lifted the atmosphere: Edward Fenwick, Lodowick's brother. He was formerly an officer in the Duke of Hamilton's regiment but now discharged. The poor brother of a knight, a nephew of a gentleman of great estate, educated, and seemingly honourable. Unfortunately, he had little but his breeding to prove that he was worthy of attention. Nonetheless, his company seems to have improved Dame Mary's mood, making the weekend together a very pleasurable late summer excursion out of the city.

At some point during the weekend, Mary was with Mr Turnour and Edward Fenwick when, in a playful moment, her servants brought her an old wedding veil. Mary was still in mourning, dressed in her widow's weeds and she pushed the veil away, not wishing to be part of the game. Yet, changing her mind in a flash, she turned to the men in the room, and asked Mr Turnour what he thought about her remarrying. She then looked to Edward Fenwick and said, according to Mr Turnour: 'I will tell you what husband I should like best. He must be a Roman Catholic, a well bred man, one of middle age. If he were a well bred man … she did not care whether he had a farthing in the world.'[12] It is a statement that needs to be served with a handful of salt, describing Fenwick almost too perfectly. Turnour was not a neutral bystander, even when standing in the witness box and having sworn to tell nothing but the truth.

After the weekend in Essex, Dame Mary returned to London, where her chaplain set about preparing the servants who were to travel with them. Dame Mary was to bring her own servants: Mrs Cookson, a maid from Eaton Hall, as well as Will Jennings who had formerly served as her footman. In addition, Fenwick hired three more servants. One, Mrs Selby, was hired a week before they set off. The other two did not join the party until they were on their journey. Tom Miller was contracted in London but was told to take the coach to Dover and meet the party at the quay. Another footman, Tom Lodge, was taken on once they reached Calais. Each was an important witness to what went on next.

There were only a few final things to do in London before heading off. Dame Mary was busy with her stepsisters going about town. One peculiar point for the widow's to-do list was to have her portrait painted, and she commissioned Michael Dahl. Born in Stockholm, Dahl came to London in the 1680s where he worked alongside Sir Thomas's portrait painter, Sir Peter Lely. Converting to Catholicism during a trip to Rome did not necessarily seem to hamper his career. Rather, he gained a reputation for his series of eight full-length paintings, later called the 'Petworth beauties', as they were commissioned by the Duke of Somerset and placed in his new home at Petworth, Sussex, which displayed some of the leading ladies in Tory society. He was on the verge of becoming the favoured painter of Prince George of Denmark, husband of Princess (soon to be Queen) Anne. Who better to capture Dame Mary at this moment of self-invention?

Who is the woman in the painting? She is literally shrouded in grief. She appears to be trapped within her widow's clothes. A heavy black hood covers her head, while a white ruffled cap encircles her face. The viewer is drawn to her eyes, searching for signs of the person within, and she seems to be looking back at us, but giving away little. Her mouth remains closed, in silence. Her right hand emerges out of the black cloth, fringed, once again, by white ruffles, but is empty, neither resting nor pointing. Somehow, Dahl struggled to find the widow's spirit. One of the criticisms of his work was his failure to capture the baroque sense of movement and dynamism. Was it unfinished? There is no background, placing Dame Mary within a place or a symbolic constellation. Did he miss Dame Mary's determination to find a new life for herself? The result is enigmatic. Dame Mary is both the mourner and the mourned. She is preparing for a voyage, but parts of her have already departed.

Finally the day of departure, near the end of October. A small sending-off party was arranged at Millbank. Dame Mary, Lodowick Fenwick, Mr and Mrs Turnour and their child, Mary's three stepsisters and brothers-in-law, various Fenwick relations: Francis Radcliffe, a Mrs Foster, a Mrs Buckle, and Edward Fenwick, who had travelled up to London from Essex. The party appeared to be jolly, but at one point, Dame Mary, observing that Mr Fenwick was talking to her stepsister, Mrs Seymour, remarked that she might get jealous of the attention he was giving her. At least two witnesses later suggested that she attempted to persuade Mr Fenwick to follow the party to Paris. Such apparent favours can be interpreted in any number of ways, and used in the future to substantiate one narrative or another. As one lawyer weaved it: Dame Mary 'gave so great intimations to him and distinguished him from all the rest with her favourable carriage that they all did see she encouraged in what he had begun.'[13] But eventually, the party seemed to go off with a cheer and Radcliffe and others watched from the riverbank as the party crossed the Horse Ferry towards Lambeth and took their coach towards Dover.

* * *

Once in Paris, rooms were arranged at the Hôtel Grand Monarque in Faubourg St Germain, on the left bank of the Seine. They stayed at least ten weeks here, and in that time they explored the city as well as socialising with the English community in the French capital. In particular, they mixed with the Catholic exiles, the Jacobites, that had gathered as part of the court of the defeated James II. Since 1688, when he had been forced to flee London, James had been given a chateau at Saint-Germain-en-Laye, and now survived on hand-outs from his cousin, Louis XIV, while cherishing ever-receding dreams of regaining the English throne. Unsurprisingly, as a result, the city was a nest of spies, intrigue and rumour, and the newly arrived tourists needed to be vigilant about who to trust or believe.

By 1700, the 'Great Century' of Parisian preponderance was coming to an end, outshone by the new sun of London. But until this moment, Paris had been the capital of the seventeenth century, reigned over by the absolute monarch Louis XIV, who had been in power since 1643. During this period, the city had been governed and developed in a way that Charles II or James II had never been able to achieve in London. The Bourbon kings, since Henri IV, aspired not just to survive but to obtain 'la gloire', and this was displayed in the fabric of the city itself. New neighbourhoods in the modern style had emerged on both sides of the river, as well as elegant bridges, theatres, and impressive places of worship with domes rising into the urban skyline. It was the national centre for trade and industry. However, it was no longer the locus of political power, since Louis XIV had moved to nearby Versailles in the 1680s. As a result, the city felt more a vestibule than a powerhouse.

Dame Mary and her party hired a coach and horses to take them around the city. From the Grand Monarque, they would have travelled northwards towards the river, Notre Dame on the Île de la Cité dominating the skyline, as well as the other monuments to the medieval city: the Sainte-Chapelle, the Conciergerie and the Hôtel Dieu, which in recent years had been transformed into one of the first state-run asylums for mentally disturbed patients. Despite the recent innovations in London since the fire, they would have still marvelled at Paris's modern architecture. The Collège des Quatre-Nations stood on the south bank of the Seine, bequested by Cardinal Mazarin in the 1660s and designed by Louis Le Vau, whose signature could be found across the modern cityscape. Crossing the Pont Neuf, they may have noticed the Place Dauphine, the inspiration for the familiar squares that were emerging in London at that time. Continuing over the Seine, they would have found it impossible not to wonder at the palace in front of them, the Louvre. For sheer size, the palace was unlike anything that the visitors might have encountered before. They would have marvelled at the recently completed colonnade that ran along the eastern façade. Designed by a committee of architects including Le Vau, Charles Le Brun and Claude Perrault, it was a shining example of modern classicism on a vast scale. Louis XIV had wished to build a new Rome and here one might imagine that he really was the 'Sun King'.

One of the first people that Dame Mary was introduced to in Paris was Mr John Errington, a Northumberland relation of the Fenwicks, who introduced the party to the exiled Jacobite community. Now, eleven years after the Glorious Revolution, only the most dedicated or desperate remained in Paris to support and plot the return of James II to England. Only three years earlier, Louis had made peace with William and James's political games were over.

By 1700, the ex-king himself seemed to have given up hope and spent more time in prayer than in conspiracies. Nevertheless, a community of chancers, Catholic fundamentalists and mercenaries flapped around the court like moths around a guttering candle. As the British ambassador reported: 'they see every day new faces, who come to make their court there [but] there are few of note that go.'[14]

Dame Mary also met, or remade her acquaintance of, William Delaval, a soldier who had once been quartered at Chester, knew Sir Thomas and was occasionally mentioned in Bishop Cartwright's diary. A Jacobite, Delaval was now in Paris waiting for muster, kept alive with a pension from the French king. A Francis Moore also later mentioned in his diaries that he often saw Dame Mary within the company of known leading Catholics. Mary also paid a visit to Lady Manchester, the ambassador's wife, to pay her respects. A Joseph Byerley seemingly had some contacts with the exiled court. Dame Mary was keen to meet the young, supposed Prince of Wales, James II's son, and she asked this gentleman to show her where the Prince went hunting so that they could follow the chase. On another occasion, he invited Dame Mary to dine, but Fr Fenwick politely declined the offer, suggesting that they have a cold supper together instead. Instead, Byerley escorted Dame Mary to Versailles to see the departure of the Duke of Anjou. This was an event that sent waves across Europe, and by chance impacted Dame Mary's future as well.

That year, far away in Madrid, Carlos II of Spain was dying and the continental royal houses were preparing to pounce on the empty throne. At the time, Spain owned lands in Italy, Holland, America and East Asia, and whoever held the throne tipped the balance of global power. As a direct family relation, the Habsburg Emperor Leopold in Vienna considered his line the rightful heirs, in particular his younger son, Charles. Unsurprisingly, Carlos's brother-in-law Louis XIV also showed an interest. At the same time, William III in England as well as the Dutch Republic felt that they needed to be part of the debate as they could not allow Louis XIV to become even more powerful without a fight. England, Holland and France started to negotiate over dividing up the spoils.

Rather than split it up, the Treaty of London gave it to the Viennese Archduke Charles. However, as the Spanish king breathed his last, he was persuaded to change his will and passed the title to Philippe, the Duke of Anjou, Louis XIV's seventeen-year-old second-eldest grandson.

On 16 November, at Versailles, Louis XIV proclaimed his grandson the new King of Spain. It was a deal that had been conducted in secrecy but was announced with a fanfare. And so in the shimmering Hall of Mirrors, Louis, with his grandson by his side, met with the Spanish ambassador and announced 'Monsieur, here is the King of Spain.' The ambassador then knelt and kissed the Duke's hand and spoke in Spanish, to which Louis replied, 'It is for me to speak; he does not understand Spanish.'[15] The British ambassador reported back that the news caused a stir within the Jacobite community as they scented advantage: 'there is great joy at Germain. The late king [James II] goes this day to visit on the Duke of Anjou.'[16] Messengers had also been sent to Scotland to rally supporters. Could this be enough cause for another insurrection?

A few weeks later, Dame Mary and Mr Byerley were there at Versailles when the Duke of Anjou, now Philip V, set off to his new realm. In André Le Nôtre's elegant gardens, the water fountains and spouts had been turned on, and so the Grand Canal became a circus of rainbows, sprays and gurgling music. A suitably impressive retinue of over forty coaches was assembled and in his departure speech Louis portentously announced, 'There are now no Pyrenees; two nations that have for so long been rivals will in future be a single people.' It was easier said than done; in less than six months, war beckoned and Philip had already sworn: 'I would rather go back to being Duke of Anjou, and I can't stand Spain!'[17]

It was also time for Dame Mary and her party to move on to Rome. Not all of the party planned to continue the tour, and so it was time for farewells. Firstly, as promised to her husband, Mrs Turnour and her daughter were to return to England. And so they departed after the child was taken to Saint-Germain-en-Laye and ritually touched for the evil by James II. Furthermore, Dame Mary was persuaded by Fenwick to let go of her own cook-maid and footman. The departure of the maid, Mrs Cookson, was unusual. It is suggested in later testimony that Dame Mary had got it into her head that her maid should go to a nunnery, which Mrs Cookson was in no way inclined to do. However, to satisfy her mistress, she spent a handful of nights in an Augustine convent but then came out. Dame Mary was enraged by this act of defiance and sent Mrs Cookson back to England. The footman Will Jennings went with her. There was now no one left in the party who had known Dame Mary from Eaton Hall and her old life. So, in the first weeks of 1701, Lodowick Fenwick, Dame Mary, the maid Mrs Selby, a French footman and Tom Miller all set off southwards towards Lyon, Genoa, and to Rome.

* * *

Dame Mary was not alone in heading towards the city at the centre of the Catholic Church, for 1700 had been proclaimed a Jubilee Year by Pope Innocent XII. This was an important event in the Church calendar that offered pilgrims to St Peter's special blessing and absolution. A Jubilee was intended to be held every fifty years or so, but often new Popes called for the celebration to mark their inauguration or when the Church needed to fill its coffers with pilgrims' coins. There had been one in 1650 and in 1675. Clearly, Dame Mary had missed the 1700 celebration by the time she arrived in March 1701, but fortunately, Innocent had died the previous November, and was replaced by Clement XI, who commanded that the Jubilee continue for a further year. And so, when the English party eventually arrived beside the River Tiber, the city was still in the midst of a mass pilgrimage.

Another traveller, under the anonymous title 'An English Gentleman', penned an account of his travels on foot from London to Rome in 1700. Even before he had reached the city, he found himself within a mob of penitents making their way to the Vatican: 'the whole world were jogging on in disorder towards a general tribunal, Bishops in coaches, poor priests in foot, Gentlemen on horses, beaus upon mules, pilgrims upon asses and they moved on higgle-de-piggle-de, like Don Quevedo's Revel-rout, when they were running headlong to the devil.'[18] The catalogue of sites visited by the author is probably similar to that of every visitor to the Eternal City: he was stunned by the ancient ruins as well as the more recent attempts to fashion a baroque metropolis. There seemed little time for actual religious observance amongst the sightseeing.

On the first day of the Jubilee, struck with infirmity, Innocent XII was too ill to open the gates to St Peter's himself and let the pilgrims in. Church bells rang. Cannons were fired. A Bull written by the absent pontiff was read out. A cardinal took a ceremonial hammer to the gates which only fell on the third attempt 'as flat as a flounder' and entered the cathedral, followed by the sea of pilgrims. The city was now filled with an 'innumerable concourse of strangers ... so incredibly great, that the country adjacent is scarce able to supply them with provisions, and the poorer sort are almost ready to petition the Pope to feed 'em by a miracle.'

Into this bustle arrived Dame Mary and Fenwick. The city had recently been further agitated by the recent coronation of the new Pope Clement XI. Whatever else Dame Mary did in Rome is sparsely noted; nonetheless, she wrote to her banker in Paris, Mr Arthur: 'I am come safely and well here, tho' the fatigue of the journey was tedious and strangely troublesome ... I have seen all the fine churches, palaces, and Gardens, and the Pope and his travelling equipage ... I have bought some pictures and feel foolish to loose my money, however, I like them tho' not much worked.' Like all tourists in Rome, she also admitted exhaustion. There is truth in there being too much of a good thing; she signs off: 'I am clogged with Princes and palaces, I hope to dye a country farmer with four or five servants in grief.'[19]

Dame Mary socialised with the leading Catholic exiles in the city. The English exiled community was particularly agitated at the time as they were hoping to ensure that the new Pope endorsed James II, and not William III, as the rightful King of England. She took lodgings near Trinità dei Monti, at what would later be at the top of the Spanish Steps, and visitors paid their respects and later took note of her behaviour. Mr Thomas Price, who visited along-side a Mr Whitley, found Dame Mary 'disordered in her mind'.

Later they attended a music concert together and Dame Mary 'talked very loud and extravagant, and disturbed the company'. Price was surprised to note that Fr Fenwick rebuked her roughly as he attempted to calm her down. The servant Tom Lodge also saw his mistress unwell for the first time. According to him, 'she ran out very much and talked of strange things.'[20] She claimed she was richer than the king (which, if she meant James II, was probably true). Was this the return of Mary's disturbances of mind? Was the strain of travel getting too much? Or perhaps Mary was discovering that no matter the distance travelled one could not escape grief.

During this period, a letter arrived for Dame Mary from Edward Fenwick. Depending on who was later being interrogated, this had, or did not have, a profound impact on the widow. According to Mrs Selby, there had been a previous letter in Genoa, but this one in Rome was different. Mary bounded into her chambers, clutching the note and told her maid to read it. As she told the lawyers: 'I found the intents of Mr Fenwick a great way towards courtship to my lady.'[21] Mary swore Mrs Selby to say nothing about this to Fr Fenwick. But she did start thinking of returning to Paris. On the other hand, Tom Miller, the footman, had no recollection of a letter at all.

By this time, Edward Fenwick had made it to Paris. After waving his brother off from Millbank the previous October, he had gone to Yorkshire to stay with family. After that, he had been persuaded by his relation Francis Radcliffe, who had been at the party too and had observed the chemistry between him and Dame Mary, that he should follow her to Paris and pursue a possible courtship. Hadn't there been something in Parndon, when they first met? Didn't Dame Mary also pay him attention at the leaving party? Radcliffe was keen to encourage his cousin to believe that there had indeed been a spark, and that it was worth risking it all to go to France. Fenwick had as much right as any other man to be loved by the wealthy widow. But once Fenwick made it to Paris, he discovered he was too late. He thought about continuing on to Rome but he did not have the money. Instead he remained and became a tutor to a rich young

English traveller, and waited for the party to return. In the meantime, he wrote two letters to Dame Mary. The first that arrived in Genoa, the second in Rome.

Whatever was in the letter, and regardless of whether it had changed her mind, Dame Mary was not well and it was agreed to leave Rome sooner rather than later. The British Catholic Bishop Ellis was there to see them off and they made their way via Loreto, Mantua and Modena to Lyon. Here, Mary's condition was so bad that the party had to halt their journey and, just before the feast of Corpus Christi, they took rooms at 'L'Ecu de France on Lanthorn St'. The landlady, Margaret Pevet, later reported what a state Mary was in: she was 'disturbed in her mind, and in a delirium, so that a bathing tub was brought to bathe her by the prescription of physicians that came to visit her'.[22] After three days, she was moved to another hostel at 'the sign of the Savage', on Place des Terreaux.

What happened over the next few weeks in Lyons as Dame Mary recovered is contested. However, both sides would later agree that she was ill and needed the attention of physicians, to make diagnoses and prescribe drugs and potions, and surgeons, to administer bleedings to purge the heat from her blood. Mrs Selby suggested that her mistress had been disturbed by the journey, but that she had taken her medicine without fuss and by the end of three or four weeks the party was ready to move onwards to Paris again. The footman, Miller, also attested that Mary had been ill in Lyons for four or five days, but throughout the ordeal remained rational, took her medicine without complaint and spoke clearly.

Nonetheless, access to her rooms was now rigorously policed by Lodowick Fenwick, who did not want Dame Mary to be disturbed. Other reports suggested that during this period of bed rest, she had tried to escape. On one occasion, she had launched herself at the window and thrown all her money out into the street below; in another account it was only a gold snuff box that was defenestrated. In a further version, later gathered by investigators, she had even attempted to throw herself from the window, but was held back by the chaplain and the footman. Fenwick was forced to nail the windows shut after this episode. Tom Lodge recalled that she had at one time tried to escape into the street dressed in a waistcoat and smock. As a consequence, she was dosed with medicine to cure and calm her. She was also bled both in her arm and her feet.

Her defence lawyer offers an even more stark account of what happened: at times she was held down by force in her bed as her fits took hold of her. Furthermore, her room was filled with fine china, and on one occasion 'all of which must be upon a frolic destroyed'. Then 'she fancied she could fly, and thought she could throw herself out of the window and do no hurt – and would have done so had she not been prevented.'²³

Nonetheless, Dame Mary did appear to recover and the party started on the journey again to Paris, via Roanne and Orléans. In total, the trip took another three weeks and so, on the evening of Sunday 12 June 1701, the party reached the Hôtel Castile on Rue Saint-Dominique. Dame Mary made her way to her rooms, facing the gardens, and took straight away to her bed, exhausted and the worse for wear from the journey. Meanwhile, Lodowick Fenwick busied the servants and footmen with sorting out all the goods and luggage. News of their arrival had been sent ahead to contacts such as Dame Mary's banker, Mr Arthur, and Edward Fenwick. The grand tour was nearing its end, and some in the party may have been hoping to see England again soon and to return to regular living after so many dramas and travails.

* * *

There is a document in the Eaton Archives, put together by one of the defence lawyers in 1703, setting out the chronology of events of what happened in the week after the 12th, for their case. This is where the lawyer and the historian diverge, even if the methods are similar. The sheet is the size of an open elephant folio volume, folded into eight sections. Two handwritten columns snake across the page, stitching together the witness statements from the various characters involved. Errors or inconsistencies are cross-referenced. Lacunae are explained away or widened. Counterfactuals are challenged with alternative interpretations of the same facts. An argument is constructed architecturally, building a world in which the actions happened like this, or that, to the exclusion of all other possibilities. Can a historian be so certain?

Section from the 1739 Turgot map, showing the Rue Saint-Dominique

The historian uncovers the sequence of events, creating a timeline upon which the known events are ordered, to discern what is important and what is of lesser impact. And from this chronology an understanding of the past emerges, a proposal of what happened is formulated, what it all signifies is argued. New documents, new revelations alter the timeline, the meaning is contested, the significance of each part and how it relates to the others is a matter of debate; the job is never complete.

The work of history is never finished, it remains shrouded in doubt. But the historian is also a detective. There is a determination in this to uncover or construct the truth: it is, in the end, only a very contingent estimation of what happened. The forensic investigations of the sleuth must sift through the rooms, objects and artefacts of the event, and also listen to testimony. This means not just marking down the words spoken, but the bearing of the speaker, what they saw and what they missed out of their account. The timeline is no longer just a chronology but a filigree mesh of causes, intentions, happenstance, as well as lies, subterfuge and disguises.

History also layers the sensibilities of one age upon the other. The researcher looks back in time towards another moment where things were done differently, feelings were expressed in ways we no longer fully appreciate, actions are judged by new standards. But can we withdraw all moral judgement on these historical figures because they are in the past? Dare we attempt to impose psychological states upon their actions, even if they themselves would not have recognised them? Is this a story we can thread together without also bringing to bear contemporary concerns of power, gender, #MeToo? Is it possible to be truly impartial?

What actually happened, day by day, in the week after Dame Mary arrived at the Hôtel Castile will never be completely known. It is a story that is constructed from many voices: a narrative that needs to be told more than once, from different viewpoints, before we can even weigh up the chances of what occurred in those rooms, over three hundred years ago. More importantly, it emerges despite the silence of the woman at its heart, Dame Mary. This raises questions of who speaks for whom. Does one perspective carry more weight than another? And what imbalances of power does this reveal?

After the late arrival on the Sunday evening, Dame Mary remained in her chamber on Monday. She was tired after her long journey, and did not want to be disturbed. She refused to see anyone, except the servant Mrs Selby, who unpacked her things and arranged the rooms. She had argued with Lodowick Fenwick on the final stage of the trip over a dog, but he now acted as gatekeeper, restricting access to his mistress. He undoubtedly was in contact with Mr Arthur, the banker, who came to ensure that all was in order. The priest had probably enquired about a good doctor within the English community that could attend to Dame Mary, who was once again showing the same signs of mental strain she had displayed in Rome and Lyons. Mr Arthur gave the recommendation of a Dr Ayres. Edward Fenwick was also keen to come and pay his respects. He wrote a note that was delivered to the hotel, but he was told – probably by his brother but in Dame Mary's voice – that she was 'tired with her journey' but to come tomorrow, when she may be feeling better able to receive guests. So, Monday passed without much drama, and plenty of rest.

Tuesday morning was also quiet. More rest. At midday, visitors arrived and Dame Mary received them in the garden beyond her rooms. In the early afternoon, Edward Fenwick arrived and joined the party. Seemingly, he was welcomed by Dame Mary, who was pleased to see him. Mrs Selby watched, spied perhaps, from inside the house as the events unfolded outdoors. Soon, the couple were left to themselves and shared three or four hours together. That evening they dined with Mr Arthur and Lodowick Fenwick. That night, Dame Mary went to her chambers and appeared to sleep well.

Wednesday 15th started with activity. At some point in the day Dr Ayres was called for and came to the rooms. At first he was sent away but he came back in the afternoon and discussed Dame Mary's condition with the chaplain. The doctor prescribed an emetic of 1 oz of crocus metallorum. This common purgative, made from antimony and sodium, was used to cause expulsion and vomiting in the patient, ridding the body of an excess of phlegm. The procedure was intended to expel the impurities from the blood, and to dispel Dame Mary's lethargy. The medicine was left with Fr Fenwick and Mrs Selby to dose the patient at the appropriate moment. This was offered that night in a drink but not taken. Edward came again that evening and spent some time with Dame Mary.

On Thursday, at about eleven in the morning, Dame Mary requested 'a drinke and a crust', and the emetic was poured into a glass and given to her, disguised in the wine. According to the landlady, Madame Dufief, this was strong medicine. She found 'madam upon her belly, on the bed'; she 'mashed her teeth and was in a sort of convulsion.'[24] Dame Mary was screaming that she felt like death and demanded any relief from this torture. The doctor was hastily recalled, and was shocked to see the patient's condition. He arrived via the apothecary with medicine to treat an 'over purgation'. He told the landlady to prepare milk with a dose of violets. When she did not have any, she used honey instead, and then administered it herself to Dame Mary as a 'clyster', to wash out the emetic.

This calmed Dame Mary's stomach but she was still fitful and distressed by the experience. In response, Dr Ayres prescribed 'chicken water' laced with laudanum, opium dissolved in alcohol, purchased from the apothecary on Rue de Buci. The doctor requested that the drug also be ordered in pill form, each lozenge containing two grains of opium each. For the rest of the day, Dame Mary refused to take any more medicine, probably suspecting another purgative, although it may have been put into her wine that evening. Mr Arthur came to visit but was kept waiting. In contrast, Edward Fenwick came too and, as Mrs Selby was keen to note, he was allowed in without hesitation.

Friday began with the doctor arriving at the rooms at the Hôtel Castile once more, this time with his surgery kit. It had been decided to bleed Dame Mary in order to rebalance her humours, which were now dangerously out of kilter. Dr Ayres claimed that the patient was still disturbed but calm, and remained in bed throughout the procedure. He cut her right arm and took about 10 oz of blood. He also prescribed the laudanum, advising no more than eighteen drops every four hours. Clearly, after she had lost so much blood, she needed something to restore her, but this needed to be disguised. Chicken water was once again suggested. And she was offered laced wine. Furthermore, at lunch she was cooked a pair of poached eggs, on which was sprinkled the laudanum pill. She was only able to finish one of the eggs and send the half-finished plate back to the kitchen.

That afternoon, Edward Fenwick came to visit again, and there were some private discussions between the pair. The later silences of the main figures within the narrative – Dame Mary, Edward, Lodowick – mean that any kind of true account of the events of what was said between the pair is beyond reach. Cicero's dictum, *Cui bono?* – who stands to benefit? – may be our only guiding light through the labyrinth. Mrs Selby was certain that the subject of this exchange was marriage. According to the maid's testimony, Dame Mary then spoke to her chaplain and told him that he should marry the couple. In another overheard conversation, this one with Edward, he stated that he was not in a position to marry, yet hoped she would consider it: 'he was the younger brother and had no other proposal to make than that of being a very good husband for her and her persuasions were such as he hoped to receive a favourable answer.'[25] He left at about seven or eight o'clock that night, making his apologies, which irked Dame Mary, who rebuked him: 'nobody should do this but him.' Whatever 'this' was: leaving, asking for her hand, making demands?

But that was not the end of it. After supper, a plate of strawberries was brought to the table and placed in front of the chaplain and his mistress. In the fruit on the side of the plate facing Dame Mary, according to one of the servants, the stalks had been pulled out and a grain of laudanum carefully placed inside the hollow, and the stalk then replaced. There is no record of how many strawberries were eaten that night. Yet later that evening, Dame Mary was still up, and deeply agitated. She called for her servants and demanded that the footman, Tom Miller, go to the Grand Monarque, where Edward was staying, and bring him back here to her rooms immediately.

The distance between the two hotels is unclear, but Miller went out in the city night, and returned empty-handed. He could not find Fenwick. Rather than accepting this situation, Dame Mary sent Miller out again. He must find Fenwick, she demanded, come what may. Again, Miller ventured out but came back some time later with bad news. Fenwick could not be found anywhere. By this time, it was close to eleven o'clock, but Dame Mary was determined, and so commanded the French footman to go out and find the object of her desire. Eventually, he was found and came to the hotel, where he was met by his brother and taken to Dame Mary's rooms.

What happened next is as uncertain as any other episode in the story. Mrs Selby could not say whether Dame Mary was asleep at the time Edward met Lodowick and together they entered her rooms. Mrs Selby sat up outside her mistress's rooms until two in the morning and did not see him leave, and so went to bed herself. The next morning, when she went into the room she found Dame Mary in bed with Edward beside her. What had happened during the early hours of the morning?

Was Mrs Selby complicit in this compromising situation? What should a maid have done in this scenario? Do as she was told or protect her mistress and face the consequences? Within a couple of hours of Mrs Selby discovering the couple in the same bed, she was called again into the room to be a witness for their marriage. The footman, Tom Miller, was also called in and told to take part in the ceremony. Both were rewarded with two louis d'or for their service. Meanwhile, Lodowick Fenwick, dressed 'such as other gentlemen wear' rather than in a priest's habit, spoke the sacred words of union. The chaplain prayed in Latin and, when rehearsing the vows and calling the two servants to bear witness, in English. This seemed to everyone involved a most informal ceremony, tawdry even. Hasty. Driven by passions. Not respectable by any definition.

Mary remained propped up in her bed throughout the whole ceremony and whispered her lines, while Edward perched on the bed in his clothes. The chaplain asked the supposed bride to speak up. When asked why she muttered so softly, she said that she 'spoke no louder when she married Sir Thomas'. But this murmur can be interpreted a number of ways. Then, in 1677, she had been a twelve-year-old girl, possibly scared, doing the bidding of her family without knowing what was happening. Is this what she meant? Or was it meant to indicate that this union, unlike the former, was a love match, her voice broken with emotion? Or was she in a daze, being commanded to speak, and repeating what she heard, without understanding its meaning?

After the brief ceremony and benediction, the two servants were told to leave the room, leaving the new husband and wife in bed. They spent the rest of the day in the room together, dining at four o'clock. When it came to ten, Mrs Selby reported that she put her mistress to bed and then 'told Mr Fenwick my Lady was in bed and he went too'. And she then saw nothing further of them until she found them again in bed the next morning, Sunday.

That morning, Dr Ayres came to visit and was surprised to find the couple married, but offered his best wishes. He would later suggest that, rather than ill, she was in love: 'I was mistaken of her illness, which then I believe was nothing else but a strong love passion.'[26] As he stood above the bed, with the couple still under the covers, he suggested that they celebrate with a customary sack posset, a spiced sherry laced with cream. But Dame Mary demurred and requested a hot chocolate. It seemed a convivial episode and as a consequence Dr Ayres considered his patient well enough that he did not need to visit again. Love, it seems, was the greatest medicine.

Events become ever more blurred from then on. If the situation was so blessed, how can one explain what happened next? In the early days of a marriage, it is assumed that the married couple spent time together, that they were enthralled in their own company. But later that morning Edward returned to the Grand Monarque. The marriage had, seemingly, been spontaneous and the new husband was compelled to gather his things before he could start this new joyous chapter in life. But Edward never did move from the Grand Monarque, and that Saturday night and Sunday morning was the last he spent in privacy with Dame Mary. Why?

Later that morning, back at the Hôtel Castile, a confrontation occurred at the front gates. At some point Dame Mary left her rooms and attempted to prepare her coach and horses to take her to Saint-Germain-en-Laye. She was somewhat agitated, according to the servant Tom Lodge. She wanted to go and see the queen, 'and complain how she was abused'.[27] However, Lodowick Fenwick was quick to come out of the house and bar the gates. He then started to remonstrate with Dame Mary, telling her to return to the house. He then picked her up in his arms and brought her back inside. She was returned to her rooms and Lodge was told to take up some bread soaked in wine. Once again, most likely, laced with laudanum.

Later that day, or the day after, the coach and horses were assembled and a trip was arranged. The destination was unclear. For some, it was a visit to some local friends, either Mrs Conn or Mrs Davis, to share their joy in the new marriage. Another story tells how Dame Mary, Mrs Selby and Lodowick Fenwick planned for a longer trip and an overnight stay, as they went to see the Dauphin's new apartments a few miles outside the city. It was intended as some kind of honeymoon, and Mrs Selby had packed Dame Mary's nightwear. When the coach reached the Grand Monarque, Tom Lodge was commanded to go upstairs and fetch Edward, and when the new husband came down, his brother descended from the coach and let him in. The coach then went off with only Mrs Selby, Dame Mary and her new husband. Unexpectedly, however, the coach returned to the Hôtel Castile later that night, and Dame Mary returned to her rooms to find Lodowick Fenwick asleep in her bed.

None of these events can be satisfactorily explained. The witness statements do not give enough detail, and come freighted with suspected partiality. Why did the coach rush off once Edward had climbed in, leaving the chaplain behind? That the coach went off seems like a trap to ensure husband and wife slept the night together. What happened during the afternoon that Dame Mary decided to return to Paris? Lodowick was not expecting the couple back but that does not explain why he was discovered in Dame Mary's bed.

For whatever reason, the relationship soured from this moment. Reports note that Dame Mary and the chaplain appeared to be in constant argument. Furthermore, Edward Fenwick did not visit the Hôtel Castile again. Tom Lodge reported that 'I was in the room when [Lodowick] Fenwick was with My Lady talking and My Lady fell out into a great passion and said that she was not married, and knew nothing of it.'[28] Despite this, there seems to have been at least one other episode during the following week, a dinner at Mr Arthur's, when all the participants were brought together. There were other guests as well, including Francis Radcliffe and Mrs Davis. Radcliffe recalled that it was a pleasant evening. He did not remember the seating arrangements, who sat next to whom, but he did note that Dame Mary drank to Mr Fenwick's health and he drank to hers. 'I never saw a woman in my life in better humour' rounds off the recollection with a somewhat hollow ring of overstatement.[29]

Elsewhere, in Paris, the news of the wedding had started to cause a stir within the English community. Mr Lewis, the secretary of the British ambassador in Paris, wrote that he had heard from 'severall witnesses, and talked of, particularly in the chocolate and coffee houses that Dame Mary Grosvenor had lately received ill-usage from Lodowick Fenwick, and persons about her.'[30] The ambassador himself sent word to London to warn Mary's relations that she needed their aid, although the same letter also suggested that she may be a Jacobite spy. Mary also complained about her situation to those who would listen. Radcliffe admitted that he had heard her denying the union. He had tried to dissuade her from going to the ambassador, ominously responding 'that Mr Fenwick had friends who would stand by him'.[31]

After a couple of weeks, plans were made for Dame Mary to return to London. Again, the episode is hazily recorded, but on the day, the wife and her servants, Mrs Selby and Tom Miller, set off on the road back to England. At the suburb of St Denis, the coach was halted by Edward who followed on horseback. Tom Lodge watched as his new master climbed up into the coach, in order to say one last word, one last defence of his actions. But to no avail. He disembarked and the coach moved on, leaving the supposed husband in Paris. They never met again.

'Let Him Prove the Marriage'

I F IT IS mentioned at all, in Grosvenor family lore this episode is referred to as 'the tragedy'. Yet, what was the actual tragedy? Was it what happened that morning in the Hôtel Castile, or what happened once Dame Mary made it back to London? The classical definition of a tragedy is the fall of a hero as a consequence of their flaws. Oedipus is undone by his desire for revenge. Othello was jealous. Hamlet indecisive. And in the final act, the drama offers a catharsis to the viewer. What kind of hero was Dame Mary? What was her fatal flaw that condemned her to this ordeal? Was it her fragility of mind? Her need for security in the wake of the loss of a beloved husband? Perhaps it was her haste in falling in love with Fenwick too quickly. Maybe her inheritance itself was the flaw that made tragedy inevitable: the legacy a curse, that once appeared a freedom.

Dame Mary's coach arrived back at Mrs Tregonwell's house on Millbank on 7 July 1701, less than three weeks after that fateful night at the Hôtel Castile. What kind of relief did she feel as she stepped down from the carriage and entered familiar hallways and corridors? She had been away for nine months, but it would have felt like the world had changed, collapsed into itself. Her mother was there and would have listened to her daughter's distressed, agitated account of the events in Paris. Mrs Tregonwell may already have heard rumours but now she heard it in Dame Mary's own words. As the daughter later plaintively wrote to another friend, 'as to the main point of the pretended marriage, I positively deny it … for I never saw book, or heard marriage words, nor said any.'[1] Mrs Tregonwell immediately called for assistance from lawyers and friends, as well as contacting the Cholmondeleys in Cheshire. Anne, now a year old, was also brought to her mother, possibly with the hope that the presence of the toddler might bring sense and calm to the disturbed widow.

In the sanctuary of her family home, Dame Mary started to rid herself of the Fenwicks. She dismissed both Mrs Selby and Tom Miller, but not before both servants were interviewed by a family friend, William Dockwra, to get their side of the story concerning the supposed marriage. How and when the ceremony occurred, who was in the room, its legitimacy. In later testimonies, Dockwra confused some of the facts of the events in Paris. He became convinced that the couple married on the Friday night, rather than the Saturday morning. Maybe in the jumbled telling, Dame Mary could not recall the sequence of events herself. This may have acted as a warning to everyone involved that there was a storm coming.

But how could one judge Mary's ability to give an accurate description of the events? According to accounts, her mind was now more disordered than ever before. She was wracked with anxiety. For another family friend, Richard Dockwra, she spoke incoherently about her daughter, Anne. This was not the child of Sir Thomas, Dame Mary confessed, but of another: 'one night when Sir Thomas was out of the way, King William came to bed with her and begot that daughter and that she was to be married to the Prince of Wales.' To Dr Nicholls, who had treated her in the 1690s, she claimed that she was to marry the Duke of Anjou, now King of Spain, and that the daughter was his child and 'heir to three crowns'. According to the doctor, these 'romantic fantasies are a sign of her continued madness'.[2]

She recalled this story to Richard Dockwra, as she sat alone in her petticoat and stuff gown, and started to pick the fabric to shreds. William Dockwra also gave an account of watching this distraught woman methodically stripping the clothes off her body. This manic behaviour, today called psychomotor agitation, is typically found in a major depressive disorder or bipolar condition. The compulsive repetition of destructive actions appears to be purposeless, but becomes the only release from the inner turmoil. Mary seemed trapped within her despair. Despite being once again surrounded by family and those who knew her, there seemed to be no relief. She even started to accuse them of betrayal; that they were trying to poison her. Hadn't those who said they loved her in France done the same thing?

William Dockwra recalled how Mary felt unsafe, even within the family home. The Fenwicks, she feared, were coming to get her. (And again, her anxiety proved accurate despite being seen as the paranoia of a lunatic.) Firstly, arrangements were made for her to stay at the old family home where she had grown up on Millbank, Peterborough House, with Lady Peterborough. When this did not prove a sanctuary, she demanded to move close to her lawyer, Mr Andrews, on Golden Square in Soho. After arrangements were made, she travelled to the lawyer's house in a sedan, but once there she refused to get out. Her mother was called, but still she refused, claiming, 'why do you lie? … You are not my mother. I can prove that you are none of my mother.'[3] In the end she was forced to return to the family house. She no longer felt at home, safe, anywhere.

Where Dame Mary was most coherent and persistent was in her refusal to admit to the marriage. She was clear that no union had taken place. That she had been poisoned and drugged. Those around her were keen to protect her from the potential calamity that they foresaw; yet there was no agreement on what to do next. For Thomas Cholmondeley and the trustees of the Grosvenor Estate, this was an existential threat. As he wrote to Mrs Tregonwell, 'I think that it will not be long till her pretended husband seizes her.' Nonetheless, he argued, Fenwick deserved an audience to air his side of the story. And possibly Mrs Tregonwell might observe 'the pretended husband and my Lady together, and hear what was said, and see my Lady's carriage to him.'[4] But was it not dangerous to allow Fenwick into the family home, to invite him in and allow him to persuade or, worse, abduct his vulnerable lover away once again? How best to protect both Dame Mary and, more importantly, the estate?

It was not long before what they most feared came to pass. Edward Fenwick returned to London and began to claim that he was now Dame Mary's rightful husband, and the new landlord of the Manor of Ebury. From impoverished Catholic ne'er-do-well to major landowner: he had come to London to collect his prize. One day in early August, he came to Mrs Tregonwell's house at Millbank and demanded to see his wife. Mrs Tregonwell refused to open the door to him; instead, Dorothy Brough, the maid of Dame Mary's stepsister, answered the door and informed him that no one was at home. He was also told that he was not recognised as Dame Mary's legal husband. Such a closed door was no more than a delay to the inevitable resort to lawyers. Also, with Dame Mary safely inside the house and Edward Fenwick outside at the front gates, this moment of rejection was probably the closest the pair were to each other ever again in their lives.

On 12 August, a lawyer, George Pinkard, arrived at Mrs Tregonwell's house and offered a citation from the Spiritual Court of the Dean and Chapter of Westminster. The notice demanded that Dame Mary herself appear before the court on 30 October and 'show cause why Edward Fenwick should not have the benefit of his conjugal rights'.[5] This sent a shudder through the family, who were concerned that Fenwick might take possession of Dame Mary and use the ecclesiastical court to legitimise the marriage. They had to get her away from Fenwick and whatever associates he may have. They decided in haste that they had to get her out of London, beyond the court's jurisdiction.

And so on the next day, 13 August, Dame Mary took her carriage once more, alongside her lawyer, Andrews, and a maid, and headed to Chester and the imagined safety of Eaton Hall. They took a coachman, who steered the vehicle, and a postilion, who rode one of the tethered horses, as added security against any surprises on the route. Once they got to the family home, the steward, Mr Piggot, later testified that Dame Mary was extremely agitated. She continued to pace the corridors until five o'clock the next morning, when she ordered dinner. Later 'she made and remade her bed half a dozen times and swept the room. She [then] locked herself in the closet.'[6]

And here at Eaton Hall, Dame Mary remained throughout the ensuing dramas that continued in London. The family home was meant to be a sanctuary, away from the threat and turbulence of legal wrangling. Away from Fenwick. Distant from the gossip and scandal. While she remained the object of these stories and arguments, she was no longer a part of them. They happened in her absence, although the outcome was set to determine the course of her life, and the fate of her family fortune. Instead, Piggot, who had worked at Eaton Hall since the late 1680s, and had seen her when she was happy, as well as when she had suffered, reported that his lady 'never found her composure of mind since coming home'.[7]

* * *

Over the next year and a half the case of Dame Mary's marriage to Edward Fenwick flowed and eddied through the courts of London and Paris: the ecclesiastical court of the Westminster Diocese, the Court of Common Pleas, the Queen's Bench, the Chancery, the Court of Delegates, as well as the court of popular opinion. This was like a complex board game, in which the customs and precedents of common law determined the moves, while the progress of the contest was driven by unpredictable forces both at home and abroad. Such debates and legal machinations illuminated only the entwined politics of private property, marriage and the woman's body.

Why did Fenwick first go to the Bishop of Westminster in order to make his case? The ecclesiastical court was a local jurisdiction, only in control of the Diocese of Westminster, but its main areas of interest were questions of marriage, divorce and probate. The court was a hangover from the pre-Reformation era when canon law and common law were distinct; the former laid down by papal proclamation, the latter dedicated to the king's peace. At the Reformation, the authority of the Pope was dismissed but the court survived to look over cases that did not fit the other courts. It was now a civil, non-criminal court and so, at this stage, Fenwick was claiming only marriage rather than any property or profit. It was only judging the legal status of the holy words spoken on that Saturday morning, 18 June 1701. Establish the legitimacy of the marriage first, and then use the slower, riskier common law courts to capture the estate. Both parties, Fenwick and Grosvenor, were called to make their case before the bishop's representative on 30 October.

By this time, Dame Mary was safely in Cheshire. However, her lawyers were busy at work. On 14 August, the day after she left the capital, George Middleton of Symonds Inn on Chancery Lane was in touch with the barrister Nathaniel Lloyd to get his legal opinion on a series of questions. The note gave a short outline of the events:

> A popish priest having a brother of a desperate fortune, whom he is resolved to advance, insinuates himself into the good opinion of a wealthy widow, and gains much credit with her, that she trusts him with the conduct and government of all her affairs spiritual and temporal, he inveigles her abroad beyond seas (where he had more power than she) from her native country and relations then sends for his brother thither, but when he found that by false applications and addresses he and his brother could not work upon the lady's affections, their means failing, resolves upon artifice and force ...[8]

From this précis, the line of defence that the Grosvenor family were going to present was clear. Dame Mary was the victim of a vile conspiracy. She was a vulnerable widow, systematically detached from anyone who could look after her interests, and the Fenwick brothers took advantage of her frailty. The plot may have started as early as that first meeting in Parndon, but it was definitely in play during the fateful week in Paris. In addition, on the day of the wedding, she was not '*compos mentis*, with the potions given her'.

Despite this, the lawyers recognised that a counter-narrative would be presented by the monk, footman and maid, who were witnesses to the marriage. This was followed by three questions: What defence can be made against these witness statements? To which the lawyer suggested that each witness could be discredited for their involvement in the plot and therefore their testimony undermined. Secondly, was a marriage conducted abroad legitimate at home? Yes, if done willingly. And, finally, is it possible to argue that she was inveigled abroad? No, because she left London willingly.

However, Lloyd did give some useful advice. Dame Mary should make a statement as quickly as possible to set out the narrative of a forced marriage. That they should pursue a case through the ecclesiastical courts and contest the marriage rather than go to the common law courts to argue over property. Finally, to act quickly. The worst-case scenario was for Fenwick to wait until all witnesses were dead, and even Dame Mary had passed, and then go after the heirs.

Middleton attached his own note to this memorandum, raising the question of who was going to pay for all this. He suggests that the trustees pick up the tab: 'It is the duty of the trustees to defend any suit that may be prejudiciall to that they're interested for and its plain if Fenwick gets the lady he'll force her to settle her lands of intermittence on himself which otherwise is like to come to Sir Richard.'[9] This complicated matters for, if the trustees were to pay on behalf of the future heirs, they did not necessarily represent Dame Mary's best interests, but her sons. Who was to speak for her?

Mrs Tregonwell wanted her daughter back with her. She also hinted that she might consider a deal with Fenwick. Dame Mary was keen herself to ride down to the capital and clear her name. In response, Sir Thomas Cholmondeley counselled caution. Firstly, it was not safe for her to travel, nor to stay in any of the houses she might call home in the capital. In a later letter, he again argued that she remain in Cheshire, and far away from the witness box. In his opinion, she was not in a fit state to conduct her own business, and could even make matters worse.

Unfortunately, Cholmondeley then died, in the midst of these negotiations, and the Trust was passed over to his brother Sir Francis, who nevertheless continued to argue for caution. This could not have happened at a worse time. When Dame Mary most needed a guardian, she had lost a true friend. More importantly, the steady payment of receipts was temporarily halted, and this had a deleterious effect on progress, especially in France. In October, it had been decided that the lawyer George Middleton was to travel to France. One imagines an eighteenth-century private investigator knocking on doors, paying bribes, jogging memories and prising open confessions in pursuit of the truth.

* * *

Meanwhile, back in London, there was another, related, case going through the courts. This time, Dame Mary's tenants, those who rented the various properties across the Manor of Ebury, were concerned about who exactly was their landlord or landlady. They did not want to find themselves in the situation where they were forced to pay two accounts. Or worse, that they pay one account and find themselves ejected from their tenancy by the other. And so on 25 October, twenty of the tenants, led by Lady Peterborough, placed a petition with the Court of Chancery, stating that 'they did not know to whom they might pay the same with lately for it is, may it please your lordship, that one Edward Fenwick doth plead that he is legally and truly married to the said Dame Mary Grosvenor and by virtue thereof pleased that in her right he is.'[10]

The Court of Chancery was another court outside the common law. Originally set up as a court presided over by the Chancellor, the Keeper of the Great Seal, it was there to adjudicate upon cases that stood outside the norm. It did not plead in front of a jury but 'ad personam'; according to legal scholar J. H. Baker, 'each case turned on its own facts rather than precedent'[11] and the judgment was solely up to the conscience of the judge. On this occasion, the Keeper of the Great Seal, Nathan Wright, judged that, while legal proceedings continued through the other courts, all rents were to be paid to him. The income from the estate now was to be looked after by the state until the true landowner of the Manor was decided.

Fenwick hit back with his own account on 29 November. He suggested that there was a conspiracy against him that involved Mrs Tregonwell, the family trustees Francis Cholmondeley and Sir

Richard Myddleton, as well as Lady Peterborough. He demanded the court make an account of all Dame Mary's property, land, plate, rings, watches, tapestries and hangings, including any jewellery that she had recently sold or pawned, to whom and when. He was convinced that there was a plot to channel everything of value away from the widow should the case came to judgment. They could then argue that she owned nothing of value.

Such actions prove that Edward Fenwick was starting to assert his rights as Dame Mary's husband over her property even before he had proven his case in court. In preparation of the suit in front of the ecclesiastical court on 30 October, he presented a witness statement that gave his side of the story. His narrative was structured in such a way as to convince the hearing that this union was a love match. The account opens with the first encounter between the couple at Mrs Turnour's house at Parndon. Dame Mary was involved in a conversation about what kind of man she was attracted to, when she professed that, 'provided he was a gentleman (of no estate), she would marry him.' Furthermore, at the leaving party at Millbank, he noted that 'she was observed to distinguish him by several … obliging expressions.'

Persuaded by friends and family to follow the party to Paris, Fenwick found that Dame Mary had left the French capital already. When she returned on 12 June, the relationship was rekindled, so that by Friday, 'he had been with her most part of the afternoon yet he was no sooner gone out she sent one of her servants hence to order not to return without him … and having sometimes together they then agreed to be married next day.'

Despite Fenwick's suggestions on that Friday night that they wait a day to make proper arrangements for the union, Dame Mary forced the issue, and persuaded a cautious Lodowick Fenwick to read the vows. And so they were married the next morning, spent the Saturday night together and on Sunday morning were greeted by Dr Ayres. And 'after dining that morning they went abroad together in her coach to visit a gentlewoman … That they afterwards dined together and were after dinner several hours retired alone in her bedchamber, and in the evening they went out together to take the air, and to all appearances they could not be a more happy couple.'

Fenwick was adamant that the marital joy was mutual. But he was also honest about what happened after. That Sunday evening, Dame Mary requested that she sleep alone and Fenwick go back to his lodging at the Grand Monarque. The next morning, he returned to the Hôtel Castile and found his new wife 'treating him as if she remembered nothing of what had past so lately betwixt them and utterly denying their marriage'. From that moment on, she had treated him poorly, perhaps when she realised that she was now 'oblig'd to obey whom she had so lately commanded'. And as a consequence, she 'began to contrive how to disengage hereby from her new conjugal state by persuading the world into a belief that she was not marry'd'.[12]

This was the case that Fenwick intended to present to the ecclesiastical court on 30 October. In response, lawyers on behalf of Dame Mary decided against posing a counter-narrative of the events but rather sought legal solutions. They did not debate the nature of the marriage or its legality, rather that the court of the Bishop of Westminster had no jurisdiction over the case when the Grosvenor home was at Eaton, Cheshire. Fenwick's lawyers charged that she had a house in Millbank that fell within the diocese, and that clearly this was a family home when it was draped in mourning at Sir Thomas's death.

The court was to meet again on 12 November and respond to these obstacles, demanding that Dame Mary attend. When she did not, Fenwick's lawyer, Mr Alexander, fixed a subpoena on the railings that encircled Mrs Tregonwell's home, commanding her to appear. In defiance, Dame Mary's legal team refused, hoping to stall the case. However, on 11 December, Dame Mary's solicitor wrote in exasperation, 'we are pressed on all sides very warmly, in the Ecclesiastical court, Chancery and Common Law!' The situation was getting increasingly tricky. The New Year passed with the mounting array of arguments, witness statements and court hearings. Motions were tabled and heard, counterarguments proposed. Delays enforced, demands ignored and lawyerly sleights of hand conjured. In the meantime, the story continued to bubble through the court of public opinion. From Eaton, Dame Mary wrote twice to Queen Anne to ask for her intervention, exhorting that she had been badly treated, dosed with a 'great quantity of opium and other intoxicating things'.[13]

She defended herself in another letter on 19 January. In her account to her lawyer, Andrews, she vehemently repeated:

> I deny it, and will forever, and will never own any such thing … After I came to Paris from Italy, Mr Lodowick Fenwick persuaded me to be blooded and to take physic, and keep my bed a few days, to refresh me after so long a journey before I went to Brussells … Dr Ayres, who they sent for me, gave me something, made me very sick, but what I know not. I thought I had died. After some time I fell asleep and when I waked found Mr Fenwick in my Bed. How he came there I know not, they did afterwards persuade me to marry him which I would not doe, so the priest brought me to my mothers and there left me at Milbank [*sic*], and I have never seen him since.[14]

These were the early rounds of sparring, but there was preparation to be made for the eventual confrontation. The arguments had been narrowed to three questions: did the Fenwick family unfairly plot against Dame Mary? Was Dame Mary *compos mentis* during the marriage? Was the marriage itself legal? Issues of class and gender also swirled through the speculations: why would a rich heiress marry a man without estate? What were two men, unrelated to the woman, doing in her rooms late at night? Was she really mad or just a victim of a frailer nature? On both sides, the harvesting of witness statements became increasingly urgent.

The lawyer George Middleton was already in Paris by October and had started his work immediately. He visited the Hôtel Castile in Paris and talked to the landlady, Madame Dufief, to find out what she saw and heard. He met Dr Ayres and got his side of the story, as well as from the others who were witnesses to the events before and after 18 June. He also made his way to Lyon and found out as much as he could on Dame Mary's medical condition when she was recuperating there, following her long journey from Rome. There were stories that had not yet been uncovered and Middleton was determined to excavate the truth. However, such sleuthing needed a steady flow of cash to keep witnesses talking.

The family archives are filled with short notes, signed off by Dame Mary's Paris banker and then forwarded on to lawyers, Bartholomew Showers, in London, for small sums paid to grease the memories of witnesses and officials. On 5 November, Middleton made his way to the Hôtel Castile and spoke to Madame Dufief. He kept assiduous notes, recording that: 'one day [Dame Mary] made it out into the garden to take the air and made it as far as the gate, when the Priest grabbed her by the hand and brought her back in, but she refusing, he took her up in his arms and carried her by force into her bed chamber, where she started to scratch him. He had her in his arms.' Later, Dame Mary said 'that she felt like a prisoner, by two villains, [and] wept at their barbarous behaviour'.[15] Middleton also ventured to Lyon and interviewed four witnesses there.

On 18 January, he wrote once again to London for more money and claimed that he needed only three or four more statements to complete his task. But he was finding it difficult to get people to open up. The English community in Paris, especially amongst the Catholics, was reluctant to talk without cause. They did not want to criminalise one of their own, especially one in holy orders. At the same time, Edward Fenwick had also made it back to Paris with the same intentions of securing the truth, finding witnesses and gathering statements that might promote his side of the story.

Middleton appealed to the French authorities to aid him to gather together the witnesses and force them by warrant to give their accounts of what happened. And so the Lieutenant-Criminal, based in the Châtelet prison in Paris, summoned them to him under oath in March. Henry Parry, an officer from James II's army, reported that he had met Fenwick who, after the marriage and once Dame Mary had fled Paris, had confessed, it would be 'very ridiculous for me to marry a mad woman, one who was out of her witts'.[16] There were also statements from William Delaval and Joseph Byerley; both spoke of the rumours of the marriage plot. The apothecary Frederick Charaz, from the Rue de Buci, told of Dr

Ayres's prescription of 'an ounce of emetic ... 20 grains of laudanum ... an ounce of salt prunello, for the same person'.[17]

Anne Bracey, who worked in her husband's coffee house in St Germain, and had got to know Dame Mary during her stay, recalled how dismayed her friend looked on her return from Rome, and how she complained of Lodowick Fenwick's 'strict hand over the said Lady, whom she kept in her chamber, and suffered none to speak to her'.[18] The chaplain's cruel treatment of his mistress came to dominate the statements. Various servants at the Hôtel Castile concurred that the priest rigidly policed access to Dame Mary. Kitchen porter Thomas Le Cleve also recalled that Fenwick 'put certain small black grains ... Sometimes with poached eggs, and at other times strawberries'.[19]

These statements were so shocking that the Lieutenant-Criminal issued a warrant for the arrest of Edward Fenwick, who was then brought up in front of the judge to explain himself on 8 April. In the cross-examination, Fenwick continued to profess his innocence, despite the gathering threat of punishment. Surely, Middleton and Dame Mary's faction had their quarry in the snare at last. If Fenwick was charged and found guilty in Paris, there was no case in London. The supposed husband might even face execution for the coerced marriage according to French law. There was no one else who could pursue his cause. But, within weeks of the hearing, events took an unexpected direction.

Since the elevation of the Duke of Anjou to the throne in Madrid, the threat of war had simmered across the continent. William III had created an alliance of nations against the preponderance of the French interest. Then, in September 1701, the exiled king, James II, died at Saint-Germain-en-Laye, and yet Louis XIV refused to recognise William III as the rightful monarch. Instead, Louis placed his blessing upon James's son, James Stuart. The first skirmishes of the War of the Spanish Succession were about to be launched. Such high politics might appear distant from the goings-on between Dame Mary and her supposed husband, but they had a direct impact on proceedings. A fog descended in the English Channel and it was impossible to communicate between London and Paris. Middleton was no longer able to receive his instructions, and even more dangerously, the flow of cash slowed to a trickle.

As a consequence, Middleton lost the advantage. In July 1702, Edward Fenwick was able to skip jail. The solicitor reported that 'an English monk' paid 2,000 pistoles to spring the accused from the Châtelet. This sent the Dame Mary party into a panic. One wrote: 'nothing but want of money on your side could give the opportunity to Mr Fenwick to get out of prison. He is now at large and Mr Middleton has not so much money as will pay bailiffs and catch-poles to apprehend and imprison him again.'

Worse, it was reported that Fenwick was on his way back to London: 'If he comes amongst you and can by any pretence get then possession of my Lady Grosvenor's estate, you must attribute it to those that keep her purse and made so ill use of it to shut it in a conjuncture when both her honour and fortune were at stake.'[20]

* * *

Meanwhile, back in London, the case continued through its rivulets and tributaries towards a trial. In June 1702, the case before the ecclesiastical court had been successfully moved to the Court of Delegates, the leading court of appeal for spiritual causes. This was a serious ratcheting up of the stakes, as it involved a bench of bishops and legal experts to examine written statements from both sides. Therefore, the two factions set about putting together copious documents of testimonies, legal arguments and clarifications.

This started with another round of interviews, and during this summer, Dame Mary's team took statements from a number of English witnesses to add to the French affidavits gathered by Middleton. This list included those who knew Dame Mary before Sir Thomas's death and could vouch for her distressed behaviour in 1698. There was also Mrs Selby, the maid who travelled with her, as well as other English witnesses in Paris. The most revealing statement came from Bishop Ellis, the Catholic bishop who had met Dame Mary in Rome, who was willing to weigh in on the legitimacy of the marriage itself. In his written statement, Ellis showed his disdain for Lodowick Fenwick, whom he criticised for travelling in secular disguise. He commanded the monk to dress in future in his Benedictine habit. On the nature of the marriage itself, Ellis denied that Fenwick had the authority to conduct such a ceremony, calling it 'a scandalous abuse'.[21]

In the meantime, the action moved to the Queen's Bench, the leading common law court, based in Westminster Hall. What both sides wanted more than anything was a date for a hearing. But such a thing was difficult to pin down, especially in the circumstances of war when it was going to be difficult to guarantee safe passage for the witnesses to come over from France. More money was needed, and there were even rumours of the Fenwick faction obstructing the passage of some witnesses.[22] The presiding judge turned down a request to delay the case.[23] There are letters from Mrs Tregonwell to the court saying how two friends of Dame Mary, including Mr Byerley, had been waylaid in Brussels.[24]

In response, Fenwick conducted a two-pronged strategy in order to break the deadlock. On the one hand, his relation Francis Radcliffe offered an olive branch to the Cholmondeleys. Firstly, he wanted to sow doubts about the efficiency of Middleton in Paris. Was the solicitor as honest, or as competent, as he appeared? Maybe this was just a matter of misunderstanding. This was followed by a more conciliatory turn: an offer to make an accommodation between the two parties, even at this late stage in proceedings. Radcliffe reminded Sir Francis that Fenwick was always ready 'to comply with any terms of accommodation that be consistent with his honour and conscience' as long as Dame Mary was willing to admit her fault, and her family were to stop their intriguing: 'A friendly end of this matter depends together upon my lady … she will at least have nobody but herself to blame for all consequences of her obstinacy'.[25]

The Grosvenor faction was not convinced and the lawyers were adamant that Dame Mary was at risk from the Fenwicks. They cautioned that she remain in Cheshire through the summer, writing in March 1702:

As for your Ladyship coming to London I am very clearly of the opinion it is not advisable for you to come until the trial is past, you have always too many causes upon account of this unfortunate business, you have one suit going on in the Queen's Bench, another in the Ecclesiastical Court and a third in the Chancery and should your ladyship come to town it is possible that you would not be long without another prosecution … Mr Fenwick and his agents would venture to take out a warrant against any one that would entertain you to charge them criminally as detaining his wife from him, and possibly if he could meet with an opportunity would use violence to seize your person.[26]

But another way to make peace was to threaten war. And so, on a second front, Fenwick was making plans to ensure that matters came to a head. This was only going to happen in a judgment from the Queen's Bench, a common law court that had a specialism in private cases dealing with trespass, and ejectment – in other words, questions of land. This was not a place to debate the puzzle of the supposed marriage, so Fenwick had to find another cause that might bring the case to resolution.

Therefore, on 12 June 1702, nearly a year after he had met Dame Mary at the Hôtel Castile, he rented out a plot of land later measured as '50 messuages, 50 gardens, 50 orchards, 50 stables, 300 acres of land, 300 acres of meadow, 300 acres of pastures and 200 acres of fresh marsh' for a term of seven years to a certain Richard Burnaby.[27] This was an odd lease as it was negotiated for such a short period: a tenant rarely agreed to such terms. Even more strangely, the land named in the contract was a part of Dame Mary's inheritance, the Manor of Ebury.

As the question of the legitimacy of the marriage itself seemed lost in the machinations of the Court of Delegates, Fenwick now wished to test the legitimacy of his conjugal rights. If he was indeed married, Dame Mary's inheritance was now his, by couverture. Let them prove him wrong. By pressing the issue, he was creating a case that was based not solely on the whispered words in a hotel room but on the actual management of property. Furthermore, following the lease of the land to a tenant, Burnaby started to eject the current tenants from the land, in particular John Orton, Edward Phipps, Anne Axtell and Thomas Franklin, who all had legacy leases negotiated with Sir Thomas Grosvenor. On 18 June, the anniversary of the marriage itself, Burnaby entered his new property and 'by force of arms' caused £10 worth of damage, as he seized possession.

This was further challenged in September when another note was delivered to a tenant in Chelsea, which made the dilemma even clearer: '[Edward Fenwick] is become master to the said Dame Mary's estate and to the rents and profits of all her manor, messuages, lands and tenements. These are therefore in the said Mr Fenwick's name.' And therefore, the tenant was not 'to pay any of the rent thereof or arrears to the said Dame Mary Grosvenor or any other person or persons by her authorised, and to pay the said rents only to said Mr Edward Fenwick or whom he shall appoint'.[28]

This was cause enough for a court case fit for the Queen's Bench. An accusation of unlawful possession of land, of violence, and ejectment. Furthermore, it was a case that did not necessarily involve either Dame Mary or Edward Fenwick. In a letter sent a fortnight before the trial, Dame Mary tried to persuade her mother that she should defend herself. In its small details of her life it is worth quoting in full:

> I like the stuff very well for the child's coat and give you thanks for choosing it. Sir Richard gives his duty and many thanks for his shoe buckles … Mr Cholmondeley hasn't been here yet, I expect him this week and if he thinks it proper I had rather come up to the trial and answer for myself. If he don't approve ont I will let it alone, but I am very weary here, for I take them all to be maddish … God send me among Senceball peeple [sic].
> Your dutiful ob. Daughter.
> M Grosvenor
> Mr Massey got ye first race at (Farndon) last week, and Sherwood the second.[29]

However, Mary was finally dissuaded from coming down to London.

Instead, on the morning of 3 April 1703, the case finally made it to the bench under the title:

Richard Burnaby
Against
John Orton, Edward Phipps, Anne Axtell, Thomas Franklin
In ejectment
Held at Queen's Bench brr.Westminster Hall, before the Lord
Chief Justice Holt, and the rest of the judges of the court ...[30]

But, as everyone in Westminster Hall that morning knew, the case itself turned on the facts of 18 June 1701, the events that happened at the Hôtel Castile – whether a marriage took place, or not. If it was legitimate, Fenwick had every right to lease out his new wife's land as his own. And if not, Dame Mary had been telling the truth all along.

'One Degree of Madness to Marry a Man Not Worth a Groat'

WESTMINSTER HALL STILL stands today, less than a mile downriver of Millbank. The ride from Peterborough House to New Palace Yard on 3 April 1703 was a familiar route for Mrs Tregonwell and her family, but we have no idea whether she made it on that day. The Hall ran along the south side of the broad public space, in front of the old Palace and the Thames. To the west ranged the Abbey and, in front of the towering buttresses, sat St Mary's Church where Alexander Davies was buried. Ahead was what was once the Palace of Whitehall that had burned down five years before in a catastrophic fire; all that was saved was Inigo Jones's glistening, modern Banqueting Hall. Elsewhere, London had modernised following the 1666 conflagration and become a new city, but not here. In truth, Westminster was a cluster of proud, ancient institutions swimming in marshy 'labyrinths of lanes and courts and alleys and slums, nests of ignorance, vice, depravity and crime'. The major loci of power – the Houses of Parliament, the discarded Palace, the law courts – barely functioned within the old structures, 'a stately veneer for the hovels crouching behind'.[1]

From the outside, the tall, leaded roof of the Hall rose like an elephant above the houses, shambles and booths that huddled alongside the exterior wall. According to a 1647 sketch by Wenceslaus Hollar, houses, taverns and shops clustered around the Yard, filled with bustle. Beyond the daily chaotic churn, many tumultuous events in British history had taken place here. Within the last century, there had been famous executions – Guido Fawkes, caught in his attempt to burn down the Palace, and Sir Walter Raleigh for treason. At the start of the Civil Wars, crowds thronged here day and night in order to cajole the MPs to defy the king. After the Restoration, the embalmed heads of the regicides Oliver Cromwell, Ireton and Bradshaw were impaled on stakes and raised to the roof of the Hall. Cromwell's head remained there for twenty-five years until it was finally blown off in a storm, and stolen. During the Exclusion Crisis of the 1680s, the Catholic plotter Titus Oates was forced to stand in a pillory in front of the Hall wearing a hat with the sign 'Titus Oates, convicted upon full evidence of two horrid perjuries'.

Westminster Yard as drawn by Wenceslaus Hollar, 1647,
with the Hall on the left

The Hall was one of the most noble buildings in the city, but had been mightily abused for centuries. There had been a hall here since the era of the Danish King Canute, huddled upon an island within the boggy estuary where the River Tyburn flowed into the Thames. It was William II, commonly known as William Rufus, who started work on the Hall we see today, intended as the main banqueting area within a larger palace. For a king who was always on the move, the Hall was a statement of his royal permanency. Running from east to west, it was 224 feet long and 66 feet wide. The roof, 90 feet tall, made it the largest hall in England, if not Europe, during the Middle Ages. The walls were whitewashed and daubed with 'rich and minute paintings', as well as hangings.[2] A large stained-glass window was added in the twelfth century to the east end, above the main entrance. At first, the central space was divided by a series of pillars creating a central nave and two aisles, but after a fire in the 1390s, these were replaced by an exquisite hammerbeam roof that spanned the entire space of the Hall.

The royal space was originally built for the Whitsun feast, but it soon took on other ceremonial duties. As a place where the king met with his barons and earls, it became a site for the resolution of legal disputes. When the king was present, the grandees made their pleas directly to the throne and the bench of his advisors, the *curia regis*, that sat at the elevated west end of the room. After the 1170s, when the king was away, it became customary that his power remained in his chair, and six judges were selected to adjudicate in his place. Thus began the court of the King's Bench, which was predominantly focused on questions of property.

At the same time, commoners who wished to make their cases to the king came to the Hall to seek his judgment. They were kept closer to the entrance, but their complaints were heard in the Court of Common Pleas, in front of representatives of the throne. Over the next centuries, the Court of Exchequer, when Henry II moved his financial dealings from Winchester to London, and the Court of Chancery were added into the space of the Hall. And each court slowly established its own authority beyond the *curia regis*. This was made starkly apparent in 1649 when Charles I was judged by his own Bench to have broken the law, and executed on behalf of the people. After this, the King's Bench itself was physically destroyed and buried under the steps at the west end, but the legislative power of the court remained. By the time of the 1703 trial, all four courts functioned in the four corners of the Hall: the Chancery in the south-west, the Queen's Bench in the south-east, the Court of Common Pleas to the west of the entrance, and the Exchequer at the top of the stairs above that. On such haphazard arrangements the law of the land, and Dame Mary's fate, was balanced.

On that morning in April 1703, like every morning, Westminster Hall was abuzz with activity and noise. According to one later account:

> men on the one side with baubles and toys, and on the other taken up with the fear of judgment, on which depends their inevitable destiny. In this shop are to be sold ribbons and gloves, towers and commodes by word of mouth; in another shop land and tenements are disposed of by decree. On your left hand you hear a nimble-tongued painted sempstress with her charming treble invite you to buy some of her knick-knacks, and on your right a deep-mouthed cryer, commanding impossibilities, viz., silence to be kept among women and lawyers.[3]

Amongst this hubbub gathered the lawyers from both sides of the case; as well as witnesses, some who had made a torrid journey

The Trial of the Seven Bishops by John Rogers Herbert

from Paris, sometimes in fear that they may be threatened or delayed en route. There is no record of family members – Fenwicks, Tregonwells, Grosvenors – sitting anxiously in the stalls.

The court of the Queen's Bench itself was divided away from the rest of the Hall by panels. In a painting of the 1688 trial of the seven bishops who refused to accept the king's call for toleration of dissenters and Catholics, imagined by the Victorian John Rogers Herbert, the space is crammed with a sea of roiling Hogarthian spectators. There is drama, movement, tension in all corners of the scene. The jury sits in a panelled box, their hats resting on pegs high up on the wall. In the front row of seats, the seven accused Church worthies in plain habits who had defied James II await their judgment. A line of lawyers sit, stand and gesture behind them, sober in black, making their arguments, scrolls of evidence unfurling over the edge of the desks in front of them. Along the side wall, above the jury, runs a public gallery. For a popular trial such as this, some of the householders whose properties huddled along the outside wall of the Hall offered viewing access through the windows for eager spectators who could not get a seat inside the chamber. And at the west end of the room, up high on a platform, beneath a wooden canopy, sat the bench of judges in their finery.

The judge on that day in April 1703 was the Lord Chief Justice, John Holt, the leading legal mind of his generation. In a forty-year career he had worked on both sides of the King's Bench, first as a barrister and then judge, and had a reputation of being scrupulously fair-minded, representing Whigs and Tories with equal passion. He had defended the right of the king to act against civic institutions, but he also ruled in 1688 on the legal justifications for the revocation of James II's right to the throne. He was interested only in the law, was always above politics, and never showed prejudice towards the accused or the victim. In one famous instance, he ruled on a treason case a day before the law changed; in his summing up he noted: 'we are to proceed according to what the law is, and not what it will be.' Elsewhere, in 1701, he made the judgment during a case of a slave who had come to England that, 'as soon as a negro comes into England, he becomes free: one may be a villein in England, but not a slave.'[4] He did not, however, challenge the sale of the same slave in Virginia, arguing that it was a separate jurisdiction over which he had no purview. In a portrait from that period he sits in his elegant red silk gown with fur trim. His heavy chain of office rests across his collar, circling his inquisitive face. He holds a lawyer's cap in hand. He is silent but appears about to make his observations known to the viewer. He is the idea of the law personified.

Once Lord Chief Justice Holt was seated, the trial started with the opening statements on behalf of the plaintiff: 'May it please your Lordship and Gentlemen of the jury ...'. The lead barrister Sir Thomas Powys quickly made it plain that this was not a trial about ejectment, criminal damage to property, or even Richard Burnaby. Rather, the case was to judge the marriage between Dame Mary and Edward Fenwick. For 'these lands are part of my Lady Grosvenor's and the wife of Mr Edward Fenwick and by his marriage with her now become his right, and if therefore such a marriage which I take will be the question betwixt us, then the ejectment is brought by him.'[5]

Sir Thomas Powys was a leading courtroom lawyer, formerly James II's Attorney General, with a reputation of representing members of the court party. In the 1680s, he defended a Catholic officer's right to be in the army, and was the chief prosecutor at the trial of the seven bishops in 1688. In the reign of William III, he then went on to defend those who came under attack from the state, such as Sir John Fenwick, leader of the supposed Jacobite plot in 1696. He was much in demand and regularly earned £4,000 a year from fees.

His opening statement continued, laying the foundations of his argument in the minds of the jury of why the marriage was legitimate while also undermining the defence case to come. His account of what happened started at the death of Sir Thomas. Almost immediately after that tragic event, Dame Mary wished to visit Rome and persuaded Fenwick and Mrs Turnour to come with her. She first met Edward at Parndon, where a mutual attraction was formed, and he gained the impression that she invited his addresses. At the gathering at Millbank before her departure, in front of many, she picked him out and encouraged his interest in her. So in all things, Dame Mary was not a victim of any plot but very much the pilot of her own destiny. Secondly, this courtship was not a hasty, sordid assignation in Paris but had its roots in those first encounters in Essex and London.

This was a love match, Powys confirmed. Edward Fenwick was not a hawk preying on a vulnerable widow; in fact, he was ideally suited as a partner for Dame Mary. After all, he was 'a gentleman of good quality ... [from] a very noble and distinct family and in his person such as was not disagreeable and in his education'. They had plenty in common too: both were Catholic and liked to travel. The only difference between them was the estate.

This being so, Powys wanted to turn the regular seduction narrative on its head. It was Dame Mary, not Fenwick, who was in command of the events on the evening of Friday 17 June. It was she who sent her footman out three times to find Edward; and when he did eventually arrive, it was she who insisted on a quick marriage. In contrast, Edward wanted to slow things down. Furthermore, Lodowick Fenwick also counselled hesitation and sober contemplation before taking the momentous steps towards matrimony. But Dame Mary refused! And so they married, in front of two witnesses. And afterwards they behaved together as husband and wife.

Nevertheless, it had to be admitted, problems arose after the marriage, Powys explained. 'She had a noble fortune, the joynture, and inheritance, both together and not worth more than £3,000 per annum. When it came to be considered that these would fall under this gentleman's power which was a mischievous thing, and no terms made before marriage how this should be ... There comes to be a dispute.'[6] And this was the seed for the current case, not the marriage itself. Yet such regrets could not be the legal basis for a denial that the marriage ever occurred.

Powys then paused and maybe surveyed the room to ensure that his words had sowed doubt into the minds of his audience. He then handed over to his colleague, the Solicitor General Simon Harcourt, considered by some as one of the finest orators of his age.[7] His opening gambit was to repeat that the marriage was the result of Dame Mary's wooing: 'If there is anything that distinguishes between this and other marriages it is this: the first steps begin with the man's part, but in this we shall plainly prove to your lordship it began with our Lady.' Furthermore, Harcourt extended the argument, Dame Mary was far from mad. In fact, as witness statements later in the proceedings attempted to prove, she behaved throughout 'in the greatest easiness imaginable'.[8]

The opening statements on behalf of the plaintiff ended with a short interjection by the third lawyer, Daniel Sloane, who turned his attention to the witnesses that were to be presented over the course of the ensuing hours. Many of those presented by the defence had been brought over from Paris by the Grosvenor party. Could they be trusted, when it was obvious that they had been paid for their testimony? It was estimated that over £1,000 was spent on getting the right story. Wasn't George Middleton, the solicitor who went over to Paris and had treated Fenwick so badly, now in prison for his dealings? The court would not hear his testimony as a result. (It was later suggested that he had been jailed for bad debts with the help of Fenwick's friends to stop him from speaking in court.) How could you trust anything that the other side had to say?

Meanwhile, the defence team stayed grounded in their seats. And so the first witnesses were called. In this opening round, the task was to normalise the marriage: to prove that this union was nothing out of the ordinary. And, in the most English manner, this meant that it was foremost a question of class. Was Dame Mary too high to marry Edward Fenwick? Not one bit of it. Fenwick was a gentleman but, as revealed in the cross-examination of a tenant, Robert York, Dame Mary came by her inheritance because Alexander Davies was 'a servant to one Mr Audley that was but an inferior man'. This lowly station was repeated by a second witness to ensure that everyone noted it. Dame Mary, this seemed to prove, despite her wealth, was only one generation away from the ink pot and was now marrying a gentleman. This was therefore an ideal match: 'she wanted blood and we have blood but we wanted an estate, and she hath an estate, these two together make an extraordinary good mix.'[9]

So the marriage made social sense, but was there the emotional fire that made it a long-standing attraction? Mr Turnour was then called to the witness box to repeat the events he observed that weekend at Parndon. He remembered how Dame Mary noted what kind of husband she might consider in the future, that, 'if he were a well bred man ... she did not care whether he had a farthing in the world or no.'[10] This was then followed up by other witnesses who were then at Millbank when the party left for France. Mr Radcliffe, Mrs Foster and Mrs Buckle all recalled how Dame Mary looked jealously at her stepsisters as they spoke to Fenwick, and how she coquettishly warned that, 'If you take too much notice of my sister, I shall be jealous.' All this, the lawyers emphasised, happened even before the party left for Paris. There was, *ipso facto*, no plot cooked up by the Fenwicks, nor was it the result of a spontaneous passion; rather, the union was a deep and sustained love match.

So far, the evidence had been to establish circumstances around the courtship; now, it was time to focus on the actual events in the Hôtel Castile: the marriage itself. Only those who were in that room could have seen what actually happened. Edward Fenwick did not give evidence, although he may have been in the courtroom; perhaps he was not seen as a sympathetic witness. Lodowick Fenwick was definitely not there, the lawyer reporting: 'he cannot come by the laws of the Kingdom – and it is a great part of our misfortune that we cannot have his evidence.' As an exposed Catholic in holy orders, he was likely to face persecution. Instead, the jury had to parse the truth through the memories of the two other witnesses, the servants Mrs Selby and Tom Miller. The threaded chain of questions aimed to spin a narrative, subtly nudging in one direction, focusing in on one detail, while obscuring all other alternative possibilities. In this manner, the lawyers created a braid of coincidences in which only one sequence of events, and one interpretation of how these things happened, was plausible.

Mrs Selby was the first to give her account. She had been hired a week before the party left for Paris, but had only met Dame Mary at Dover. She therefore had not been witness to any of the events at Parndon or Millbank. She had attended to her new mistress in Paris, alongside Mrs Cookson, and was with her, alone, on the trip to Rome. She was the only witness to her mistress's emotional joy at receiving the two letters from Edward Fenwick while on the road. At Genoa, Dame Mary 'read the letter twice over and seemed to have a great deal of satisfaction', and then later in Rome where it appeared the courtship had blossomed further, despite the distance between the lovers.[11] There was already talk of marriage, she told the court. And during this same period, Dame Mary started to feel ill.

Was her mistress's illness a love passion? That's what Mrs Selby's answers seem to suggest. Two or three times, Dame Mary in her sickness asked for Edward in Lyons, and once they had made it back to Paris, he was one of the first visitors to the Hôtel Castile. Mrs Selby had watched through the window their reunion in the garden and noted that Dame Mary was 'uneasy' when Edward was not there. And then on the night of Friday 17th, her mistress had called for Edward three times and when he eventually arrived, Dame Mary confessed: 'I am glad you are come for I cannot sleep without you.'[12] The next time Mrs Selby saw the couple was when she was called to be a witness at the wedding.

The legitimacy of the wedding ceremony was the fulcrum on which the whole trial turned, so it was essential to substantiate that the ritual was followed according to all conventions. 'Were they married in French or English?' the lawyer asked, to ensure that Dame Mary was not fooled by some foreign ruse. 'These were in English,' replied Mrs Selby. Were her lady's replies to the vows correct? 'She spoke very low and the priest asked her to speak louder.' And then the witnesses were sent away again, and the newly married couple spent the rest of the day together. And then afterwards, they continued to act as one might expect of a man and his new wife.

It was now the turn of the defence barrister, Mr Hooper, to approach the witness box and probe Mrs Selby's account. He swiftly raised a number of quickfire questions to test the rigidity of the narrative so far presented to the court. How long did Mrs Selby know Lodowick Fenwick before setting off? Did she know Edward Fenwick's handwriting? Did she understand all of the marriage vows? Where was Fenwick on the Friday night when the footman was sent to find him? None of these questions tested her testimony, but small cracks could be seen to appear in their foundation. She had known the Fenwick family for ten years. She did not know if it was Edward Fenwick who wrote the letters that arrived in Genoa and Rome or not. She did not understand the Latin in the Mass.

Hooper then opened a new front in his assault, switching subjects without preamble. The murmurs of the room halted and all eyes turned to the witness box.

- *Had she taken any physick?* inquired Hooper.
- *None that I know of.*
- *When did Lady Grosvenor take any laudanum?*
- *I know of none she took.*
- *No? No other physick?*

Here, one imagines, there was a pause as Mrs Selby gathered her thoughts and eventually responded: 'I do not say that she took no physick, she took some physick.'[13]

At this point, Powys jumped up and complained about this line of inquiry. 'Everybody that asks a question on the other side must not ask such as is impossible for the witness to answer.' But he was told to sit down by the Lord Chief Justice. Hooper pursued his questioning: 'Who was it gave her the powder? I ask you whether any laudanum was given?'

Mrs Selby then recalled what she had so assiduously omitted from her initial account. Dame Mary was prescribed physick by Dr Ayres and this was administered on Wednesday, Thursday and Friday 'to the best of my remembrance'. This included eggs sprinkled with laudanum, and the strawberries. The liquid form dropped into the glass of wine and the chicken broth. All brought to her mistress. But did Dame Mary know of her medicine? *No.* Did you tell her? *Again, no.*

The sowing of doubt was reaping a bountiful harvest. Hooper then returned to events in Lyons, where Dame Mary had been willing to take medicine and it had not been hidden from her. But it was disguised in Paris, and administered without her knowledge or consent. Why? Here, even Lord Chief Justice Holt pointed out the contradictions in Mrs Selby's testimony, and Sloane attempted to come to her rescue by suggesting that Dame Mary's malady was only an 'obstruction of nature'. But instead of searching for clarity, the confusion hung in the air, and the barrister moved on.

And what of the wedding itself? In fact, the lawyer proffered, the ceremony was not as perfect as it originally appeared. There was no evidence of a ring. The priest, Lodowick Fenwick, was not dressed in his order's habit but in regular dress 'such as other gentlemen wear'. Dame Mary remained in bed throughout the whole ritual. The questioning switched again but it was now established that this was an unusual union.

Mrs Selby's cross-examination ended where it had begun, with the question of how long she had known the Fenwick family. She responded that she was a relation, and had known them for over ten years; yet they were distant relations and she had never exchanged more than ten words with Lodowick before the trip to Europe. This confession allowed Hooper to leave a question unanswered, as the next witness was prepared: whose servant was she, Dame Mary's or the Fenwicks'?

Next up was the footman Tom Miller, whose testimony chimed almost exactly with Mrs Selby's and was ably guided by the plaintiff's lawyers. Although Dame Mary's servant, he was not privy to the same intimacy with his mistress as Mrs Selby, so he knew nothing of the letters in Genoa or Rome. Once they had returned to Paris, he noted that Dame Mary 'seem'd very well pleas'd while in [Fenwick's] company and very uneasy when she was not'.[14] Furthermore, he had no recollection of the medicine during that week, despite waiting at the table during the meal when the strawberries were served. He was, therefore, the perfect witness, and was able to leave without the scrutiny of the defence team.

The testimony of the next witness, Dr Ayres, however, opened almost immediately with a revelation. Although called to the Hôtel Castile on the Tuesday, he had never actually examined the patient. Instead, he had been led into the antechamber where he spoke to Lodowick Fenwick and Mrs Selby. They told him that if he had been seen by Dame Mary, she might 'take no physics of me'. Nevertheless, he prescribed the emetic and gave the instruction to infuse it in wine. Was this ethical? The doctor explained that, 'as a child that is sick, I make my judgment upon the description that the nurse makes.'

On the following day, Wednesday, the doctor was shocked to hear that the purgative had worked 'so hard' that he rushed to the apothecary and ordered the laudanum to calm the attacks. The dosage of the drugs was important, and the lawyers and the physician went into detail about the right amount and the frequency of application. He told them that they should not give more than eighteen drops at a time, every four hours. He reported that they had in fact given Dame Mary far less than that, a dose 'not intoxicating enough to send a baby to sleep'.[15]

In his mind, Dame Mary suffered from an emotional sickness, and marriage appeared the best medicine. When he came to visit on the Sunday morning after the marriage, he found that the patient had fully recovered. He ended with a defence of his own professionalism: 'I appeal to the whole college of Physicians whether any such quantities of laudanum as she took could intoxicate her head as early lay a child to sleep'.[16]

And that is what the lawyers then did, calling a Dr Ridley and a Dr Clear, who concurred that such dosing was entirely safe. Only one objected to the fact that Dr Ayres prescribed such a strong draught without inspecting the patient. Apart from that, the professional witnesses noted, he behaved within common practice. Therefore, they confirmed, the proposition that Dame Mary was drugged into submission could be dismissed.

Proceedings were then handed over to the defence team of barristers led by Mr Hooper. With his opening statement, he wished to reset the clock, to return to the events that the plaintiff's lawyers depicted as so innocent. This was not a worthy marriage; breeding did not disguise the truth that 'this person who makes suit to her hath not one groat.' Instead, it was a plot from the outset, marshalled by Lodowick Fenwick from the moment of Sir Thomas's death. In order to substantiate this, however, it was important to reveal what the family may have wanted to keep secret: the truth of Dame Mary's disordered mind. And to make her the victim of the worst machinations of the Fenwick family.

This logic was summed up in a line that an inattentive juror could have missed: 'it is one degree of madness to marry a man not worth a groat for one that hath £3000 per annum.'[17] In effect,

Dame Mary had to be mad in order to marry Edward Fenwick because it was an economically irrational act. The relationship between the idea of private property, reason and Dame Mary's body was brutally exposed, almost in passing.

Secondly, that the marriage itself was a sham by both French and English laws. And that the events afterwards proved that the marriage was the sum of a plot, and as soon as Dame Mary came to her senses, she refused to acknowledge her supposed husband. These threads were then taken on by Hooper's colleagues, Mr Conyers and Mr Hollice. Like the plaintiff's lawyers, they retraced the narrative from the death of Sir Thomas all the way to the Hôtel Castile, but they also showed that she was ill before this time. And with this the witnesses were called.

William Rippon and Rob Davis, both servants at Eaton Hall, supplied a patchwork narrative of Dame Mary's first collapse in the summer of 1696 and 1697, where she started to see apparitions and witches. And the event where she had to be saved from throwing herself out of the window. A nurse, Mrs Catherine Evans, who had known Dame Mary since that period, added to this portrait. Her mistress veered from melancholy to violent mania: 'she would bite anything and fling about anything that was next to her.' By this time, Evans informed the court, the patient was in need of constant company. This was substantiated by Dr John Nicholls, who had cared for Dame Mary since 1698, and spoke of her madness 'at a very high degree'. However, he suggested that laudanum was not the correct medicine for such a condition.

When Dr Nicholls was asked whether he had seen Dame Mary since her return from France, he observed that her condition had worsened. He spoke of Dame Mary's romantic fantasies about her love affair with the Dauphin or the King of Spain, and the identity of the father of her child, Anne. This drove Powys on the plaintiff's bench to lurch forward and object to this line of questioning. What was the relevance of this information to the matter of the case? But Hooper was allowed to continue with the examination.

Similar observations were then delivered by the next witness, William Brerewood, who had cared for Dame Mary at Eaton Hall. After her return to London, Brerewood continued, Dame Mary had become a broken figure, one who came down to dinner 'with flowers in her hair and feathers in her sleeves to fly with.'[18] This pathetic image of the supposed wife desperately hoping to escape by building a pair of wings from pillow down was shocking, and hopefully effective in driving home in the conscience of the jury how unfairly this frail woman had been abused.

Now, the ill intentions of the Fenwicks were brought into the narrative. And through the testimony of other witnesses, their part in the deterioration and manipulation of Dame Mary's mental health was laid bare. Charles Maddison claimed that Lodowick was plotting from the outset: 'her distemper evidently showed itself to grow worse and worse, especially upon the coming of Fenwick the Priest who with his lies and vanities he had [her] exceedingly much worse than she was before he took her up to London.'[19] A Mrs Finham claimed that before she went to France, in London, 'I never saw her composed half an hour' and when she returned Dame Mary exhorted her to believe that she had not been married. The steward at Eaton Hall, Mr Piggot, remembered how, since she had returned to Eaton, she had never found her composure again and was 'as mad as anyone could be'. And that Fenwick the priest had abused her in France. Maddison, again, reported that despite her derangement and constant distractions, Dame Mary was consistent in her avowal that the marriage never took place.

But what of Dame Mary's mental state during the trip to Paris itself? Will Jennings had been a footman at Eaton Hall and had travelled to Paris alongside Mrs Cookson, the lady's maid. However, he observed that Dame Mary was unwell during that first leg of the tour: 'she would be very ridiculous. She would throw herself about and then fall a crying, and then fall into a spleen of laughing.'[20] He also described how the chaplain got rid of all Dame Mary's personal servants before the party headed to Rome. It appeared as if anyone from her past was dismissed in order to isolate her for the next stage of the plot. This was corroborated by Mrs Cookson herself who recounted the strange tale of Dame Mary attempting to place her in a nunnery. Either this was a signal of her growing disorder or proof that she was being manipulated by the chaplain.

This was followed up with the statement from Tom Lodge, the servant hired at Calais. And here, as a defence witness, he offered an alternative narrative to the events at the Hôtel Castile. It was in Rome that he first saw her sick: 'she ran out very much and talked of strange things', that she was as rich as the King of Spain. In Lyon, her condition deteriorated and he witnessed her being bathed and bled. He was there when she attempted to throw a gold snuff box out of the window.

Once they had arrived in Paris, Lodowick instructed Lodge that he should restrict access to his mistress only to 'Mr Edward Fenwick, Dr Ayres, Mr Ratcliff [*sic*] (a relation) and Mr Arthur (Dame Mary's banker)'.[21] Other friends were to be turned away. It also meant that Lodge was meant to keep Dame Mary in, and he recalled the moment when his mistress tried to leave the hotel to complain to the queen at Saint-Germain-en-Laye of her treatment, and the chaplain was forced to pick her up in his arms and carry her back inside. Lodge was unsure of when this was, before or after the wedding, but it suggests the events of Sunday 19th, the day after the wedding.

However, Lodge did remember more clearly how bread was soaked in the emetic and served to his mistress by the French footman. He was again in the kitchen when the poached eggs sprinkled with laudanum were returned and he was convinced that she had eaten at least one of them. He saw the strawberries being prepared: 'they pulled the stalks off and put the pills then and they put in the stalks again and they were carried to her ladyship.'[22] After the supposed marriage, he was present when Dame Mary and the chaplain argued whether there had been a wedding. Finally, he offered a garbled account of the trip on the Sunday night, when Dame Mary and Mrs Selby went with Edward Fenwick to Sooe. Lodge was sent from the carriage to fetch Edward from his hotel rooms and had been left behind as the coach rushed off without him. The party then returned unexpectedly that night, to find Lodowick in his mistress's bed.

Almost as an afterthought, Lodge announced that he had been threatened with arrest before he came to court that day. Did someone not want him to testify? Certainly, his testimony contradicted the narrative weaved by the other servants, Mrs Selby and Miller. They would need to come back to give their own accounts of these overlooked scenarios. Who could one believe? But it did start to appear that the Fenwicks and their servants had some kind of understanding, isolating and manipulating their vulnerable mistress in order to take advantage. But to what effect? And how did this conspiracy impact on the actual wedding itself?

Next up was Madame Dufief, the landlady of the Hôtel Castile, whose first observation exposed the power the chaplain had over his mistress. She had been there when Dame Mary had suffered from the emetic and she had brewed up the glister of honey to calm her stomach. She had then accused the doctor and Fenwick of administering sufficient medicine 'for a horse', as she cradled the victim in her arms for four hours. She was in the kitchen and looked on over the following days as the poached eggs and strawberries were served.

And here she offered a new perspective to the story. After the strawberries, Dame Mary went to bed and slept. This suggested that she had ingested some of the drugged fruit. This was also, supposedly, the time that Dame Mary called for Edward Fenwick three times. But was this what had happened? So far only the servants Mrs Selby and Tom Miller had spoken of the evening's events; were they telling the truth? At some point, the landlady had observed Lodowick and his brother tiptoe upstairs and into Dame Mary's chamber. At that point, Madame Dufief went to bed, but after a few hours, she was woken by loud noises, the scraping of chairs and shouting as 'people do when they used to quarrel, and not only madame but others too speak very loud'.[23] Three voices were heard, and this continued for two to three hours into the morning.

In a flash, lawyers on both sides rose to examine this new account. If this was the night before the wedding, why did Dame Mary then wake up next to Edward Fenwick and take the vows the following morning? Perhaps there was a confusion here. Was there an argument on Friday? Maybe the landlady had her days wrong. Did Dame Mary sleep through Friday night, drugged with the strawberries, to find Edward in her bed the next morning? And, in her panic, was she rushed into marriage? If so, there cannot have been any arguments that night. Perhaps the argument was the following night, Saturday, after the wedding. Were the lady's cries of distress in response to Edward forcing himself on his supposed wife? It is appalling to consider that while this trial focused on the nature of the marriage, an alternative crime scene was swiftly passed over: rape.

We can only surmise what happened, but it is impossible not to look back at these distant events with contemporary eyes. Dame Mary's reaction to the events of Saturday morning seem to be intricately wound up with the events of Saturday evening. Her response to the wedding vows was a muted whisper; but according to certain accounts, her strongest reaction to events came the following day. Had she been violated that night? We will never know, but I believe that it offers an explanation for events that are difficult to fathom. In the seventeenth century in England, rape was a serious crime, punishable by death, but it always brought the victim into suspicion. Sir Matthew Hale, former Lord Chief Justice, noted: 'it is an accusation easily made, hard to be proved, but harder to be defended by the party accused, tho innocent.'

Did Dame Mary, like so many rape victims, before and afterwards, reflect inwardly into herself for what was done to her? As her supposed husband, Edward Fenwick expected sex on his supposed wedding night; but if it was rape, does this bring into question whether it was a marriage to which Dame Mary was willing or able to give consent? If, according to Madame Dufief's account, Dame Mary had gone to bed drugged on Friday night, after a day of being bled, she had found Edward in her bed the next morning. In her confused shame, she was rushed into marriage. The violent conclusion of the plot, however, was not committed until that night. Rape is itself a form of possession, of making the body a property. The violation did what the marriage could not: it enforced total ownership, with or without consent.

This may explain Dame Mary's confused, contradictory behaviour over the next three weeks; she stayed in Paris, surrounded by those who had conspired against her. From that time onwards, Madame Dufief reported, 'it was quarrelling every day after' between Dame Mary and Lodowick Fenwick. In fact, on one evening, 'when they were at the last service of the fruit she took a china dish of cream and threw it at the priest's head, he stooped and so avoided the blow'. More telling, after that Saturday, 'I do not remember that I ever saw [Edward Fenwick] come to the house again till the lady was gone.' And the mystery continued after Dame Mary's departure. At some point, Mr Arthur and Edward Fenwick came to visit and spoke to Madame Dufief in the garden, asking what she knew about the marriage. She professed ignorance, and they 'said that she should not say that again and say that she knew about it all'.[24]

But was the marriage itself legitimate? All these witness statements were circumstantial if the ritual of the wedding was followed to the letter of the law. They offered insight only into the character and intentions of those around Dame Mary. Next in the witness box was an unnamed French minister, who spoke through an interpreter. He raised concerns about the failures to comply with French laws. There was no licence, and without that, Edward Fenwick could be charged with the crime of fornication. There was a need for a minimum of four witnesses, not two. The power to conduct a wedding comes from a bishop, and clearly Lodowick Fenwick was in no position to do this. Finally, the banns had not been published to ensure that there were no legal impediments to the wedding.

Things appeared to be going against the Fenwicks and so Powys stood up and asked that his team needed to call two or three more witnesses, which might take another three hours or so. Was this not a suitable time for a break? It is difficult to tell how long the session had been sitting, but one imagines that it was deep into the afternoon by this time. The audience in the public gallery were rapt by the rising and waning tide of the arguments. To call for a break at this point seemed to be a tactic as the defence strategy was in the ascendant. Powys might be able to regain the upper hand after a hiatus in the proceedings. The courtroom was emptied for half an hour.

When the judges were back on their bench, the jurors in their stalls and the public gallery packed with jostling gawkers, Powys knew he had to hold the listeners' attention while his team gathered together a new set of witnesses, and so he set about destabilising the opposition's argument: 'We must beg leave to give some answers to their evidence they rely on.'[25] The witnesses appearing for both sides had agreed on the sequence of medicines, he announced. The taking and not taking of the physick, the eggs and the strawberries, the liquid laudanum dropped into wine. (They clearly had not.) However, the witnesses supplied by his team had also proved that the dosage was so small as to have almost no impact. (Not necessarily.) Secondly, both sides agreed that Lodowick Fenwick had been within the Grosvenor family for some time; 'therefore there is an end of that design of his coming there but just after the death of Sir Thomas.' (This was not proof or otherwise of a conspiracy.)

Finally, reports of her earlier disorder were not proof that she was incapable of marrying on 18 June. While everyone could agree that it was an unnaturally hasty union, and one to be regretted, Dame Mary's rebuttal of the event was in fact proof of her sanity: 'to tell your lordship in the same breath that she talks like a mad woman, has all the action of the mad woman, and is very steady in that particular subject of her marriage, and that she held so.'[26] She may have often shown signs of distemper, but 'a person that was once a lunatic is incapable of marriage ever after.' Why did she not eject him from her bed? Why did she continue to hire the chaplain, Mrs Selby and Tom Miller after the plot? Why was she seen in public with Edward Fenwick? Hasn't this seemingly irrational behaviour been seen in many rape survivor's accounts? It does not make them a 'bad witness', but is an expression of the trauma that lasts long after the violation.

The baton was then passed on to Sloane, who started to brew a plot of his own: that of the trustees who wanted to preserve the estate in the Grosvenor name. Who stood to lose the most in the event of the marriage? the lawyer appeared to ask. Surely, it was in the interest of the Cholmondeley faction to hold on to the estate in the interests of Sir Thomas's children. The plot therefore started after Dame Mary had made it back to London. And the witnesses produced by the defence overstated her mental incapacities. Only William Dockwra had suggested that she should be commissioned as a lunatic, and then did not do it for the sake of the children.

Was this *compos mentis* argument impossible to judge, and just hearsay?

Finally, it was time to call the last round of witnesses. The most eminent visitor to the witness box was the Duke of Hamilton, who was called to speak of Fenwick's reputation. Edward had been an officer in the aristocrat's cavalry during the reign of King James, but had then been disbanded. Just having such an august person in the witness box was signal enough, but the Duke, having been asked, 'What does your Grace know of his carriage in the world, and his reputation?' replied, 'I always observed he behaved himself extremely well, and on all occasions thought him to be a man of honour, and did esteem him one that was not capable of doing anything unbecoming a gentleman.'[27] Such praise counted for much, even if it said nothing about Fenwick's behaviour in Paris.

Next, Mr Francis Radcliffe, the family relation of the Fenwicks who was in Paris at the same time, had more to say on the actual events under examination. He had encouraged the suit, and arranged for Edward to work as a tutor while he waited for Dame Mary's return from Rome. After the wedding, when relations had started to sour, he had attempted to act as mediator between his cousin and his supposed wife. He had spoken to Dame Mary on a number of occasions but she now vehemently denied the union. He had counselled her not to go to the ambassador, as that course only threatened more shame. Yet he still felt able to impugn her character, noting that she said on one occasion, when asked why she was in bed with Edward, 'she would make nothing to be in bed with a man and run away the next day.'[28] This was a strong accusation to make against a gentlewoman.

Most of the remaining testimonies gave character references to witnesses already seen. Elizabeth Bamber and Mrs Ridley both spoke to the good services of Mrs Selby. Dr Ayres was spoken for by his brother, and a Mr Nelson also credited the character of Tom Miller. Another witness, Mr Viner, was called to discredit Tom Lodge, who was a 'lying and infamous boy'. Another, Mrs Wesley, claimed that Lodge had told her that 'his master was one of the most abused gentlemen in the world.'

Mrs Selby was called once again and shored up her narrative, claiming that her mistress 'acted as prudently and discreetly as ever I saw a woman act in my life'. She elaborated further on what happened after the supposed wedding, and how the new pair went out together often, including a dinner at Mr Arthur's. She was there in the coach as Dame Mary travelled from Paris back to London. At St Denis, Edward Fenwick had ridden up to the side of the coach and asked whether he could travel with his wife, who refused. At their farewell, 'Mr Fenwick asked for a glass of wine and wished her a good journey and said he would be in England presently after her and, says he, any thing that I have shall be at your service.'[29]

* * *

And with that, almost as a final act, the adversarial part of the trial was complete and it was left to the Lord Chief Justice to address the jury and sum up the evidence. He repeated that the case was based on the facts of the marriage in that hotel room in June 1701:

> If so be this lady was so distracted that she knew not what she did, whether she was by a disease, or made so by Art or physick, and so brought to be married when she did not know what she did, then it will be no marriage, then the issues will be the defendant's. On the other side, if you are satisfied that there was no such sort of marriage but she was in her sense when she married then the issue is with the plaintiff.[30]

He then slowly patched together a narrative from both the plaintiff's statements and the defence. This began, once again, with the death of Sir Thomas in 1700. He went into detail, sketching out a sequence of possible events and their alternatives, aiming to balance the claims of both sides. He pulled out threads from individual statements and weighed them for integrity and consistency. He held a candle to contradictions.

The heart of the debate, however, was whether a mad person was capable of marriage. Was there a plot to exploit her frailties? Was Dame Mary *compos mentis* as she spoke her vows? On this the judge paused and elaborated: 'It is not necessary that a man be a wise man yet marries, but it is necessary that they know what they do; if there be an intoxication by physick or medicines to a high degree then it would be no marriage at all.' However, 'On the other side, if you are satisfied that there was no such sort of marriage but that she was in her sense when she married, then the issue is with the plaintiff.'[31]

And so, finally, the jury was asked to stand down and agree on the case.

Reports record that the session had been sitting for over sixteen hours with only short breaks. So it was deep into the early hours of 4 April, as the lawyers and spectators in the public galleries lingered in order to hear the judgment. There was bustle and gossip as groups huddled and discussed their own hunches, picking out the convincing detail. The lawyers nervously reassured themselves, offering encouragement and congratulations, unsure of which way the twelve men of the jury might go. The wait was intolerable, but it was unexpectedly short. At four in the morning, the court was called back into session and the jury asked to make the decision known.

Later that day, the MP and historian Narcissus Luttrell sat down and wrote in his journal. Amongst various news stories about goings-on in the House of Lords and a report from Lisbon of the King of Portugal was the note: 'Yesterday was a trial at the Queen's Bench, which lasted until four this morning, between Mr Fenwick, Plaintiff, and Mary Grosvenor, Defendant; the former setting forth that he was married to her in France: the court seem'd to be of the opinion 'twas a forced marriage, but a verdict was given for the plaintiff.'[32]

'For the Good of Her Family'

'IF THE BEST comes to the best, it is not a respectable marriage,' concluded Lord Chief Justice Holt.[1] Nonetheless, in the eyes of the jury of the Queen's Bench, it was a legal union. There had been some form of wedding that morning of 18 June 1701, in Dame Mary's rooms at the Hôtel Castile. The jury had been satisfied that her faint, whispered vows, as she was sat up in bed, Edward Fenwick perched by her side, and the chaplain and two servants circled around her, had occurred as the witnesses described. Was this justice, or justice postponed? Had the jury disbelieved the narrative sewn by Dame Mary's lawyers or determined that it could not be accepted beyond reasonable doubt?

News of the catastrophe would have travelled swiftly. Within a matter of days, Francis Cholmondeley had returned to Chester from London and was approaching Eaton Hall, ready to tell Dame Mary of her fate with consoling words and a promise to pursue her cause. According to the court, she was now the wife to a man she abhorred, and who had probably abused her. How did he break the news, and how did she react? We don't know. Nor do we hear, after Cholmondeley's departure, from the steward Mr Piggot, of how Dame Mary spent that night. Nor of the atmosphere for the next days as his mistress veered between mania and melancholy. The eldest son, Sir Richard, was probably at school at Eton and would have been told by letter. It is unclear of the whereabouts of the other children, Sir Thomas, ten, Sir Robert, eight, and Anne, three. Would they have understood what was happening to their mother? Or to comprehend her misery on the receipt of the judgment? It was not just her future that was under threat; they too stood to suffer as a consequence of the events in Paris.

The future of the Manor of Ebury itself was at stake. Did this now belong to Edward Fenwick? Certainly, within the narrow confines of the trial itself, the property dispute between Richard Burnaby and the three tenants had found for the plaintiff. Burnaby had been within his rights to eject forcefully the sitting farmers who were illegally using his land, leased from Fenwick. Clearly, Fenwick had rights over Dame Mary's widow's third and any land that she oversaw as part of Sir Thomas's will. He also had a right to her jointure of £1,000 a year. This made him, on paper at least, a very rich man, at last.

And yet, it appears, following the trial, Fenwick did nothing to claim his rightful prize. He did not ride up to Eaton Hall and demand to see his wife. He did not begin to manage the estate, rewriting the leases in his own name. There are no documents in the Chancery notifying the change of ownership, demanding that the rents that had been held over until the dispute was resolved be paid to him directly. He had won at the Queen's Bench in front of the Lord Chief Justice, the highest judge in the land, and yet this did not appear enough to permit him to act.

Was it shame that caused him to hesitate? It is unlikely that this would have caused a delay. The whole of London society now knew the details of what had happened in Paris and the rumour of a Fenwick conspiracy was now widely circulated. There was also the question of Dame Mary's mental state: the court had not decided whether the widow was capable of making choices for herself, but the full disclosure of her disorder was understood. More important, however, was the nature of the trial itself. While the judgment turned on the legitimacy of the marriage, the ruling concerned the property named in the trial: the dispute between Richard Burnaby and the Grosvenor tenants – John Orton, Edward Phipps, Anne Axtell and Thomas Franklin. The marriage was legitimate enough for the case to be decided against Dame Mary. But that did not mean that the legitimacy of the marriage itself had been proven in law. Elsewhere, the appeal hearing, following on the failure of the Court of the Bishops of Westminster to make a judgment, was trundling through the ecclesiastical Court of Delegates. This forum would decide the truth of it once and for all.

Thus, the question of the laws of matrimony remained open, and whatever was decided in the Court of Delegates could overrule the judgment of the Queen's Bench. This was a reflection of the confused, overlapping hierarchy of jurisdictions where common law, civil law and ecclesiastical governance all had something to say about marriage, and the questions of property. None had a clear priority. In addition to Westminster Hall, there were the Court of Admiralty, the Court of Chivalry, as well as the Court of Oxford University that all made some demands on legitimacy. However, the Court of Delegates was seen as the highest appeals court on matters of the law of marriage. It was originally set up as a court of the papal legate, as a source of power separate from the Crown. This was one of the reasons for Henry II's ire at Thomas à Becket, who defended the jurisdiction of the court. Things changed with the Reformation, when the power of the Popes was banished, but the court itself remained a useful forum for ecclesiastical cases, especially on questions of probate, marriage and divorce. In time, the purview of the Court of Delegates was absorbed by civil courts, but not yet.

The Court of Delegates did not have a permanent home, although it more often than not met, following the fire of 1666, at Serjeant's Inn on Fleet Street. Nor was it a permanent bench of judges. A commission was recruited for each new case and mustered by the Lord Chancellor. This included a division between divines and commoners: four bishops were assigned to the case and five judges.[2] As had been judged at the ecclesiastical court at Westminster, this case was plainly focused on whether a marriage had taken place in Paris and whether Fenwick could demand his conjugal rights over Dame Mary.

The process before the hearing itself was exhaustive. Each side delivered a case for the appeal to the judges, who then accepted the assignment. Both sides were then commanded to take no action based on previous judgments. This may further explain why Fenwick was restrained from taking any action following the Queen's Bench ruling.

There remains a copy of one of these statements sent to the Court of Delegates in the Eaton Archives. It is a labyrinthine document consisting of twenty-four large pages, stitched along the top and then folded into four, like a roll. The argument is complexly structured across the page and the text scrolls across the paper in cascades of neat writing, linking arrows and architectural subsections. Nonetheless, it is so dense, it is almost impossible to follow the argument. It is perhaps for this reason that there is a large margin running down the left-hand side for note taking and remarks.

At the top of the first page runs the opening statement of the case between Dame Mary, 'widow relict of Sir Thomas Grosvenor having a fortune in land to the value of £30,000', and Edward Fenwick, 'a man of no fortune, a papist, a disbanded officer of the late king James who pretends to be married to said Dame Mary'. And is followed by the narrative account: 'The appellate having sometime in the reign of the late King James changed her religion and turned Roman Catholic from a Protestant shortly after became disordered in her mind and about the year 1697 her disorder was so great that some times she commits very extravagant acts of madness indeed.'[3]

On the second page, the Fenwick lawyers set out their case. Along the left-hand column there is an itemised list of proofs to the 'libells'. The second column then cross-references these with testimonies taken from witnesses and others. There is a deliciously revealing note from one of Dame Mary's lawyers who had carefully combed the opposition's argument and, at one point, scribbled 'insincere'[4] in pencil. His more forensic sieving of Fenwick's case continues on the back of the page. The document then returns to twenty-nine articles from Dame Mary's lawyers as a riposte to Fenwick, and then Fenwick's team responds once again. Much of the evidence rehearsed what we have already heard in the trial of 3 April 1703. But this was enough for the Court of Delegates to accept the case and commence proceedings. There was next a process of interviewing witnesses that seemingly was conducted throughout 1703, in preparation for a hearing in June 1704.

In the meantime, where was Dame Mary? Once again, we don't know; there are no records. We can only assume that she remained at Eaton Hall, looked after by Mr Piggot, while the children remained under the guardianship of Francis Cholmondeley. There were no more reports of her erratic behaviour, but that does not prove that she did not struggle with ongoing mental anguish. Did she continue to veer between mania and melancholy as the witnesses at the Queen's Bench testified? Did she still imagine that a prince might come and take her away? Did she still have Daedalus-like dreams of constructing a pair of wings to fly away from her labyrinth? Or was she once again well in the most part, only occasionally hiding away in her closet and shredding her clothes in anxiety? Those around her, her family, must surely now have judged her behaviour as that of a lunatic and treated her accordingly. What Dame Mary herself thought is lost, or was never even noted, and so we can only see her though others' eyes, for better or worse.

At some point during this year Sir Richard, now fifteen years old, left school and went on the Grand Tour. By this time, such a pilgrimage of the major cities of the continent had become a requisite part of a young gentleman's education. There is also a sense that Cholmondeley and others were hoping to keep the young heir as far away from the machinations of the case as possible. A series of letters between him and Cholmondeley set out an itinerary of his travels: The Hague, Amsterdam, Brussels, Paris (did he visit the Rue Saint-Dominique?), Geneva, Frankfurt, Venice, Turin, Florence. Here he studied in an academy, yet there also seems plenty of opportunity for more leisurely pursuits. At Ulm, Cholmondeley offered some paternal advice to the teenager, of 'avoiding all occasions of Play, because from which nothing but ruin and a broken reputation can be expected'.[5]

Cholmondeley wrote once again in early 1705 to Sir Richard, somewhere on his travels, that he continued to work on his mother's case: 'I'll try my utmost … and I trust God will sustain me in so just a design, as to detect the greatest villainy and treachery as ever was committed.'[6] Back in London, the records for the Manor of Ebury in the Westminster Archives reveal a chasm of inactivity during this period. The last contract signed was in Mary's hand in 1700, a few weeks before she went off to France. The next tenant agreement was not signed until 1705, signed by Cholmondeley on behalf of Sir Richard. But the silence of the records does not mean that Dame Mary was not concerned with her inheritance, or her fate. She had wanted to defend herself in front of the Queen's Bench in 1703 and had been dissuaded from doing so. She was once again not allowed to speak for herself in front of the Court of Delegates when they eventually convened in Serjeant's Inn in June 1704. The lack of a record of her concern is not, however, proof that she was neither concerned nor involved in any of the discussions about what was to happen in the Court of Delegates. Nonetheless, one gets the impression that there were plenty of people who were willing to speak on her account, and that she was allowed less and less purchase on her own destiny.

According to a Rawlinson portrait from a century later, the courtroom was a far less rowdy affair than Westminster Hall. There was no audience to speak of, only a few clusters of witnesses and interested parties hanging back from the drama. At the far end of the room, framed by a pair of pillars, sat two rows of benches shaped like a horseshoe. On the outer ring of benches sat the judges, dressed in gowns: 'a scarlet robe, and a hood of taffeta, if they be of Oxford; if of Cambridge, white miniver and round caps of black velvet'. There were five judges: Sir Edward Ward, Sir John Powell, Sir John Blencoe, Sir Thomas Bury and Judge John Smith. On this occasion there were also four bishops on the bench: Henry Compton of London; Thomas Sprat of Rochester and Dean of Westminster; George Hopper of Bath and Wells; and William Nicolson of Carlisle. On the inner benches sat the lawyers for both sides who marshalled the statements that had already been submitted as well as questioning the witnesses in the room.

Some of these revelations came from individuals who had so far remained silent. Dame Mary's team delivered a number of new witnesses. But the Fenwick team must also have felt confident that their arguments would be vindicated as both Lodowick and Edward entered the witness box to substantiate the truth of the events of 18 June. Unlike the trial at the Queen's Bench, we do not have a verbatim account of the hearing and have only snippets of state-ments given that day. It would be fascinating to read what the

Fenwick brothers – especially Lodowick, who remains eerily silent throughout this whole narrative despite being such a major figure – had to say about their genuine hopes for the marriage.

Robert Questel, the footman at the Hôtel Castile, was one of the new witnesses who had not been questioned before and his testimony raised some serious questions about the accepted narrative of what happened. On the previous day, Friday, 17 June, he had been sent out by the chaplain to fetch the surgeon who was to bleed Dame Mary. This had been reported before but Questel's details of what happened next were telling: Dame Mary was seriously debilitated by the loss of 'three porringers' of blood (elsewhere reported as 10 oz). 'She fainted away, and seemed weak after it,' he reported. It was in this desperate state that Dame Mary was later dosed with laudanum. Was she really in a condition to demand Edward Fenwick later that evening? Or to be *compos mentis* the following morning when she spoke the sacred vows? Questel also recalled that, on that morning, the chaplain had left early and told him to guard the door, and then came back early in the afternoon. Was this after the supposed wedding? And if so, was this to stop people coming in or people coming out?

Another new witness, Ann Bracey, described the chaplain's treatment of Dame Mary after the wedding. When the supposed bride had demanded that she be allowed to see the ambassador, Lord Manchester, Fenwick had warned her against it. He suggested that to do so might stir the anger of other Catholics in the city 'and if she meddled with any such thing she would be murdered or have her throat cut in the street, and therefore she would do better to stay in the house.'[7]

For Dame Mary's team, the arguments remained focused on the suggestion that there was a Fenwick family conspiracy, which connected the brothers with Radcliffe, the maid Mrs Selby, and the footman Tom Miller, and was supported by the wider English Catholic community in Paris. Perhaps more damning was the accumulated evidence that Dame Mary was *non compos mentis* at the time of the wedding, and had not recovered her senses since.

But what, in law, was a marriage? It was both a 'holy estate' in front of God as well as a matter for lawyers. As the event happened in Paris, did the ritual have to follow French or English law, in order to be legitimate in London? Or solely to follow Catholic liturgy? For some, it was solemnised by sex – which is what we might imagine happened, perhaps involuntarily, on the evening of the 18th. For others, wedding vows could be both in the present tense ('I marry you'), or a promise for the future ('I will marry you'). Most importantly, marriage vows had to be in public and symbolised with the exchange of tokens. Common law, as a general rule, only recognised publicly contracted vows. It was too late to influence this case but in Lord Hardwicke's Marriage Act of 1753 clandestine marriages were banned and a formal marriage cere-mony demanded to solemnise every proper union. The future fate of Dame Mary and her inheritance therefore came down to this: whose narrative account of the events of 18 June did the judges and bishops find the most compelling?

At the end of the hearing, the judges then went away to make their judgment. It took nearly seven months before the judgment finally arrived on 19 February 1705. On that day it was announced: 'The Court having heard, seen and understood, and fully deliber-ately discussed the merits and circumstances of appeal and complaint … that the said Dame Mary shall be absolved from all claim set forth by the said Edward in his libel above said, and that silence shall for ever be imposed on him touching the same.'

On the following day, the judgment was broadcast in the *News Letter*, stuck between marriage notices and the report of a ship lost near Land's End, giving more detail: 'It appearing that she was not, according to proof made, *compos mentis* at the time of the pretended marriage in France, so that the same is null and void and Mr Fenwick has lost his expectation of a rich bride.'[8]

At last Dame Mary was free of the tragedy. She had been found to be the innocent in an unfortunate affair. She was once again a widow, not a wife. But, of course, it was not her victory alone, nor was she the person who was to benefit the most from this ruling. The joy was to go to Sir Richard, on his continental getaway, who now stood to inherit the whole estate without hindrance. As Francis Cholmondeley noted in his celebratory letter to his young charge: 'I have gained the point against the villain's act, as ever was perpetuated by the worst rakes in the world, and what was never known in any court. You are all now freed from an insulting party, who I had to contest with.' Mrs Tregonwell also wrote to her grandson, while apologising for not being in contact often enough, 'to wish you joy of your mother's good success for which we have all laboured', further reminding him that: 'nobody has been so naturally concerned as myself.'[9] Both pieces of correspondence remind us that the focus of concern was, inevitably, not Dame Mary herself but her inheritance.

* * *

Now that the estate was safely in the hands of the children's guardians, what did Dame Mary's future hold? She was forty years old. A mother to three boys, and the five-year-old Anne. The court rulings had been in her favour and this once again ensured that she was a very rich woman. She could, if she wished, follow the path of widowhood set out by Lady Russell, who refused to remarry or be part of court society, and instead spent her time on improving the family estate, and the marriage prospects of her children. She could find a 'good man', or allow one to be found for her from the wide circle of Cheshire gentry, and remarry; this time allowing Cholmondeley to negotiate the terms of the union to protect her inheritance and that of her children. She might even renounce the world and return to Europe to join a convent, as she had pressed Mrs Cookson to do.

But whatever the future held, the present had to be protected. Who could say she might not go off again, and behave in a manner that put the estate once more into jeopardy? Were there other Fenwicks who might exploit a vulnerable widow? There were enough plays on the London stage about such tragedies, that were more often than not played for comic amusements. But now that Sir Richard was getting close to the age when he was expected to inherit his father's lands, this possible calamity could not be allowed to be repeated.

And so, within two weeks of the Court of Delegates judgment, a commission was set up in Chester to assess Dame Mary's mental health. The start of the process was the issuance of a writ of *de lunatico inquirendo*. This was another legal process leading to a judgment upon Dame Mary, and one that could once again dispossess her of her inheritance. But this time those who stood to accuse her were not plotters hoping to exploit her weakness, but her own family. On 2 March, a commission was collected together to judge Dame Mary's mental health and to decide on whether she should be allowed to continue to have control over her wealth and estate. Was she too mad to look after herself, and if so, who should look after her?

Such a hearing reveals the unusual social and legal position, in transition, of the mad during these early days in the history of psychiatry. Much of this history has been influenced by the work of the French historian of ideas, Michel Foucault. He proposed that from 1660, across Europe, a regime of social discipline was imposed upon the mad, that he called 'the great confinement'.[10] This saw the development of a legal system of segregation and institutionalisation between the rational world and the irrational. If this were true of France, the primary region of Foucault's study, what was going on in England was different. We should look beyond the theory to see what actually came to pass concerning both the legal treatment of the insane, and how they were treated after they had been legally identified as incapable of looking after themselves.

During the seventeenth century, the main area of care had been either the local parish through the Vagrancy Act, that included the feeble-minded and deranged under local care, or the by-now-shuttered Court of Wards. As a result, the insane were first defined as vagrants or orphans. This placed an emphasis on the patient's ability to function, rather than a psychiatric assessment. The mad were therefore treated in the community. Often the judgment was that the patient was allowed to remain free 'so long as she shall carry herself quietly or orderly'.[11] In one instance, a woman was free to live in her village but was fastened to a post when she became violent, on one occasion plucking out her own eye. Elsewhere, a villager who had left to live by himself in the local hills was brought back and cleaned up, and the parish paid for him to live with the priest.[12]

Treated as orphans, the mad also came under the purview of the Court of Wards, where Hugh Audley had made his fortune, the source of Dame Mary's inheritance. Like orphans, the patient judged *non compos mentis* came under the care of the Crown and found guardians – not immediate heirs or beneficiaries for obvious reasons – to care for them. But after 1646, once the court was finally shuttered, the management of the sick moved to the Chancery. This did not initiate a centralised state system of care and confinement, as Foucault suggested happened elsewhere. Once again, it was determined that the social question of the insane remained private, or within the local community. It was the work of Justices of the Peace and parish officials, and not high court judges, to decide whether the sovereign rights of the individual were curtailed. There was to be no legal ruling on the insane for another seventy years, when the laws of confinement first made it into the statute, as part of the 1774 Mad House Act.

The capabilities of the patient were the utmost consideration for any commission, to establish whether they could look after themselves with some help, and yet there were rarely any doctors at a commission hearing. This was not a forum for medical definitions of madness, and it was assumed that a local officer or Justice of the Peace was expert enough to tell if someone was in need of care. This was defined, it seems, by the social norms of living an orderly life.

But what was normal? This was obviously differentiated by class as well as gender. During the seventeenth century, it is estimated that more men were placed in care of some kind, but this was changing. The feminisation of madness, a diagnosis based on mental frailty, overpowering passions and hysteria, was on the rise. Men were violent, angry, manic, while women were more likely to be sad, and passive, and therefore less of a threat to others, if not to themselves. As the eighteenth century progressed, more women were diagnosed mad than men.

Therefore, the commission had to assess four questions in front of them. The first was whether the patient was mad but no harm to anyone. Secondly, whether the patient was able to look after their own affairs, or whether others should be made trustees of the property. Thirdly, whether the patient was criminally responsible for their actions. Finally, if a patient was a threat to the public order, and whether they should be incarcerated for their own good and the good of the community.

The laws of judging a person mad were still very much in their infancy. Being mentally ill was not a crime, and the regimes of punishment that later befell the disturbed had not yet been instituted, in England at least. In a trial, the prosecution had to prove criminal intent, *mens rea*, yet someone who was mad, whether temporarily or more permanently, was not considered responsible for their actions. And therefore could not be judged guilty. However, they could still be held under the Vagrancy Act that set out 'prisoning, chaining and sending them to their proper homes' as appropriate measures.[13]

As far as Dame Mary's case was concerned, she had already been judged *non compos mentis* at the Court of Delegates. And so the role of this hearing was to decide the duty of care over the patient. In particular, who was going to have control of her estate? And within weeks a dispute erupted between Francis Cholmondeley, guardian of the children's estate, and Mrs Tregonwell, making conflicting appeals to the Lord Chancellor to be the person to take care of the patient and her fortune.

Francis Cholmondeley expounded his close ties to the Grosvenor family, and his legal duties to Dame Mary's children. Dame Mary, he argued, should be allowed to stay near Eaton Hall, where:

> the lady had the satisfaction of her own fancy and contrivance when she was in her right understanding, and was the place where she took the most satisfaction in, it being amongst her husband's relations, and the place of her children's residence when from school, and under the inspection of the patina [Cholmondeley] for whom the Lady has constantly declared a great friendship and respect.

However, his most choice words were reserved for why Mrs Tregonwell should not be allowed to care for her daughter. It was a damning catalogue of maternal failings. His account of what went wrong starts after the death of Sir Thomas, when Mrs Tregonwell even failed to make enquiries of her daughter's welfare. And once

Dame Mary had come down to London, her mother did little to stop her going to France with Lodowick Fenwick, despite a supposed concern for her mental health. When her daughter had come home to London, she had lodged briefly with Mrs Tregonwell but later, during the period of the court cases, when a grandson had requested to stay with his grandmother in London, she had refused. On another occasion she had refused to look after the four-year-old Anne, claiming she was too old. Cholmondeley asked, 'if there were not rooms for two small children, how will the house be large enough for the Lady, her physicians, tenders and servants?'

He dealt the *coup de grâce* by highlighting Mrs Tregonwell's desperate need for money, and her prior willingness to sell her daughter for the sake of the estate. Her second husband 'was an extravagant man, and much diminished his estate', and with numerous children and grandchildren from her second marriage to consider, she might not be able to resist leaning on her daughter's fortune for their future comfort. She 'would seek to advance them by the Lady's, either by selling her again in marriage in some lucid interval, or by getting her in that interval to settle the lands of inheritance as Mrs Tregonwell would have them settled.'[14] No love lost there.

But Mrs Tregonwell was made of stern stuff; she had not got this far without having a survivor's instincts. She replied with a fulsome *apologia* outlining everything that she had done for her daughter. We have seen how young Mary Davies was furnished with the finest clothes, servants, a governess, a coach with six horses in the attempt to carry on with 'an air of greatness answerable to the fortune she was supposed to have'. But she also makes a mother's plea:

> The entire affection she always bore to her daughter both for her own sake and for the sake of her father who had been so generous to her, the principles of justice and honour instilled in her from her cradle, and the whole conduct of her life should, one would think suffise to screen her from any such imputation, and yet so it is that some have maliciously suggested that she join'd in selling her daughter at a certain price, and make several unfair advantages of her.

All these matters came to a conclusion in April 1705, when there was a hearing on the care of Dame Mary.[15] The options available to courts were limited, and once again go against the assumptions laid out by Michel Foucault. In his history of the great confinement of the mad, large state-run asylums started to emerge throughout the seventeenth century and dominated the methods of segregation and control of the insane. As Dame Mary's case was being debated, there were no state asylums in England. Bedlam was a charitable foundation, originating in the thirteenth century, which stood on Moorfields, north of London's wall, and the only such institution in the nation. Much is made of the fact that citizens could pay an entrance fee to come and view the lunatics, like zoo animals. It sometimes deserved its reputation as a graphic condemnation of man's cruelty to his vulnerable fellow. But this does not necessarily reflect the range of care institutions available.

In 1700, there was a pamphlet that demanded 'one general hospital erected in each county ... For the reception and maintenance of all poor lunatics, idiots, blind persons, maim'd soldiers and seamen, cripples incapable of relieving themselves by any manufacture or Labour.' But such pleas, for the time being, fell on deaf ears. The second public asylum was not founded until 1713 in Norwich, and then Thomas Guy bequeathed after his death in 1724 a ward in a new hospital to be dedicated to the care of 'incurables', including the insane.

At the same time, Daniel Defoe demanded the foundation of public asylums as a response to the unaccountable care provided by the private asylums set up across the country. Such institutions did not necessarily advertise themselves for obvious reasons, and varied hugely in the manner of their duty of care, and so the actual number is impossible to calculate. On his 1724 tour of Britain, Defoe counted twenty-four metropolitan madhouses. The nature of such institutions varied tremendously, from the care of a few parishioners by the local priest, paid for by the community, to cottage industries run by quacks who promised miracle cures. A 1714 Act specifically banned the whipping of lunatics, and in that year one keeper, Thomas Fallowes, was fined £600 for the maltreatment of his vulnerable charges.[16] His only defence was that others were worse: 'the rough and cruel Treatment, which is said to be the Method of most of the Pretenders to this cure'.[17] Legislators were reluctant to get involved with these enterprises until 1763 when an inspectorate was called for, and in 1774 the Mad House Act set out some rudimentary regulations.

However, for people of quality such as Dame Mary, institutionalisation was unnecessary. The purpose of the commission was not to protect her person, but her fortune. She already had doctors and maids to look after her. In the 1690s, there had been servants with the particular task of looking after her welfare. One of the scandals of the Fenwicks' plot had been how they surreptitiously divided the mistress from her carers. Nevertheless, the commission did decide that Dame Mary was to remain under the guardianship of Sir Francis Cholmondeley. There remains in the Eaton Archives an elaborate grant of custody. It is a contract of sorts, announcing: 'A grant of the custody of the person and estate of Dame Mary Grosvenor widow relict of Sir Thomas Grosvenor Baronet served unto Francis Cholmondeley esq'.[18]

* * *

This is one ending of the story. The estate was secure after the turbulence of the last five years, since the death of Sir Thomas. Dame Mary now no longer had any legal control over the Manor of Ebury, which was safely in the hands of the trustees. When Sir Francis died in 1713, the commission was recalled and it passed the trusteeship of Dame Mary to another relation, Sir Richard Myddleton, at nearby Chirk Castle. And when Sir Richard died, Dame Mary returned to Vale Royal and the care of Charles Cholmondeley. The grant of custody described her as: 'Dame Mary Grosvenor, she being a lunatic and unable to govern herself and to manage her said estate during the continuance of her lunacy'.

And it appears that she remained in ill health for the rest of her life, living for another twenty-five years under the care of others.

Nonetheless, elsewhere it was back to business. In 1705, months after the grant of custody, Francis Cholmondeley signed the first lease within the Manor of Ebury on behalf of the teenaged Sir Richard Grosvenor, who was still abroad on travels and remained out of the country for another four years. It was not until 1709 that it was felt safe for Sir Richard to return home, far from the scandal or, even, from kidnap.

In 1708, Mrs Tregonwell once again attempted to take control of some of the land, taking her daughter and her trustees to court. The case came to nothing but during the proceedings the grandmother reached out to Sir Richard, sending him a copy of her apologia, prepared three years earlier. However, her grandson was not to be moved. He regretted that the two sides of the family had fallen out but wrote that 'the court justly decreed the custody to an honest gentleman who, not only appeared a true friend to my mother (when she wanted) … and adventured his health, his person, and his purse too, to rescue her from a most ruinous design, when she had no other friend that would join with him in carrying on so dangerous an attack.'[19] That seemed to quiet the old woman for the time being.

In 1716, following the death of Sir Richard Myddleton, as Dame Mary returned to Vale Royal and the care of Charles Cholmondeley, the grandson considered it politic to communicate with his grandmother once again, and so sent a lawyer, Mr Meitts, to Millbank. Here, Mrs Tregonwell, now seventy-four, asked if there was any legal opportunity for her to regain control of her daughter and was told there was not. As Meitts later reported, 'But (that I may trouble you with no more of our dialogue), she at last told me she well approved Mr Cholmondeley and (though the right was with her) would give no opposition, for all she endeavoured was the good of her family.'[20]

Of course, the slow dissolve of Dame Mary's mark upon the records of the period does not mean that she herself vanished. Her retreat into the care of others was a return to the norm for most women of her period: first a daughter, then wife. It was only the brief moment of widowhood when she was in charge of her own destiny. And now she was, once again, under the charge of another man. This was, after all, a woman's burden. We should be surprised by how much of her life is in the public record rather than how little. But we should also challenge the assumption that this meant that it was not a lived life.

This silence was a form of violence imposed upon the patient. There are few records of her illness during these decades of care. Did she have both good days and bad? Did the condition get worse until she was no longer herself, or did she find an equilibrium that, with care, made the reduced circumstances of her life a whole, rich existence? Despite the wealth of material, the witness statements, the records that cover other aspects of her life, it is impossible to know, for certain, that she was ill or not, or what the nature of her malady might have been.

Was she beyond saving in her mania or melancholy? Some descriptions give the suggestion that she had bipolar disorder, a mental disease that is often managed today with a medical regime. Another interpretation might be that she was overcome by grief and that the major events in her life – her conversion to Catholicism, the episodes in the 1690s, and the trip to Paris – map onto the deaths of her two sons and her husband. In another interpretation, one could read that her disorder was interwoven with her condition as a woman unable to find her subjectivity, driven mad in desperation as she hoped to escape her state of submission. On top of this is the trauma of the night of 18 June 1701, when she was, on the balance of probabilities, violated by Edward Fenwick, and there was no means to process this in conjunction with everything else she was forced to deal with.

These are interpretations based on the scant array of documents and records that happen to have survived three hundred years. The mother was rarely, if ever, mentioned in the letters passed between siblings over the following decades. No mention of how she was faring. Where she might be. Whether they had visited her. This did not mean they did not write. There are probably many, some in Dame Mary's own hand, that told the whole story, from her perspective, that did not survive. Scrunched up and placed in the bin to be taken away by servants. Thrown upon a bonfire at Vale Royal in an effort to tidy up. Sorted and abandoned by following generations who did not see such testimony as important or worthy of preservation. Lost in the archives. Eaten by damp or beetles. This is, let us not forget, the fate of most of our nation's record.

This was not the end of Dame Mary's story, however. She would live for another twenty-five years. And the main reason why her name is so often repeated in history books on the development of London and remains relevant today is a result of events that happened in the final decades of her life, when she was far away from the capital. At the same time, the story moves from the fate of her body to the future of her inheritance, the Manor of Ebury, and the next period of expansion of the limits of London.

'An Amazing Scene of
New Foundations'

THE PRODIGAL SON, Sir Richard, returned from his years abroad at some point in 1707. It had been at least three years since he had left England; nevertheless, still only eighteen, he was a changed man. A gentleman of experience and education. At the start of his travels, Francis Cholmondeley had encouraged his charge always to carry a memorandum book with him, so that he could mark down his thoughts or observations, 'and employ your mind to make everything useful to you and easy'. His head was now so filled with continental memories that what had been happening at home may have felt distant and incomprehensible. On the cusp of his majority, he was ready to become the master of the house at Eaton Hall, as well as the heir of the Manor of Ebury.

What had he brought back in his trunk and carriage? He had collected works, books and sculptures that had been sent home ahead of his arrival, and stored in the family home. Did he now start to spread these goods through Eaton Hall in order to give it a modern look? Did he take advice on how to improve the rooms in ways similar to those he had seen in Paris or Florence? Was there a desire for something new, to improve the rooms that now reminded him of his departed father? Something befitting the new century.

In the year of Sir Richard's return, the Dutch engravers Johannes Kip and Leonard Knyff published their lavishly produced *Britannia*

Illustrata that contained views of all the major houses in the kingdom. This included royal palaces, urban powerhouses, as well as stately homes which were now all the rage throughout the counties. It was a catalogue of privilege displaying the recent supremacy of the elites and how they showed their potency through their land: the power of property. In addition, the collection marked the architectural turning point from the English baroque that had dominated thus far, towards neoclassicism. The new century demanded a new aesthetic horizon, one that returned to Vitruvian principles of order; in particular, the work of Palladio across the Veneto, which now had become an essential destination on every cultured gallant's Grand Tour.

Plate 62 of Kip's volume shows Eaton Hall. The park had now matured since being set out by Sir Thomas thirty years previously. The terraces and avenues are mathematically precise and symmetrical. This is the very essence of order over Nature. The landscape is a statement of belief in private property above all things, and the extraordinary wealth that came from it. Ownership now organised the world and gave it its rhyme and reason, a natural law as indisputable as gravity. Anything that went against this pull defied the order of the universe.

Nevertheless, it is possible to look at this image of the family estate, and to see this projection of omnipotence as a veneer; a covering that hid deeper, more disturbing turbulence. Did Sir Richard recognise the fragility submerged below the surface? On his return, he also went to see Francis Cholmondeley at Vale Royal, and undoubtedly visited his mother there. But there are no notes on what was said, or how this new relationship was rekindled after so many years and dramas. Was he able to hide his surprise at her changed condition? Did he believe her when she protested her innocence? Could he forgive her for putting his future into jeopardy?

In a portrait painted eight years later, when he was about to become a public man and follow his father as MP for Chester and mayor of the city, he gives little away. He is defined by the garments of office: the mayoral cloak, the sober black coat and the thin staff balanced in his right hand, a folded black cap in his left. There are

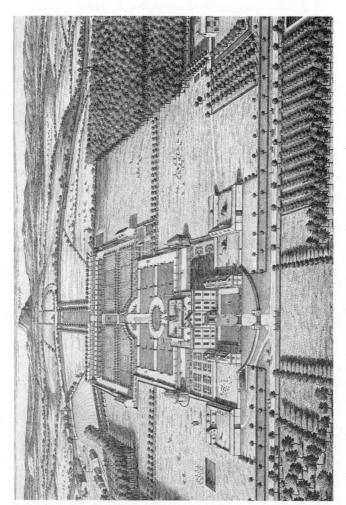

Eaton Hall from Kip and Knyff's *Britannia Illustrata*

no other signals to his position, wealth, history. The setting is nondescript, the room is panelled, he stands by a covered table; he could be in an antechamber waiting to go into the council chamber. This is a model of duty and tradition: a modern man to be judged by his seriousness and his place in the social order. This was a departure from the dashing pose of his father in his portrait by Lely in the 1670s, who wished us to see who he was through his taste and estate. Ironically, it was Sir Richard who gained the epithet 'The great builder' later in his life. There is little sign of that grand schemer here.

Portrait of Sir Richard, as a city official, soon after his arrival back in England

As well as returning home to Eaton Hall as master, preparations were made for a wedding. A question as important as Sir Richard's hand in marriage was tightly orchestrated by the trustees, but there may be suggestions that the young man had some say in his choice of wife. In 1708, he married Jane Wyndham, daughter of Sir Edward Wyndham, a leading Somerset landowner and MP. The father had died a decade beforehand and the estate had passed to his son, William, who had been at Eton College (at the same time as Sir Richard) and had also travelled through France and Italy in 1704–8. Such similar fellows found each other on the continent, and became friends.

Either way, Jane Wyndham was a fine catch. Politically, it was a Tory alliance between two major landowning families. That same year, William Wyndham married the daughter of the Duke of Somerset and soon entered Parliament; he was named by Queen Anne in 1712 as Master of the Buckhounds, leaping to Chancellor of the Exchequer two years later. By the end of 1714, he was one of the leaders of the Jacobite rebellion, and was briefly imprisoned. For such reasons, a marriage contract was necessary, especially as the status of the Manor of Ebury remained so confused. In an agreement from June 1708, a dowry of £12,000 was handed over and, in return, a jointure arranged.[1]

However, in order to sort out the complex situation over the Manor of Ebury once and for all, the family had to take the case to the House of Commons and get MPs to legislate the actual circumstances of the estate. The family needed Parliament's permission to begin the process of turning the Davies inheritance to profit. As the Act stated it was necessary for Parliament to permit the marriage 'notwithstanding the Lunacy of Dame Mary Grosvenor … and for settling the Estate in the Family, and, making Building Leases, as effectually as if the said Dame Mary was of sound Mind.'[2] To add to the confusion, Mrs Tregonwell was still thriving and in charge of her widow's third. Meanwhile, Dame Mary's inheritance was bound up with the commission of lunacy and rents continued to be collected and held by the Chancery.

The Grosvenors were now making the transition from land-owners to land speculators. The Act was finally passed as a private Bill in 1711 and, most significantly, permitted the family to start leasing out plots of land. It stipulated that this could only be for a maximum of sixty years. This meant that there needed to be special oversight of the plots developed on Dame Mary's lands, especially the Hundred Acres at the north-east corner of the Manor. The question of inheritance was also fixed. The estate was to be handed down the male line. Firstly, to Sir Richard's sons, and if childless, to his brothers and their sons. There were to be no more heiresses.

At the same time, Sir Richard was developing his interest in politics, taking up his almost-hereditary status in Chester politics as well as in Westminster. He carried the baton passed on from his father and joined the Tory faction, believing in the power of the monarchy, and the protection of the established Anglican Church. However, it appears from his political record that Sir Richard barely left a mark. One of his few decisive actions in 1715 was to attend a Jacobite meeting in Cheshire where it was voted not to be part of the rebellion in support of James II's son, James Francis Edward Stuart, who had landed in Scotland, hoping to rally an insurgent army. Nevertheless, Sir Richard's connection to leading conspirator William Wyndham meant that he was nonetheless seen as a sympathiser. After 1715, he voted consistently against George I's Whig government. However, in the next decade, his politics did not follow him into his role as landlord, where he was happy to attract tenants from both sides of the political divide.

Despite his years in Europe, Sir Richard seemed close to his two younger brothers, Thomas and Robert. Robert went up to Eton in 1707 and then on to Oxford where he matriculated on the same day as Thomas, 21 October 1712. Thomas was eighteen at the time, Robert seventeen. There seems to have been a continual flow of letters between the brothers, catching up on family news and social gossip. When in London, they tended to stay in Millbank, sometimes with their grandmother, and there was often news about their Tregonwell cousins. In June 1714, Robert reported, 'My grandmother has been much out of order, but is now pretty well; she still complains pretty much, but (I think) with little reason, for to all appearance she is as hearty now as she was ten years ago.' Elsewhere: 'I received a letter today from my sister, the family at Millbank are well.'

There was news of guests at Eaton Hall: 'Piggot acquaints me that the very merry and jocose Mr Sherborne is with you, who I know is very pleasant and diverting company, so shall not presume to say much in order to divert you.' Society weddings: 'I suppose by this time it is no news to you that old Portman Seymour is married to one Miss Fitz, a young girl under fifteen. He is three score and above two years older than his wife.' As well as nights on the town: 'we were together at the tavern on Wednesday night together with Mr Prince, the pewterer in Pall Mall, where we drank your's [*sic*] and Robin Piggot's healths; we drank pretty heartily, and parted about one in the morning.' During the 1715 rebellion, Oxford came under suspicion as a hotbed of Jacobitism, and Robert relishes the rumours that 'several swords and bayonets [were] seized here, supposed to have been intended for the Pretender's service', but turned out to be nothing of the sort. And the perennial interest of the turf: 'we had very good sport every day. The Marquis of Carmarthen won the £40 plate, Mr Holman the Bucks and Does, and Mr Oakley the Gentleman's plate worth £30. I will endeavour, if possible, to get a list of all the horses and how they came in, which if I can obtain I will send to you.'[3]

But nowhere were there mentions of Dame Mary, or questions after her health. She had, it seemed, disappeared from the conversations of others. Or did they know the answers without asking? She remained unwell. Another cloak of silence around her final years, woven by her own children.

* * *

At the same time, London was growing once again, and building soon reached the eastern boundary of the Manor of Ebury. The city's population was on the move, and the continued rise of the urban bourgeoisie increased the demand for new housing in the suburbs. Events abroad also accelerated the sense of optimism at home, acting as a catalyst for a revival of the building boom of the 1680s. In 1713, Britain withdrew from the War of the Spanish Succession through the Treaty of Utrecht to focus on more domestic affairs. And so in the second decade of the new century, a new generation of aristocratic landowners sought to profit from turning their pastureland to squares and houses.

One of the heralds of this expansion was the 1710 Parliamentary Commission that calculated that since 1660, London had grown so quickly that nearly half the population now lived in neighbourhoods without a parish church. So, the following year, the politicians set up plans for fifty new churches in the outlying suburbs to equal the number of churches rebuilt after the Great Fire. In the end, this proved overambitious and only twelve new edifices were finished, including Nicholas Hawksmoor's Christchurch, Spitalfields, St George in the East and St Anne's, Limehouse, reflecting the expansion of the city eastwards towards the docks. South of the Thames, Hawksmoor revived St Alfege in Greenwich, and worked with John James on St John Horsleydown in Bermondsey. Thomas Archer worked alone at the parish church for the new settlements at Deptford, St Paul's.

There were also significant developments to the west of the city. Again, Hawksmoor, who had done his apprenticeship in Sir Christopher Wren's office, was called on in Bloomsbury, on the edge of the estate developed by Lady Russell, developing the idiosyncratic St George's Church. Here Hawksmoor replaced the spire with a re-imagining of the Mausoleum at Halicarnassus, and then placed George I on top. Closer to Westminster, there was also work at St John's, Smith Square, the neighbouring estate to Millbank, where the Smith family were starting to develop a new well-to-do neighbourhood set around Archer's elaborate confection. Close to Piccadilly, work had also begun on St George's, Hanover Square, on another plot that rubbed up against the eastern boundary of Dame Mary's inheritance.

These projects signalled the next phase of the capital's expansion, breaking new ground to expand the girth of the city, and the consolidation of the square as the paradigmatic urban form; as Guy Miège explained in 1707: 'the nobility, and chief among the gentry, are at this time much better accommodated in fine Squares, or streets; where they breath[e] a good air, and have houses built after the modern way ... in short London is remarkable for its multitude of squares.'[4]

In 1713, work started on Hanover Square, picking up where Hinde's failed syndicate had abandoned their schemes. The landowner, Richard Lumley, first Earl of Scarborough, commissioned a survey of his plot. So far, he had had a distinguished career as a soldier, that was converted into a political career, joining the Whigs and rising to the position of privy councillor. But this had come to a halt in 1712 as the Tory party briefly ascended to power. Scarborough clearly then sought influence elsewhere. Work started on the square after the arrival of George I on the throne in 1714, and it was an act of astute fealty to name the square after the new royal house.

Scarborough's aspirations at Hanover Square were speculative. He had no new urban vision, instead following the template, form and process of previous schemes, picking up the same pattern as St James's or Leicester Squares without any modification. A central square was planned and plots leased out to leading builders around the edge. A large main house was located at the north end; the other houses, sold as plots to individual builders, were large enough to attract the leading tenants. The square was connected to already existing neighbourhoods to the north, Oxford Street and Soho to the east, and most importantly Piccadilly to the south, which linked it to the royal court and St James's Park. It was on this route, George Street, that the new resplendent parish church was placed. In 1717, the *News Medley* announced: 'Round about the new square, which is building near Oxford Road, there are so many other edifices that a whole magnificent city seems to be risen out of the ground, that one would wonder how it should find a new set of inhabitants.'[5]

It was important for the long-term prospect of such a project that it attracted the right kind of people. This was the time when the idea of a good address became as important as the house itself. Squares were cultivated as brands, for different sections of the elite. And Scarborough encouraged his close friends and comrades to populate his development. This included the Lord Chancellor, William Cowper, who had been on the privy council alongside the landowner, as well as a disproportionate number of military men: the Duke of Roxburghe, and 'The Lord Cadogan, a general; also General Carpenter, General Wills, General Evans, General Pepper, the two General Stuarts, and several others'.[6]

Only one street ran off the west side of the square, Brook Street, as far as Bond Street; and beyond, the countryside of the Manor of Ebury. For now.

Meanwhile, to the south, there was a different kind of development emerging as part of the Burlington estate. Burlington House, designed in 1665, alongside the neighbouring Berkeley House and Clarendon House, was a grand *hôtel* in the most Frenchified style. The original owner, Sir John Denham, had sold it to the second Earl of Burlington almost as soon as he started work on it. Burlington then spent another fortune on making the house a palace before dying in the 1690s. His son, the third Earl, finally inherited it on his majority in 1715, having spent much of his youth on the Grand Tour in Europe picking up a taste for the finer things. Immediately, he decided not only to update his family home but to transform the whole estate, establishing him not just as a major urban speculator but an artistic patron, offering a beacon of good taste to the rest of the nation.

Firstly, the Earl had to obtain a private Act of Parliament that allowed him to develop the land behind the house into a series of streets. But first, he started on improving the family house; and in 1717 turned to Colen Campbell to transform his dream into stone. Campbell was already established as one of the most cutting-edge designers of the era. Like many of his peers, he had travelled to Italy, and had dedicated himself to bringing neoclassicism across the Channel. In 1715, he published the first of the three volumes of *Vitruvius Britannicus*, a catalogue of the finest examples of modern design, while also launching an attack on the excesses of the baroque. It was a youthful cry of rebellion for authenticity.

However, Burlington's debts soon started to stack up and it became increasingly necessary to speculate on the land to the north of the house, that had remained garden and waste ground surrounded by new developments. The future of the site was clear. However, unlike other schemes, instead of setting out individual plots and selling them to speculators who built according to their own designs, the whole scheme was overseen by Campbell, and only the most fashionable architects were permitted to design here. Burlington himself spent much of 1718 on the development. Most of the plots were leased on a two-year peppercorn rate as the houses were under construction, and then, by 1720 or so, a full ground rent was demanded.

In 1724, the former Scottish spy and travel writer John Macky noted admirably in his *Journey through England*: 'three noble Streets finely pav'd; the Houses balustraded with Iron, and few of them under a hundred Pounds a Year Rent, most of them more'.[7] Within these relatively small ten acres, the houses themselves were still impressive. One was designed by Giacomo Leoni, while others came under the names of Nicholas Dubois, Colen Campbell, William Kent (who met Burlington in 1718 in Italy and became the close design partners), Henry Flitcroft and Nicholas Hawksmoor. One house, 29 Old Burlington Street, belonging to General Wade, was designed by Burlington himself in order to accommodate an unusually large canvas by Rubens that the soldier had picked up in Holland.

Such attention to design and detail did not necessarily bring Burlington the fortune for which he was hoping. Any time there was a prospect of cash, the aristocrat tended to spend it on his next architectural venture rather than paying off his debts. In 1727, he was forced to mortgage off the ten acres for £15,000 to a London merchant. And he was persuaded to develop more ground, adding Savile Row, connecting his estate to the Conduit Mead estate that had once been owned by Hinde and was now in the hands of the City of London Corporation. By the 1730s, the development had moved northwards so that it reached the boundary of the Hanover Estate. And while it connected to the rest of the city, it nevertheless stood apart. Burlington made no attempt at a square or to give the impression of *rus in urbe*. There were no green spaces apart from the gardens of Burlington House itself. Every vista was closed off with a cross street, so that the view northwards up Cork Street and Burlington Street ended with a neatly composed architectural feature rather than a view to the countryside beyond. This gave the effect of the estate looking in on itself, restricting through traffic, creating an elite enclave cut off from the rest of the city.

Watching such exciting ventures on neighbouring land probably spurred Sir Richard Grosvenor further to revive the spirit of his grandfather, Alexander Davies, and become a speculator himself. However, it was clear from these events that the area that might profit most from development was not at Millbank. Here,

Peterborough House, where Dame Mary had spent her first years, still remained the most westerly limit of the city. Work had not yet started on the expansion westwards from Westminster. The most profitable land was that south of Tyburn Road (Oxford Street) bordering Hanover Square, the very land tied up by the legacy of his mother and grandmother.

As a result it was not until 1717, and the death of Mrs Tregonwell, that Sir Richard was able to move forward. The formidable woman, who had held the estate together since 1665, was buried at St Mary's Westminster, beside her first husband, Alexander Davies. It was the only tomb in the churchyard, and was engraved with the epitaph: 'She was a lady of exemplary piety and charity and dyed universally lamented.' She certainly died a rich woman and shared her wealth amongst her many children and grandchildren, including the four Grosvenors.

On her death, her widow's third from the original Davies estate now passed on to Dame Mary, whose property was managed by the Chancery and the terms of the 1711 Act of Parliament. The Act stipulated a limitation upon any future leases within this property to an upper limit of sixty years, until Dame Mary's death. This posed a problem: as many previous landowners had discovered, no aristocrat was going to be willing to pay for the construction of a new house with only a sixty-year lease. It needed to be at least ninety-nine years in order to satisfy the buyer's substantial expense: 'the intended buildings being very large'.[8] Somehow, Sir Richard was going to have to find a loophole if he were to succeed. He would also spend the next decades attempting to release the cash held by the state on his behalf in order to pay for new sewers and other essential preparations for the developments to come.

The first task in hand was to find a pair of officers, an estate surveyor and estate agent, that could run the whole operation. Sir Richard was at that time an MP, as well as a major landowner in the north, and had insufficient time for the details of the London speculation. His younger brother Robert spent more time in London and appeared to be more hands-on with the development of the land, but it was clear that the successful running of this kind of scheme was no longer an elite side-hustle, but a fully professionalised operation. The management of land itself had turned into a sector that demanded a certain kind of expertise.

Originally a carpenter, the estate surveyor Thomas Barlow had gained valuable experience across many of the schemes since the beginning of the new century. However, the job that got him the most attention was negotiating with the Commission for Building Fifty New Churches on behalf of the Earl of Scarborough, on the site for St George's to best enhance Hanover Square. And he was possibly the builder of a number of houses in George Street. By 1720, he was employed by Sir Richard with a £50 golden handshake, and the promise of £50 a year income after that. According to a later agreement, he also had purview on 'all and every of the houses which shall be built on ye said piece of Ground ... so as to range in their fronts in such manner as Mr Thos. Barlow the present Surveyor of the said Lunatick's Estate, or other the Surveyor or Surveyors ... for the time being shall hereafter direct and appoint'.[9]

The estate agent, Richard Andrews, also hired in 1720, was commissioned with collecting the rents. He had previously been a steward of Dame Mary's properties but for some reason had been dismissed in 1706, possibly for malfeasance. However, he was reinstated on the request of Anne Grosvenor. He did not solely collect rents but speculated himself, picking up some of the plots and sub-leasing them. He was also open to offering mortgages to builders who had hit a difficult patch. It is uncertain whether he was putting up his own money or working on behalf of the Grosvenor family. Nevertheless, the job was profitable enough that he got his son Robert, a lawyer from the Inner Temple, into the agent's office, and together they had the operation sewn up well into the 1730s.

With these two officers running the project, the Grosvenor Estate, despite the complication surrounding Dame Mary's inheritance, was now in business. Where plots covered by the 1711 Act ran into the problem of the limitation of a sixty-year lease, a legal fudge was found. Barlow simply wrote agreements for sixty years and 'a further term of years ... as shall be agreed to be granted for building the new intended Square'.[10] In June 1721, some relief came when forty-three acres were placed in trust to Richard Myddleton, and he was able to grant longer leases, not exceeding ninety-nine years, as long as it was passed through the Chancery. Elsewhere, such as east of what became Davies Street, the surveyor tended to grant leases for only eighty years. It was a slow process but it allowed for the kind of improvements that Grosvenor desired.

At the same time, another scheme was beginning to emerge to the north of Tyburn Road, the Harley-Cavendish estate. This new settlement focused on the centrally planned Cavendish Square, designed to attract the Tory faction, in political and geographic opposition to the Whiggish Hanover Square. The aristocratic developer was Edward Harley, the second Earl of Oxford, and son of Queen Anne's first minister who had recently been imprisoned and later released by George I. The scheme quickly ran into a crisis, the result of another speculative venture. In 1720, catastrophe struck the whole enterprise with the explosion of the South Sea Bubble that engulfed many of the grandees who had invested in the estate development. The South Sea Bank had been established in 1711 by Harley's father, as a Tory alternative to the Bank of England. The Company was promised a monopoly over all trade from South America, but quickly pivoted into more lucrative slavery and taking on government debt.

In January 1720, the Company attempted to boost its own share price. Trading at £128, it made the claim that there were big profits on the horizon with its South American routes. By the next month, the stock price had risen to £175. The following month, the government accepted a proposal for the Company to take on more of the national debt and the price rocketed up to £555 in May. In June, an Act of Parliament made it law that all joint stock companies had to gain a royal charter, knocking out any potential competition. At the same time, a new market emerged to take advantage of this investor boom. London became consumed with financial speculation. That summer, the price reached a peak of £1,050.

But just as stocks rocket up, they can plummet with similar velocity. The selloff began in July as confidence started to wobble. By September, the price was back at £175. It was not just investors who lost out, but also bankers and goldsmiths who could no longer recover their loans. Even a genius such as Sir Isaac Newton was burned, forced to write off £20,000, claiming that: 'I can calculate the movement of the stars, but not the madness of men.'[11] By December, there

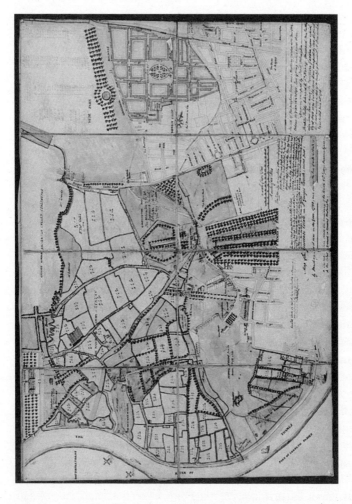

John Mackay's prospective map of the layout of the new development, 1723

were calls for a government inquiry, which inevitably uncovered widespread fraud. In the end, the enterprise was folded into the East India Company, and recorded as the first financial 'bubble'.

Such an economic bust had a huge impact on all other forms of speculation. It is calculated that there has not been such a dramatic fall in economic activity in the three hundred years since, until the 2020 'lockdown' as a consequence of the coronavirus. Work on Cavendish Square screeched to a halt.

It was in the midst of the South Sea speculation that work eventually began on Grosvenor Square. The layout of the whole scheme was devised by Barlow. The surveyor created a large map with the new streetscape, and John Mackay set this out into a compelling projection in 1723. What is apparent is that the scheme followed a standard urban grid form without addressing any topographical particularities of the site. The land itself was highest in the north-west corner and descended towards the River Tyburn that marked the eastern frontier. There was one raised area, called Oliver's Mount, which was one of the last examples of the defensive earthworks constructed by the Parliamentarians during the English Civil War. The map itself represents an urban scheme of a series of nested squares and rectangles clustered around the central *grand place*. There are no details apart from the street names, the oval garden within the square, and a chapel to the south.[12] It was Georgian urban planning by the book.

Efforts were made to link the estate with its neighbours, integrating the new project with the rest of the city. Brook Street continued over the border from the Hanover Estate, while Grosvenor Street was planned to align with St George's classical façade. Less successful was the confused junction with the Berkeley estate to the south, which turned into Berkeley Square a few decades later, and still causes traffic problems today. To the west, the fields of Hyde Park; to the north, the fields of Marylebone with views all the way to Hampstead Hill. Nevertheless the whole estate was designed to look into itself, seemingly turning its back on bustling Tyburn Road and modern-day Park Lane. The focal point of the design was the square itself that sat in the centre of the project. And the development recounted its own history through the street names: Davies Street linked the square to Tyburn Road. Audley Street ran both north and south of the west end of the square. Grosvenor Street ran to the east, connecting the square to Bond Street.

Work started at the edges of the estate in the 1720s. Firstly on Brook Street and Grosvenor Street to the east, and then a few years later to the south on Audley Street and what became the north end of Berkeley Square, and Mount Street. 'Peas, cabbages and turnips once grew where now stands New Bond Street, and a new Square; such piles of buildings now rise up and down, London itself seems going out of town,' noted Daniel Defoe in 1726.[13] Over the next fifty years it moved from the south-east to the north-west, with the last leases signed for plots in the late 1770s. This was partly to do with the complexity of Dame Mary's inheritance but also the proximity of these plots to Tyburnia, today Marble Arch, which still remained the site of regular executions. No respectable people wanted to live cheek by jowl with the carnival at the Tyburn Tree and this section of the estate was mainly home to tradesmen, rather than the elite.

In those first decades, the estate surveyor offered few restrictions on the design of the individual plots. In most agreements, buildings were to be constructed in brick and correspond with their neighbours. Beyond a stipulation to be 'good and substantial', speculators were free to follow their own commercial instincts. Brook Street and Grosvenor Street in particular were planned as boulevards, and some specifications were made on building materials, lighting and pavements so that it was a pleasant place to promenade. Entry to Hyde Park was devised through the exclusive Grosvenor Gate.

Much was made of the diversity of frontages along the streetscape, offering variety and visual interest. As one guide noted:

the fronts are far from being uniform, some of them being entirely of stone, others of brick and stone, and others of rubbed brick, with only their quoins, facias [*sic*], windows and door cases of stone. Some of them are adorned with stone columns of several orders, while others have only plain fronts. Indeed there is the greatest variety of fine buildings that are anywhere to be met in so small a compass, and are so far from uniform, as to be all sashed and to be pretty near of an equal height.[14]

This was the happy result of the impossibility of policing the architecture of the many different builders and schemers, rather than a conscious policy.

As with so many projects, one often wonders: where does the shit go? And here the Grosvenors came up with innovations. Firstly, in order to preserve the elegance of the streets, they devised a network of mews and stables at the rear of the main houses. Dung was banished from the street; instead, to be covered over or moved away into special 'sinks'.[15] For human waste, the Grosvenors themselves constructed a network of sewers that flowed out into a local brook. The investment was recouped through ground rent: six shillings per foot frontage on Grosvenor Street, five on Brook Street, and something similar on Grosvenor Square, which obviously housed larger properties. Sir Richard allowed his brother to pay only two shillings per foot. For the first decade at least, the estate was therefore run at a loss, and in 1730 Sir Richard even had to take a loan of £10,000 from one of his tenants.

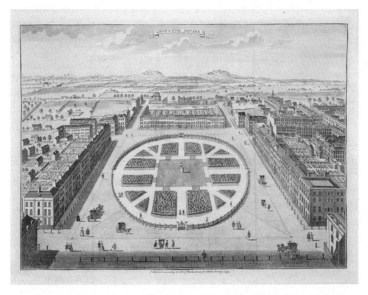

Grosvenor Square, and the oval gardens

It was the plan for the square itself that distinguished the estate from its neighbours. The '*grand place*' was plotted by Barlow to be vast: 68oft by 53oft, still the largest in the capital besides Lincoln's Inn Fields. In a seemingly geometrical tease, at the centre of the square was a 'Garden Oval'. And so, in 1725, Sir Richard contracted John Alston to landscape a 'wilderness work', and then become the official gardener at a salary of £40 a year. Rather than a wilderness as we would understand it, the garden was a sequence of geometric walks and beds, surrounded by low hedges including just under one mile of elm hedging, 4,100 turfs, 2,635 small mixed 'shrubs, plants and evergreens' and 3,000 flowering shrubs. These rural devices encircled a central equestrian statue of George I 'double gilt in gold', commissioned by Sir Richard from sculptor John Nost in 1725. Although the statue was vandalised two years later, its left leg pulled off and 'affixed with a traitorous paper to the pedestal'.[16]

The overall scheme was inspired by the work of English horti-culturist Thomas Fairchild, author of *The City Gardener*. Here he noted that the designer should avoid a 'plain way of laying out Squares in Grass Platts and Gravel Walks' in pursuit of the 'country manner'. This was a space between the city and the countryside, and described in one guide book as: 'different from all the Squares in *London,* and agreeably planted with Dwarf-trees, inter-mixt with fine Walks: It is certainly laid out in a very expensive Taste, and kept with great Decency and Neatness; and the making it octagonal is new in Design and happy in effect.'[17]

The upkeep of the gardens was managed by an annual fee of 9d for all the residents on the square, although this soon proved to be insufficient. By 1729, the costs had reach an eye-watering £2,871. Nonetheless, this presented a shared space, but only for those who could afford it, as set out in housing agreements for residents, granting 'Liberty and Privilege in Common with other Tenants fronting on the said new intended Square of walking within the Garden designed to be made in the said new intended Square and of having and keeping a Key or Keys to the Gate or Gates thereof.'[18] Here was a paradox: this was an enclosed commons for the elite only. Meanwhile, the rest of the city was allowed to enjoy the garden's pleasures through the railings.

The overpowering sense of turbulence is palpable when Daniel Defoe refers to the construction site of Grosvenor Square in 1725:

> I passed an amazing scene of new foundations, not of houses only, but as I might say of new Cities. New towns, new squares, and fine buildings, the like of which no city, no town, nay no place in the world can shew ... All the way through this new scene I saw the world full of bricklayers who seem to have little else to do but like gardeners, to dig a hole, put in a few bricks and presently there goes up a house.[19]

The square, started that year and completed around 1731, was to be the architectural centrepiece of the estate, yet was placed in the hands of a variety of architects and builders who were willing to speculate on the project. This raised an interesting tension in the development of the four sides of housing around the square, that speaks to the continued balance between commercial imperative and aesthetic considerations.

How does one follow the dictates of emerging neoclassical taste that promoted the notion of uniformity in all things – that is to say, the four sides of the square expressing a stylistic unity – and the demands of the individual developers who wanted to satisfy the tastes of their clients and the limits of their pocket books? And, on top of that, how to do so within a space so large that uniformity itself might have a deadening effect? The results were rather an image of London itself: powerful gestures of control from above demanding architectural harmony were followed when convenient, and ignored when the bottom line suggested an alternative route.

This was best seen on the east side, developed by the builder John Simmons, who had bought all the plots along this side. Next he probably engaged the architect Colen Campbell, who was at that time living on Brook Street, to produce a series of designs. The plan never made it off the drawing board, and today remains in the Ashmolean Museum in Oxford. However, the drafts offer an intriguing vision of what the square might have been. The whole elevation was a single design: a uniform and symmetrical range, in the best Palladian style. The rusticated ground floor was designed as a series of arches. These were framed by a sequence of balconies along the second floor. Columns rose to the third floor. Whether these designs were commissioned by Simmons or Sir Richard Grosvenor is unknown. Nonetheless, the designs that Simmons ended up with were a more feasible attempt at urban grandeur. As Sir John Summerson notes: he 'resorted to a plainer and more articulate symmetry, building a large pedimented house in the centre and large houses at either end'.[20] This was the first example in the city of such a monumental terrace that later became a template for other schemes.

Similar projects were in hand on the north side, under the guidance of speculator Edward Shepherd. Starting life as a plasterer, Shepherd had made a profit working in various properties on Hanover Square and flipped his craft into becoming a full-blown projector, taking on properties on Cavendish Square and becoming the architect for the Duke of Chandos. From 1723, he had picked up a handful of properties on the Grosvenor development at Brook Street and Audley Street. In 1728, he took three leases in the middle of the north side of the square (nos. 18–20 today). Here he created a uniform façade that he had originally hoped might unfold across the whole of the side of the street. It offered a neoclassical gesture without losing its popular touch. This was, after all, the home of MPs and grandees, not the cognoscenti.

In the end, the hopes of a grand scheme fell to the contingencies of the time. The building work started on the eastern fringes and worked westwards. There was a certain charm to be found in the unevenness of its 'moderate variety'. For other more severe critics, such as the Grub Street 'hack' James Ralph, the square was 'little better than a collection of whims and frolics in buildings, without anything like order of beauty'. Harsh, perhaps. Although the scheme attracted the leading neoclassical architects of the age, this style was still emergent and not a guarantee to attract the rich. The developers themselves knew that their job was to give their clients what they wanted. And here they were probably more successful than Ralph gives them credit for: 'a wretched attempt at something extraordinary'.[21]

The houses themselves did not sell quickly, costing between £1,166 and £7,500. And in 1739, they even had to sell one of the houses on the square by lottery during a lull in the market. Nonetheless, despite choppy economic waters, by the 1730s the Grosvenor Estate had become one of the premier addresses in London. In total there were 277 houses, including the fifty-one dwellings around the square, built across the estate in the first years. The first tenants included forty-seven peers and a further sixty-seven were people of title. Sir Richard did his best to attract his friends from Westminster and by 1733 there were lease agreements with thirty members of the House of Commons and sixteen peers of the House of Lords. Yet it remained a mixed estate with streets (especially those close to Tyburn) filled with tradesmen and coffee houses. The electoral roll for Mount Street named fifty-three businesses including peruke (wig) maker, greengrocer and snuff man.[22]

The social historian Julie Schlarman argues the estate was almost uniquely timed and designed for a new kind of urban living. The geographical location of the estate in relation to the royal court and Westminster was ideal, as one eighteenth-century writer noted: 'at the farthest Extent of the Town Westwards, upon a rising Ground, almost surrounded by Fields; which with the fine Air it is by this Means enjoys, renders the Situation delightful, and makes it reckoned the finest of all our Squares in Town.' It was also designed with an idea of public life. The public spaces – both the *grand place* itself as well as the radiating boulevards – all allowed for the circulation and interaction of the social elites.

A good address was more than just architecture, it was about who your neighbour was, what location said about your social standing. Unexpectedly, Schlarman estimates that a third to a half of all rate payers in the estate in its first years were women. Many were widows, dowager Duchesses, heiresses and even a royal mistress or two. She writes: 'In the spaces of the estate, social alliances were created and cemented, political influence was courted and given. For women in particular, who formed a significant number of estate residents and who were considered arbiters of taste and guardians of morals, such spaces were crucial settings for the day-to-day functioning of elite life.'[23]

It is unlikely that such things were designed by Sir Richard Grosvenor and his estate agent. Nor did he necessarily set out to build homes for what Walpole called 'abandoned women of quality'. Rather, the estate was acquired, adapted and evolved by those who sought it out. By accident or design, this became a place that could represent and nurture their interests best. The new estate was a forcing ground for new ways of living, offering new opportunities to make alliances and form communities. For some elite women, this offered a potential liberation of sorts. But this did not signal a release from the social confines of primogeniture in inheritance and the curse of couverture in matrimony. Nevertheless, there continued to be rich widows, fathers who had only daughters, and these lucky few had more space in which to articulate their subjectivity, in the realms of either consumption or political influence. The public spaces of the estate, as well as the semi-private spaces of the salon, became worlds where a Georgian woman found a place in the urban setting. This is the way that capitalism shapes everyday lives.

Within Mary Davies's lifetime, this plot of London soil went from being a field to becoming one of the centres of power, wealth and influence in the city. The shape and history of this community was determined by the now sacrosanct doctrine of private property. In the eighty years since the first experiments in aristocratic capitalism in Covent Garden and Lincoln's Inn Fields, the economics of leasehold, freehold, mortgages had become increasingly sophisticated. The financial and legal machinations formulated by the moneylender Hugh Audley had now become commonplace and the debate on debt and credit the lifeblood of the city. London was already the seedling of the financial capital we know today, linked by the docks as the gateway to global trade, the Royal Exchange, and the speculation on the ground at the metropolitan edges.

This is the birth of the modern city that we live in today.

* * *

But where does this leave Dame Mary herself? What role did she play in this last chapter of her own story? We can hardly say that she was the driving force behind this development. Rather, it happened to land that she owned, and was now in the hands of her guardian and sons. She did not transform London except for the fact that she once owned a part of it that went on to become central to the metropolitan story. It is a fleeting thought to consider whether she ever came down to London again after her trials. Did she go and see her mother at Millbank, while one of her guardians was in the capital to attend Parliament? Or maybe she was too ill to travel and only heard news of what was going on in the Manor of Ebury. The historical record does not tell us, so we can only speculate.

Sadly, her life ends in silence too. She had moved from guardian to guardian since her confinement in 1708. By 1730, she was living at Chirk Castle in Denbighshire, North Wales, with Robert Myddleton. Myddleton had remained in contact with the estate, in particular the estate agent Andrews, and papers show he granted in her name extended leases to plots that came under her inheritance throughout the 1720s. Whether he did this with Dame Mary's consent is unknown. As a guardian for the sons, he also had their interests in mind.

Are we to assume that she had become the lunatic that everyone now took her for? Who knows. In one narrative interpretation, from the moment of her confinement she did not wish to know about the world, consumed by her own distemper. Chirk Castle was a fourteenth-century castle that had been turned into an aristocratic home. The grounds had been turned into an elegant baroque garden of formal borders close to the house, leading to walks and avenues. In a 1742 engraving of the estate, one path leads to a bend in the River Ceiriog, and there stands a small, two-storey 'cold bath' house beside a pool. One wonders if this was created for Dame Mary. Myddleton has also constructed a bowling green and walled garden that contained a dovecot and a series of classical statues. Is this where Dame Mary came to organise her thoughts? To think about her children? To recall her childhood in London or, in darker times, flashes of those crazed, fearful moments in Paris, at the Hôtel Castile?

Into the same silence we can also read a more spectral existence. On one side, that the mania reported during the trials of 1703 and 1705 became a permanent fog. That Dame Mary's life was marked by anguish and struggle as she continued to fathom who she was, and what agency she had over her own life. On the other side, in this silence, she found peace and an accommodation with her history and her present. I cannot help seeing my own wishful thinking in these speculations.

She died at the age of sixty-five and was buried in the family plot at St Mary's, Eccleston, on 15 January 1730. During the last twenty years of her life, she had been more or less at a distance from the world. For a life that was marked by ledgers, leases and contracts, there was little notice of her passing. She was returned to her husband in death, in the family vault. And was also later remembered on the family plaque inside the current parish church.

Yet even then the inheritance was not settled. All Dame Mary's land passed on to her oldest son, but Sir Richard Grosvenor died in 1732. The estate was then passed on to his brother Sir Thomas, although there are some indications that there had been attempts to cut him out of the inheritance. And for good reason: Sir Thomas Grosvenor was by this time in his mid-thirties and suffering from tuberculosis. His doctors had recommended that he travel to Naples for the improving air, but he died there in February 1733. Without children of his own, the estate then moved on to Dame Mary's youngest son, Robert.

Robert moved into Eaton Hall and took on the task of running the family estate. He also stood as MP for Chester as if it were a family right. He was a high Tory and it was even rumoured, erroneously, that he rode to fight alongside Bonnie Prince Charlie in 1745 in the Jacobite rebellion. In another scurrilous caricature, Thomas Carew noted in 1747: 'It is said Sir R. Grosvenor is soon to be made a peer, but I hope without foundation.'[24] Once Robert died in 1755, it went to his son Richard, who became the first Earl Grosvenor, rising to the House of Lords. And from there, there is a direct line from this Richard to the current Dukes of Westminster. But this is not their story. Nor is it the story of how the estate grew after the building of Grosvenor Square.

For most histories of the city, the story of Dame Mary is an alluring point of interest before the narrative of the estate begins. But for us, this is where it ends. For most, Dame Mary is interesting only because of her marriage to Sir Thomas; and in similar fashion her inheritance is not of note until it is improved. This way of looking at the progression of a city as it grows is to accept the inevitability of what happened without looking at how fragile, contingent, emergent these ideas and actions were. There was never anything inevitable about the fate of Dame Mary and her inheritance. The modern world was coming into view as she grew up, as she attempted to take hold of the world and then finally was defeated by it. She is not a feminist heroine but her history is important to mark. Nor should she just be seen as a tragic victim of the system set against her sex.

She deserves more than a passing reference in other people's stories. We can learn much from looking at her life as if it were more than an anecdote or footnote to a bigger history. This narrative is, in so many ways, the beginnings of the same world that we are living in today. And as a result, Dame Mary's struggles feel so relevant, so contemporary. A consideration of her life shines a light on the interlaced threads of the relationship between private property and politics, gender and economics, land and the city. These are our struggles too. It raises questions of the nature of madness. Of how trauma manifests itself. And finally, of whose story deserves to be told.

Afterword

WALKING THROUGH GROSVENOR Square today, one is treading the same paths as many of the figures who have crossed this narrative. But one is also navigating a completely different city. Today, Mayfair is in zone 1, now considered the centre, rather than on the periphery of the metropolis. It is where people come to from the suburbs for work, shopping, entertainment – the benefits of urban living. However, this is also an exclusive neighbourhood, an enclave with invisible borders that stands back from the rest of the urban bustle. So much seems to have changed since the 1720s about this place, yet there are some aspects of its form, flow and function that remain the same, as intended, and managed.

Step away from the churn of Oxford Street and you can find yourself within a different version of the city. The crowds recede, the pace slows, the noise moves into the background. For many, this space may appear exclusive, and excluding. Even without barriers, Mayfair can feel as if it is not a place for everyone. The urban adventure on offer here is only for a very particular type of person. A home to discreet hotels with liveried doormen, hedge funds, expensive clothes shops, art auctioneers, sellers of gin palaces and gunmakers. If you wanted to live here, it offers some of the most expensive real estate in the city, if not the world. In 2017, it was estimated to be worth £21,000 per square metre.[1] The successful preservation of Mary Davies's inheritance over three hundred years tells us much about how the city has developed over the centuries. But just as those origins were contingent, uncertain and fragile, so it is today.

I started the journey of this book asking the question of who owned London, and the answers were not exactly as I expected. This situation was made particularly stark when, in my initial research, I came across this striking claim in Simon Jenkins's 1975 *Landlords to London*: 'It may well be that the days of private land ownership, at least in the central areas of a city like London, are over.' The combination of local authority controls over development, the rise of tax on profits and even the threat of compulsory purchase suggested that 'the age of private property development will have come to an end.'[2]

Clearly not. Today, I live in what the urban geographer Rowland Atkinson calls the 'Alpha City'. London has become the home to the super-rich, and as he shows, the city boasts 431,000 property millionaires. More billionaires call London home than any other city, apart from New York.[3] Politicians, financiers, lawyers, developers and estate agents have become enablers to the city's transformation into an elite playground. It welcomes oligarchs, warlords, and 'non-doms' who use the system to avoid paying tax, as well as speculators who wish to play the London property game; a real-life, real-time Monopoly. It is no accident that Mayfair and Park Lane are the most expensive locations on the board. And just as in that game there are winners and losers in the real city too.

So who does own London? It is surprisingly difficult to find out. There are plenty of people who do not want the public to find the names on a particular lease. According to a *Private Eye* investigation, over 42,000 commercial and residential properties in London were purchased through offshore tax havens.[4] As a result, the records of ownership are fiendishly difficult to uncover and a Freedom of Information request to the Land Registry will produce little beyond a company name based on an island often thousands of miles from the Thames. There are many reasons for people to hide their identity and their wealth in such ways.

Nevertheless, it is still worth asking who are the largest owners of the capital. Until the beginning of the twentieth century, land remained in the hands of aristocratic landlords, developed into what made up the Great Estates. This changed throughout the twentieth century with the rise of large-scale development companies on the one hand, usually as the result of aristocrats selling off their property to speculators. And, on the other hand, the increased public ownership of public housing and the welfare state following the Second World War. A dramatic shift occurred near the end of the century when London property became attractive to international speculation. In 2017, in another survey from *Property Week*, the league table of major landlords, ranked by size rather than value, reveals a perhaps unexpected top 10:[5]

1. Canary Wharf Group Investment Holdings 21,452,796 sq ft
2. The Mayor and Commonalty and Citizens of the City of London 17,447,701 sq ft
3. Transport for London 14,889,025 sq ft
4. Aviva 8,964,857 sq ft
5. BNP Paribas 7,457,253 sq ft
6. The Crown Estate 7,266,023 sq ft
7. Legal & General Group 6,782,525 sq ft
8. SEGRO 6,589,014 sq ft
9. British Land Company 6,410,015 sq ft
10. Network Rail 4,903,713 sq ft

The gold medal goes to the sovereign fund of Qatar which bought up over one million square feet of Canary Wharf in 2015 and added five five-star hotels, the Chelsea Barracks and the Shard as well as the former American Embassy on Grosvenor Square. With the Kuwaiti and Emirati sovereign funds at no. 16, this signals a dramatic transformation of the city's landscape in less than a decade. The geography of London is now in the hands of people who see the city as an investment rather than a place to live or work. The city is a financial instrument. This is consolidated with the proliferation of ownership in the hands of insurance, pension and finance companies – Aviva, BNP Paribas, Legal & General. Large property development companies such as SEGRO and the British Land Company, both founded in the twentieth century, reflect the move from state or council ownership towards private dominance of the capital's evolution.

Note that none of the Great Estates makes the cut. This may surprise many people. The Crown Estate, which by law actually belongs to the state, is the only remnant of former times. In fact, the Grosvenor Estate comes in at no. 20, one spot behind Tesco. Have the days of the great aristocratic control of the city come to an end? This transformation of the city is not reflected in the dominance of the Crown and the aristocracy over the rest of the country. In 2018, the Grosvenor Estate, which includes lands in Cheshire and Scotland, on top of the 300-acre London properties, was calculated to reach 140,000 acres.[6] But it does demand the question: what kind of city does this new, global financialised land system offer us today, and in the future?

While who owns the city may have changed, the system of development and private property remains resolute. What is different is that land value has seemed to be detached from the soil itself. Is this a city that the erstwhile property developer Sir Richard Grosvenor might recognise? There is plenty that would appear familiar. Recently, Peter Wynne Rees, the former head planner of the City of London, noted that we are currently living through a second Great Fire moment. The fabric of the city is changing at a rate that has not been seen since the late seventeenth century. He was probably right, but Wynne Rees was not just concerned about the speed of change but what shape the new city was taking.

Instead of the historic fabric, he observed, London was becoming overrun with what he termed 'safe deposit' towers: 'These towers, many of dubious architectural quality, are sold off-plan to the world's "uber-rich", as a repository for their spare and suspect capital.'[7] Wynne Rees's remarks recombined the 'what' and the 'how' of urban development: the architectural form as indistinguishable from its financing.

Such sentiments could easily have been expressed by Nicholas Barbon, who wrote in *An Apology for the Builder* in 1685: 'To write of Architecture and its several parts, of Situation, Platforms of Building, and the quality of Materials, with their Dimensions and Ornaments: To discourse of the several Orders of Columns, of the

Tuscan, Dorick, Ionick, Corinthian, and composit, with the proper inrichments of their Capitals, Freete and Cornish, were to transcribe a Folio from Vitruvius and others; and but mispend the Readers and Writers time.'[8] Speculators were not aesthetes, after all.

Barbon was also drawn into another of the essential debates of the age. In 1695, he got into an argument with the philosopher John Locke on the nature of money. Locke proposed that money's intrinsic value was in its coinage; the silver determined the coin's worth. Barbon pushed this aside, claiming that money was anything that the law said it was: 'it is not absolutely necessary money should be made of gold or silver; for having its sole value from the law, it is not material upon what metal the stamp be set.'[9]

Looking once again at the skyline of the contemporary city, perhaps this is Barbon's greatest legacy. Long after he died, on the verge of bankruptcy, refusing to pay any debts but the cost of his wife's funeral, this is what he really left the city: the idea that the city can rise on nothing but imaginary money. As one estate agent, interviewed by the *Financial Times* in 2015, noted: 'A lot of these buyers are effectively taking a financial position rather than buying a property.'[10]

Where does this leave our twenty-first-century cities as places to live, and potentially to thrive?

* * *

In opposition to this seeming dissolution of the relationship between ownership, investment and land, there has been a popular movement towards what developers and planners have called 'place-making'. Simply put, this is an acknowledgement that much recent development was created without consideration of the people who live there. It promotes the involvement of those who might be called 'stakeholders' in the design decision-making. It is also an acknowledgement that a place does not stay static once it has been built, but develops over time. And that this process can be predicted, managed and encouraged. In particular, there is an emphasis on public engagement as an integral part of the development process.

The public, however that is defined, takes part in co-creating the public realm, whatever that might be.

In recent years, Grosvenor Square has been dominated on its western edge by the modernist American Embassy, designed with all the subtlety of a hub airport dropped into the centre of the metropolitan churn. But since the Embassy staff moved south of the river in 2018, there has been an opportunity to rethink the square: what it is and what it is for. The garden at the centre of the square is to be redesigned and the Grosvenor Estate office spent the spring and summer of 2020, despite the lockdown, engaging with the public about what the square could be like, who it was for, how a green space in the city might be used. This was developed out of a more long-term project, launched in 2012, titled 'Living Cities'.[11]

The first report had a strong environmental message, recognising the problem that cities are centres of pollution and energy use, and that the poorly designed built environment itself has deleterious climatic impacts. But it also highlighted the potential for city-making to be the best response to these challenges. Environmental concerns quickly lead on to social questions of who is the most vulnerable to these effects. This has resulted in a series of place-making schemes across the estate. In 2009, the influential Danish planner Jan Gehl was engaged to look at ways to make certain corners of the estate – Brown Hart Gardens and Mount Street in Mayfair – more accessible to pedestrians in the hope of making more people-centred spaces. The Beaumont was turned from a car park for nearby Selfridges into a boutique hotel, including the iconic Antony Gormley 'feature room' on the south corner. The Gagosian Gallery, designed by Caruso St John, was added on Britannia Row.

These sites mark out places for the global 1 per cent. The public consultation on the square, on the surface, looks different. The work is planned to continue over the next few years, but the aim is described thus on the project website: 'Together with our neighbours and other London communities, we will embrace contrasting perspectives and create a space that has something to offer everyone. We will bring together the best knowledge to create a new kind of urban square that encourages discovery and fosters wellbeing.'[12]

This appears to be chapter and verse out of the place-making hymnal. It echoes the words of New Yorker Jane Jacobs, seen by many as the patron saint of modern urbanism: 'Cities have the capability of providing something for everybody, only because, and only when, they are created by everybody.'[13] And this is clearly the lesson being put to the test with the current development of the square and its concerted programme of public engagement. This has included a running blog, an Instagram feed and a Twitter account, socially distanced events in the square and, during lockdown, a series of Zoom webinars where experts and stakeholders have discussed ideas of urban nature, community building, well-being and sustainability. There has also been a wide consultation on design; for example, by 14 August 2020 the website noted that it had held eighteen events, reached 1,066 people and collected over 3,000 pieces of feedback.

These notes have been integrated into the design work of landscape architects Tonkin Liu's master plan. The brief includes both an open garden framed by new and historic trees, as well as corner gardens and more secluded places of contemplation. There is a desire for encounters with Nature, rather like John Alston's 'Wilderness worke', but with a very twenty-first-century feel, featuring an emphasis on calm spaces, biodiversity and education. This is clearly a very well-thought-through project with the best intentions. But this also closes off another way of thinking about a public space. Co-creation creates a place that people feel that they have a stake in, but it remains private land that is open under certain rules. The barriers around the green space are no longer hedges and spiked fences, as in 1720, but can be just as exclusionary, by other more invisible means. Will the estate feel that they need technological surveillance or guards in hi-vis vests in order to protect these tranquil spaces? What kind of activities will be allowed, and what prohibitory signs will go up at the gates? Who will be made to feel that this is not a place for them, so that it can be one for someone else?

The architectural writer Juliet Davis has written on the Grosvenor Estate's particular commitment to long-term 'steward-ship'. This notion that the land is not owned by any particular generation but held for the benefit of the future offers a resilience that sees beyond short-term fluctuations in fortune.

One current point of contention is the rise of 'ghost houses': the phenomenon whereby the most expensive housing in the city is often left empty. The global elite invest in property but rarely are there to use it. Thus, the lights within buildings are rarely illuminated at night, and as a consequence the local economy is no longer sustained by the local population. Another is the needs of new residents who want to convert their houses for more modern tastes. This often forces major excavations of the spaces below the property, because of the difficulties of altering the fabric above ground, due to preservation orders and local restrictions.

In the face of these disruptions to the private spaces, the estate has needed to invest in the public realm in order to maintain a vital sense of urbanity. As Davis notes, 'this had involved developing strategies for cultivating life and density in the face of deadening forces. It had focussed managers' attention on the public realm, enhancing the retail environment and the adaptation of certain buildings to accommodate public uses such as markets or galleries.'[14] And with the departure of the Embassy, the new vision of the square appears at the heart of this new approach to bringing people from the outside into the estate. But as Davis also points out:

> However, ultimately, resilience-building was directed towards one primary purpose: securing the inheritance of the Grosvenor family by securing the long-time economic value of the estate as an asset. It was to make the family's position, power and assets resilient long-term. Clearly such economic resilience is very different from the 'urban resilience' with its emphasis on communities and participatory planning processes.[15]

* * *

In the end, it comes back to land. Because of the imperatives of ownership as consolidated during the period covered in this book, the priorities of the estate, while they may often coincide with the needs of the city that encircles it, are not necessarily synchronous with them. At times in its history, Mary Davies's inheritance has stood in contrast to London, and perhaps just as importantly has not been a place with Londoners in mind. This tension is not exclusive to this singular relationship between the estate and its city; it is deeply baked into the current form of the private property system that first started to take shape over three hundred years ago.

And there does not seem to be any chance of it changing over the near future. Simon Jenkins's expression of the potential of the nationalisation of private land in the 1970s seems an impossibility today. Then, the fear was that the imposition of a tax regime might make landowning an unprofitable burden. According to the Land Registry, the average property value in London in 1977 was £13,180. In the subsequent forty-three years it has grown, by March 2020, to £485,794.[16] This rise had mainly been as a result of rising urban land prices rather than just the bricks and mortar above ground. This is proof of economist Thomas Piketty's historic argument in *Capital in the Twenty-First Century*, that capital has always had the advantage over income.[17] At the same time, it has become increasingly difficult to regulate, or even register who owns what, and where.

* * *

'Buy land', joked the American humourist Mark Twain. 'They're not making any more of it.' This is very true of private land in our cities, but what we are also seeing is a dangerous loss of public spaces. As Brett Christophers notes in his book *The New Enclosure*,[18] we have seen a sell-off of publicly owned lands from the streetscape, squares, playing fields, forests, hospitals, housing estates and parks. In the 1970s, public agencies owned twenty per cent of all land; this has now halved. This comes to an estimated value of £400 billion. This appears to have occurred as a response to rising land prices, rather than a means to control it. The state has seemingly encouraged, and benefited from, this escalating value of land, rather than seeing it as a problem. It reflects that political move away from the city as a public, open space to a private, mediated zone. And has had a profound impact on the experience of urban living.

If there has been an opportunity to challenge this in recent years, it has been missed. In 2019, the Labour Party produced an independent report on how to address the current inequalities in land ownership: *Land for the Many*,[19] by a group of radical thinkers and campaigners led by George Monbiot. It offers an envigorating suite of recommendations: the transparent registration of all land ownership, stabilisation of prices, tax reform and stronger controls on banking, as well as more public scrutiny of development. It also includes a variety of alternative forms of ownership that range from increased access of the right to roam, to the encouragement of community land trusts. This might make it easier for a community to own and manage property for the benefit of the group: a modern framework for the idea of the commons.

Anecdotally, many landowners read this report and feared for their future. But with the defeat of the Jeremy Corbyn project in the General Election of December 2019, these progressive debates about the future of the ground beneath our feet are unlikely to be revived any time soon.

And so, for the moment, the interest of land wins. It is what drives the modern city, and without addressing the question of land itself, the city cannot change.

Acknowledgements

THE BOOK WAS completed in strange circumstances. As I was working on the final chapters, the pandemic arrived and the normal course of things halted. In particular, libraries and archives were closed. So much information can be found online today but this does not replace the actual physical encounter of historical documents. I missed my days in the basement of the London Library, the National Archives, the Westminster Archives and in Chester City Archives. In particular, I would like to thank Louise Benson at Eaton Hall; Gillian Butler at Westminster; and the Grosvenor Estate for permission to access these invaluable resources. Thanks especially to Jeremy Newsum who has been constantly supportive of the project.

Nicola Barr and the Bent Agency have been the perfect team. Nicola is a good friend and a wise guide. To everyone at Oneworld, it has been an absolute pleasure to be welcomed into this bold, independent house. Firstly, Sam Carter for taking a punt on a fellow editor. Rida Vaquas who was an acute reader of the text. Kathleen McCully was a hero with the copyedit, saving slips and blushes and improving the text with acupunctural precision. Paul Nash has guided the production, from my Word doc to the gorgeous object that you have in your hands, alongside the team of Laura McFarlane, Jon Bentley-Smith, Ben Summers, Juliana Pars, Lucy Cooper and proofreader David Inglesfield. This is proof that a book is always a collaboration, involving many experts. I am the amateur amongst these professionals, and so the faults are mine alone.

Notes

Introduction

1 Gatty, C. T. *Mary Davies and the Manor of Ebury*, Vol. 2, Waverley Book Company Ltd, 1921, p. 69

2 Ibid., p. 70

3 Ibid., p. 72

4 Thornbury, W. 'New Palace Yard and Westminster Hall', in *Old and New London*, Vol. 3, Cassell, Petter & Galpin, 1878, pp. 536–44

5 Grosvenor Papers, Eaton, PP4/82, p. 50.1

6 Christophers, B. *The New Enclosure: The Appropriation of Public Land in Neoliberal Britain*, Verso, 2018

7 Hollis, L. *The Phoenix: The Man Who Made Modern London*, Weidenfeld & Nicolson, 2008

8 Gatty, C. T. Vols. 1 and 2

9 Jenkins, S. *The Selling of Mary Davies and Other Writings*, John Murray, 1993

Chapter 1

1 Thornbury, W. 'Fleet Street, general introduction', in *Old and New London*, Vol. 1, p. 32

2 Pepys, S. *Diary*, 23 January 1663, https://www.pepysdiary.com/diary/1663/01/23/

3 Anon. *The Way to be Rich, according to the practice of the great Audley, who begun with two hundred Pound, in the year 1605, and dyed worth four hundred thousand Pound this instant November 1662, etc. (with notices of other usurers)*, E. Davis, 1662

4 Ibid., p. 3

5 Ibid., p. 20

6 Ibid., p. 10

7 Ibid., p. 17

8   Linklater, A. *Owning the Earth: The Transforming History of Land Ownership*, Bloomsbury, 2014, p. 15

9   More, T. *Utopia*, 1516, Book 1

10 Meiksins Wood, E. *Liberty and Property*, Verso, 2012, p. 8

11 Jervis, M. A. 'The Caroline Court of Wards and Livery, 1625–41', p. 29, PhD thesis, http://etheses.whiterose.ac.uk/14219/1/546817.pdf

12 Anon. *The Way To Be Rich*, p. 12

13 Ibid., p. 15

14 Grosvenor Papers, Westminster Archives, 1049/1/1/63

15 'The Great Remonstrance', in Gardiner, S. R. *The Constitutional Documents of the Puritan Revolution, 1625–1660*, Clarendon Press, 1906, p. 208

16 Diprose, R. *Some Account of the Parish of St Clement Danes Past and Present*, Diprose, Bateman & Co. 1876, p. 115

17 Anon. 'Pedigree XII: Hugh Audley "The Userer"', Audley Family History website, https://audley.one-name.net/wp-content/uploads/Publishedinfo/AudleyPedigrees/Chapter12.pdf

18 'Gold mourning ring of 17th c lawyer, sheriff, usurer found', *The History Blog*, 17 April 2014, http://www.thehistoryblog.com/archives/30117

19 Considine, J. 'Sir Thomas Davies', *Oxford Dictionary of National Biography*

20 Grosvenor Papers, Westminster Archives, 1049/1/1/161

21 Gatty C. T. Vol. 1, p. 132

22 Audley Family History website, www.audleyfamilyhistory.com

23 Grosvenor Papers, Westminster Archives, 1049/1/1/124, 1049/1/1/127

24 Ibid., 1049/1/1/154

25 *A Plan of the Manor of Ebury c. 1663–1670 (with accompanying text, from Additional MS. 38104 at the British Museum)*, London Topographical Society, 1915

26 British Library, Crace.1.33, 'A map of London, designed to help country men to find their way around the city, 1653'

27 Thorold, P. *The London Rich, The Creation of a Great City, from 1666 to the Present*, Penguin, 1999, p. 1

28 Evelyn, J. *A Parallel of the Ancient Architecture with the Modern*, 1664, p. 2

29 Quoted in Hollis, L. *The Phoenix: The Man Who Made Modern London*, Weidenfeld & Nicolson, 2008, p. 73

30 Dasent, A. *Piccadilly in Three Centuries*, Macmillan and Co., 1920, p. 4

31 Scott Thomson, G. *The Russells in Bloomsbury 1669-1771*, Jonathan Cape, 1940, p. 52

32 Grosvenor Papers, Westminster Archives, 1049/01/145, 1049/01/51

33 Ibid., 1049/1/1/166

34 Ibid., 1049/1/1/168

35 Ibid., 1049/1/1/159

36 Ibid., 1049/1/1/162–164

37 Ibid., 1049/1/1/181, 1049/1/1/185

38 Walford, E. 'The City of Westminster: introduction', in *Old and New London*, Vol. 4, pp. 1–13

39 'St Margarets Westminster, St Margarets Street', *British History Online*, accessed at https://www.british-history.ac.uk/london-hearth-tax/westminster/1664/st-marga-rets-westminster-st-margarets-street

Chapter 2

1   Quoted in Leasor, J. *The Plague and the Fire*, Allen & Unwin, 1962, p. 42

2   Grosvenor Papers, Westminster Archives, 1049/1/1/179

3   Ibid., 1049/1/1/180

4   Boghurst, W. *Loimographia: An Account of the Great Plague in the Year 1665*, 1894, p. 13

5   Defoe, D. *A Journal of the Plague Year*, Penguin, 1988, p. 34

6   Ibid., p. 64

7   Vincent, T. *God's Terrible Voice in the City*, 1667, p. 29

8   Quoted in Rideal, R. *1666: Plague, War and Hellfire*, John Murray, 2017, p. 32

9   Vincent, T. 1667, p. 30

10 Defoe, D. 1988, p. 28

11 Vincent, T. 1667, p. 30

12 Defoe, D. 1988, p. 98

13 Grosvenor Papers, Westminster Archives, 1049/1/1/190

14 Gatty, C. T. Vol. 1, p. 169

15 Defoe, D. 1988, p. 99

16 Jordan, D. *The King's City: London under Charles II*, Abacus, 2017, p. 185

17 Grosvenor Papers, Westminster Archives 1049/1/1/161

18 Erickson, A. L. *Women and Property in Early Modern England*, Routledge, 1993, p. 153

19 Bacon, J. L. 'Wives, widows and writings in Restoration comedy', *Studies in English Literature, 1500–1900*, Vol. 31, no. 3 (1991), p. 435

20 Gatty, C. T. Vol. 1, p. 174

21 Fraser, A. *The Weaker Vessel*, Knopf, 1984, p. 1

22 Ibid., p. 10

23 Erickson, A. L. 'Couverture and capitalism', *History Workshop Journal*, Vol. 59 (Spring 2005), p. 4

24 Churches, C. 'Women and property in early modern England: a case study', *Social History*, Vol. 23 (May 1998), p. 165

25 Hanson, N. *The Dreadful Judgement: the True Story of the Great Fire of London*, Corgi, 2002, p. 61

26 'Sir John Tregonwell', History of Parliament website, https://www.historyofparlia-mentonline.org/volume/1660-1690/member/tregonwell-john-1632-82

27 *House of Commons Journal*, Vol. 8, 9 November 1666, pp. 647–8, https://www.british-history.ac.uk/commons-jrnl/vol8/pp647-648

28 Goring, O. G. *From Goring House to Buckingham Palace*, Ivor Nicholson and Watson Ltd, 1937

29 Pepys, S. *Diary*, 12 July 1666, https://www.pepysdiary.com/diary/1666/07/12/

30   Taswell, W. 'Autobiography and Anecdotes by William Taswell, DD', ed. G. P. Elliott, *Camden Miscellany*, Vol. II, 1853, p. 11

31   Ibid.

32   Pepys, S. *Diary*, 2 September 1666, https://www.pepysdiary.com/diary/1666/09/02/

33   Vincent, T. 1667, p. 62

34   From a letter from William Sandys, quoted in Bell, W. *The Great Fire of London*, Bodley Head, 1923, p. 316

35   Corsellis, N. 'Experiences in the Great Fire', ed. L. C. Sier, *Essex Review*, Vol. 51, 1942

36   Vincent, T. 1667, p. 63

37   Evelyn, J. *Diaries*, 3 September 1666

38   Taswell, W. 1853, p. 11

39   Quoted in Bedford, J. *London's Burning*, Abelard-Schuman, 1966, p. 135

40   Taswell, W. 1853, p. 13

41   Stow, J. *A Survey of London*, ed. C. L. Kingsford, Clarendon Press, 1908, p. 345

42   Evelyn quoted in De La Bédoyère, G., *Particular Friends. The Correspondence of Samuel Pepys and John Evelyn*, Boydell Press, 1997, p. 337

43   John Evelyn, quoted in Hollis, L. 2008, p. 144

44   Bell, W. 1923, p. 253

Chapter 3

1   Hollis, L. 2008, p. 67

2   Ariès, P. *Centuries of Childhood*, Pimlico, 1996

3   Reeves, M. 'A prospect of leaves: concepts of childhood and female youth in seventeenth-century British culture', in Cohen, E. S. and Reeves, M. (eds.), *The Youth of Early Modern Women*, Amsterdam University Press, 2018, p. 36

4   Pinckbeck, I. and Hewitt, M. *Children in English Society*, Vol. 1, Routledge & Kegan Paul, 1969, p. 19

5   Cunningham, H. *The Invention of Childhood*, BBC Books, 2006, p. 77

6   Locke, J. *An Essay Concerning Human Understanding*, 1690, Book 1, Chapter 3

7   Pollock, L. *Forgotten Children: Parent–Child Relations from 1500–1900*, Cambridge University Press, 1983, p. 243

8   Coudert, A. P. 'Educating girls in early modern Europe and America' in A. Classen (ed.), *Childhood in the Middle Ages and the Renaissance*, Walter de Gruyter, 2005, p. 401

9   Cunningham, H. 2006, p. 88

10   Pollock, L. 1983, p. 242

11   Grosvenor Papers, Eaton, Box Q2, bundle 8/1

12   Ibid.

13   Ibid.

14   Ibid.

15   Waller, M. *1700: Scenes from London Life*, Hodder & Stoughton, 2000, p. 225

16   Pepys, S. *Diary*, 10 August 1660, https://www.pepysdiary.com/diary/1660/08/10/

17   Walford, E. 'Hyde Park', in *Old and New London*, Vol. 4, pp. 375–405

18   Clinch, G. *Mayfair and Belgravia*, Truslove and Shirley, 1892, p. 31

19 Johnson, B. H. *Berkeley Square to Bond Street, the Early History of the Neighbourhood*, John Murray, 1953, p. 38

20 'Moll Davies', Pepys Diary online, https://www.pepysdiary.com/encyclopedia/9899/

21 Quoted in Hollis, L. 2008, p. 126

22 Ibid., p. 161

23 Grosvenor Papers, Eaton, Box Q2, bundle 8/1

24 Fraser, A. 1984, p. 32

25 Habakkuk, J. *Marriage, Debt and the Estate System*, Clarendon Press, 1994, p. 194

26 Grosvenor Papers, Westminster Archives, 1049/03/1/16

27 Pepys, S. *Diary*, 17 February 1665, https://www.pepysdiary.com/diary/1665/02/17/

28 Johnson, B. H. 1953, p. 49

29 Pepys, S. *Diary*, 3 December 1664, https://www.pepysdiary.com/diary/1664/12/03/

30 Evelyn, J. *Diaries*, 25 September 1672

31 Grosvenor Papers, Westminster Archives, 1049/1/1/210

32 Habakkuk, J. 1994, p. 144

33 Gatty, C. T. Vol. 2, p. 189

34 Habakkuk, J. 1994, p. XX

35 Locke, J. *Two Treatises of Civil Government*, 1689, Chapter 5 'Of Property', sec. 27, https://www.marxists.org/reference/subject/politics/locke/ch05.htm

36 Grosvenor Papers, Westminster Archives, Tregonwell Leases: 1049/3/1/

37 'Sir Richard Grosvenor', History of Parliament website, https://www.historyofpar-liamentonline.org/volume/1604-1629/member/grosvenor-sir-richard-1585-1645#footnote53_3dynmh4

38 Gatty, C. T. Vol. 1, p. 204

39 Ibid., p. 215

40 Ibid., p. 209

41 Ibid., p.213

42 Grosvenor Archives, Eaton, Box Q2, bundle 5/4

43 Grosvenor Papers, Westminster Archives, 1049/1/1/227

44 Ibid., 1049/1/1/233

45 Waller, M. 2000, p. 226

Chapter 4

1 Fraser, A. 1984, p. 4

2 Erickson, A. L. 1993, p. 58

3 Drake, J. *An Essay in Defence of the Female Sex*, 1696, https://archive.org/details/essayindefenceofooaste/page/n8/mode/2up

4 Ibid., p. 54

5 Ibid., p. 22

6 Erickson, A. L. 1993, p. 102

7 Cliff, J. T. *The World of the Country House in Seventeenth-Century England*, Yale University Press, 1999, p. 68

8 Ibid., p. 66

9   Redmill, J. 'The Grange: Hampshire. A house ahead of its time', *Country Life*, 8 May 1975, pp. 1166–8

10 Gatty, C. T. Vol. 1, p. 227

11 Ibid.

12 Ibid., pp. 277–8

13 see Laurie, I. C. 'Landscape gardeners at Eaton Park, Chester, I', *Garden History*, Vol. 12, no. 1 (Spring 1984)

14 Floud, R. *An Economic History of the English Garden*, Allen Lane, 2019, p. 81

15 Fraser, A. 1984, p. 34

16 Gatty, C. T. Vol. 1, p. 287

17 Ibid., pp. 287–8

18 Handley, S. 'Sir Thomas Grosvenor', *Oxford Dictionary of National Biography*, https://doi.org/10.1093/ref:odnb/11674

19 Hodson, H. *Cheshire 1660–1780: Restoration to Industrial Revolution*, Cheshire Community Council Publications Trust Ltd, 1978, p. 72

20 Bryant, C. *Entitled: A Critical History of the British Aristocracy*, Doubleday, 2017, p. 169

21 Sir Thomas Grosvenor, History of Parliament website, https://www.historyofparliamentonline.org/volume/1660-1690/member/grosvenor-sir-thomas-1655-1700

22 Phillips, P. 'St John Plessington, Priest and Martyr', *Rescusant History*, Vol. 28, no. 3 (May 2007), p. 425

23 Barrow, J. S., Herson, J. D., Lawes, A. H., Riden, P. J. and Seaborne, M. J. V. 'Churches and religious bodies: Roman Catholicism', in Thacker, A. T. and Lewis, C. P. (eds), *A History of the County of Chester: Volume 5 Part 2, the City of Chester: Culture, Buildings, Institutions*, Victoria County History, 2005, pp. 162–5

24 Bossy, J. *The English Catholic Community 1570–1850*, Darton, Longman & Todd, 1975, p. 122

25 Phillips, P. 2007, p. 247

26 Hodson, H. 1978, p. 11

27 Ibid., p. 14

28 Gatty, C. T. Vol. 2, p. 20

29 Bossy, J. 1975, p. 158

30 Ibid., p. 159

31 Cartwright, T. *The Diary of Dr Thomas Cartwright, Bishop of Chester*, Camden Society, 1843, p. 23

32 Ibid., pp. 23–4

33 Hodson, H. 1978, p. 15

34 Cartwright, T. 1843, p. 23 [footnote]

35 Sir Thomas Grosvenor, History of Parliament website, https://www.historyofparliamentonline.org/volume/1660-1690/member/grosvenor-sir-thomas-1655-1700

Chapter 5

1   Hollis, L. 2008, p. 298

2   Morton, H. V. *Mayfair*, Marshalsea Press, 1927, pp. 9–11

3   Kennedy, C. *Mayfair: A Social History*, Hutchinson, 1986, p. 25

4   Fraser, A. 1984, p. 288

5   Scott Thomson, G. 1940, p. 74

6   Ibid., p. 34

7   Walford, E. 'Bloomsbury Square and neighbourhood', in *Old and New London*, Vol. 4, pp. 535–45

8   Ibid., p. 173

9   North, R. 'Life of the Honorable Sir Dudley North', in *Lives of the Norths*, G. Bell & Sons, 1890, p. 55

10   Brett-James, N. G. *The Growth of Stuart London*, Allen & Unwin, 1935, p. 330

11   Barbon, N. *An Apology for the Builder*, Cave Pullen, 1685

12   Barbon, N. *A Discourse Shewing the Cause and Effects of the Increase in Building*, 1678

13   Survey of London, Vol. 33, *St Anne's Soho, pt. 1*, 1966, p. 30

14   Johnson, B. H. 1953, p. 77

15   Evelyn, J. *Diaries*, 19 June 1683

16   Ibid., 10 September 1683

17   Ibid., 12 June 1684

18   Johnson, B. H. 1953, p. 103

19   Ibid., p. 111

20   Kennedy, C. 1986, p. 23

21   Hollis, L. 2008, p. 301

22   Walford, E. 'The City of Westminster: introduction', in *Old and New London*, Vol. 4, pp. 1–13

23   Grosvenor Archives, Eaton, PP4/73

24   Ibid., p. 289

25   *Calendar of State Papers Domestic, 1689–90*, p. 238, http://www.british-history.ac.uk/cal-state-papers/domestic/will-mary/1689-90

26   Gowing, L. *Common Bodies: Women, Touch and Power in Seventeenth-Century England*, Yale University Press, 2003, p. 121

27   Ibid., p. 126

28   Ibid., p. 127

29   Wilson, A. *Ritual and Conflict: The Social Relations of Childbirth in Early Modern England*, Ashgate, 2013, p. 158

30   Howard, S. 'Imagining the pain and peril of seventeenth-century childbirth', *Social History of Medicine*, Vol. 16, no. 3 (2003), p. 367

31   Ibid.

32   Ashbury, L. 'Being well, looking ill: childbirth and the return to health in seventeenth-century England', *Social History of Medicine*, Vol. 30, no. 3 (2017), p. 504

33   Ibid., p. 505

34   Stone, L. 1990, p. 270

35   Gatty, C. T. Vol. 1, p. 285

36   Stone, L. 1990, p. 286

37   However, the fifth edition of the *Diagnostic and Statistical Manual of Mental Disorders* (*DSM*) issued in 2013 introduced the new category of 'Complicated Grief Disorder'.

38 Grosvenor Archives, Eaton, PP4/82, p. 20.1 (NB: the verbatim court papers are bound in a single volume but only every fifth page is numbered, so I have noted them here as 22.1, 22.2, 22.3, 22.4 etc.)

39 Ibid., p. 20.2

40 Ibid., p. 23.2

41 Ibid., p. 21.4

42 Burton, R. *The Anatomy of Melancholy*, B. Blake, 1838, p. 90

43 Ibid., p. 171

44 Porter, R. *Mind-Forged Manacles: A History of Madness in England from the Restoration to the Regency*, Penguin, 1990, p. 47

45 From 'The anatomy of the brain … ' by Thomas Willis (1667) in Ingram, A. (ed.), *Patterns of Madness in the Eighteenth Century: A Reader*, Liverpool University Press, 1998, p. 19

46 Showalter, E. *The Female Malady: Women, Madness and English Culture 1830–1980*, Pantheon Books, 1985, p. 3

47 Houston, R. A. 'Madness and gender in the long eighteenth century', *Social History*, Vol. 27, no. 3 (October 2002), p. 310

48 Grosvenor Archives, Eaton, PP4/82 p. 21.3

49 Ibid., p. 23.4

50 Ibid., p. 24.3

Chapter 6

1 Lancaster, H. O. *Expectations of Life: A Study in the Demography, Statistics and History of World Mortality*, Springer, 1990, p. 8

2 Cressy, D. *Birth, Marriage & Death: Ritual, Religion and the Life Cycle in Tudor and Stuart England*, Oxford University Press, 1999, p. 429

3 Ibid., p. 454

4 Ibid., p. 454

5 Grosvenor Archives, Eaton, PP4/76

6 Grosvenor Papers, Westminster Archives, 1049/3/2/96

7 Gatty, C. T. Vol. 2, p. 55

8 Grosvenor Archives, Eaton, PP4/82, p. 22.2

9 Ibid., p. 23.2

10 Grosvenor Archives, Eaton, PP44/77

11 Ibid., p. 38.2

12 Ibid., p. 4.4

13 Ibid., p. 2.3

14 Grew, E. and Grew, M. *The English Court in Exile: James II at Saint-Germain*, Mills & Boon, 1911, p. 415

15 Dunlop, I. *Louis XIV*, Chatto & Windus, 1999, p. 359

16 Grew, E. and Grew, M. 1911, p. 416

17 Kamen, H. *Philip V of Spain: The King who Reigned Twice*, Yale University Press, 2001

18 An English Gentleman, *A Pilgrimage to the Grand Jubilee at Rome, in the Year 1700*, 1701, p. 85

19 Gatty, C. T. Vol. 2, pp. 65–6
20 Grosvenor Archives, Eaton, PP4/82, p. 27.3
21 Ibid., p. 6.4
22 Gatty, C. T. Vol. 2, p. 93
23 Grosvenor Archives, Eaton, PP4/82, p. 17.4
24 Ibid., p. 32.2
25 Ibid., p. 3.1
26 Ibid., p. 15.1
27 Ibid., p. 29.1
28 Ibid., p. 29.3
29 Ibid., p. 45.1
30 Gatty, C. T. Vol. 2, p. 69
31 Grosvenor Archives, Eaton, PP4/82, p. 45.2

Chapter 7

1   Grosvenor Archives, Eaton, adds 2795/14
2   Grosvenor Papers, Eaton, PP4/82, p. 21.3
3   Ibid., p. 33.4
4   Gatty, C. T. Vol. 2, p. 71
5   Ibid., p. 72
6   Grosvenor Papers, Eaton, PP4/82, p. 23.2
7   Ibid.
8   Grosvenor Papers, Eaton, 'A discussion of the case of Lady Grosvenor, with advice from Nathaniel Lloyd …'
9   Ibid.
10 Grosvenor Papers, Eaton, adds 2795/13
11 Baker, J. H. *An Introduction to English Legal History*, Butterworth & Co., 1979, p. 90
12 Grosvenor Papers, Eaton, adds 2795/13
13 Gatty, C. T. Vol. 2, p. 81
14 Grosvenor Papers, Eaton, adds 2795/14
15 Grosvenor Papers, Eaton, adds 2795/13
16 Gatty, C. T. Vol. 2, p. 84
17 Ibid., pp. 86–7
18 Ibid., pp. 87–8
19 Ibid., p. 88
20 Ibid., p. 97
21 Grosvenor Papers, Eaton, adds 2795/15
22 Farresley, T. *Modern Cases Argued and Adjudged in the Court of Kings Bench at Westminster in the Reign of her Late Majesty Q. Anne*, 1716, pp. 70–1, 121
23 Farresley, T., 1716, p. 121
24 National Archives, Kew, PC/1/1/267
25 Grosvenor Papers, Eaton, adds 2795/16

26 Ibid., adds 2795/14-15
27 Grosvenor Papers, Eaton, PP4/82, p. 1.1
28 Grosvenor Papers, Eaton, adds 2795/16
29 Gatty, C. T. Vol. 2, p. 151
30 Ibid.

Chapter 8

1   Inglis, L. *Georgian London: Into the Streets*, Viking, 2013, p. 84
2   Hollis, L. *The Stones of London: A History of the City in Twelve Buildings*, Weidenfeld & Nicolson, 2011, p. 42
3   Thornbury, W. 'New Palace Yard and Westminster Hall', in *Old and New London*, Vol. 3, pp. 536–44
4   Halliday, P. 'Sir John Holt 1642–1710', *Oxford Dictionary of National Biography*
5   Grosvenor Papers, Eaton, PP4/82, p. 2.1
6   Ibid., p. 3.3
7   Handley, S. 'Simon Harcourt, First Viscount Harcourt', *Oxford Dictionary of National Biography*
8   Grosvenor Papers, Eaton, PP4/82, p. 3.4
9   Ibid., p. 4.2
10 Ibid., p. 4.4
11 Ibid., p. 7.1
12 Ibid., p. 7.4
13 Ibid., p. 8.4
14 Ibid., p. 12.2
15 Ibid., p. 15.1
16 Ibid., p. 17.1
17 Ibid., p. 17.4
18 Ibid., p. 22.3
19 Ibid., p. 24.2
20 Ibid., p. 28.1
21 Ibid., pp. 28.1–2
22 Ibid., p. 29.2
23 Ibid., p. 33.1
24 Ibid., pp. 33.3–4
25 Ibid., p. 39.3
26 Ibid., p. 40.1
27 Ibid., p. 43.1
28 Ibid., p. 44.3
29 Ibid., p. 49.3
30 Ibid., p. 56.2
31 Ibid., pp. 55.3–4
32 Luttrell, N. *A Brief Historical Relation of State Affairs from September 1678 to April 1714*, Vol. 5, Cambridge University Press, 2011, p. 265

Chapter 9

1   Gatty, C. T. Vol. 2, p. 152
2   See Duncan, G. I. O. *The High Court of Delegates*, Cambridge University Press, 1971
3   Grosvenor Papers, Eaton, adds 2795/19
4   Ibid.
5   Gatty, C. T. Vol. 2, p. 201
6   Ibid., p. 176
7   Ibid., pp. 178–9
8   *The Manuscripts of His Grace the Duke of Portland*, Vol. 4, Eyre and Spottiswoode for H. M. Stationery Off., 1891–1919, p. 166 (see https://catalog.hathitrust.org/Record/000239326)
9   Gatty, C. T. Vol. 2, pp. 181–2
10 See Foucault, M. *Madness and Civilization: A History of Madness in the Age of Reason*, Routledge Classics, 2001
11 Macdonald, M. 'Women and madness in Tudor and Stuart England', *Social Research*, Vol. 53, no. 2 (1986), p. 265
12 Porter, R. 1990, p. 120
13 Ibid., p. 114
14 National Archives, Kew, C 211/10/G18
15 Gatty, C. T. Vol. 2, p. 193
16 Ackerknecht, E. H. 'Private institutions in the genesis of psychiatry', *Bulletin of the History of Medicine*, Vol. 60, no. 3 (1986), p. 390
17 Porter, R. 1990, p. 139
18 Grosvenor Papers, Eaton, adds 2795/25
19 Gatty, C. T. Vol. 2, p. 192
20 Ibid., p. 194

Chapter 10

1   Grosvenor Papers, Eaton, Chest B, bundle 6, 12 June 1708
2   Private Act, 9 Anne, c. 18
3   Gatty, C. T. Vol. 2, pp. 203–7
4   Longstaffe-Gowan, T. *The London Square: Gardens in the Midst of Town*, Yale University Press, 2012, p. 43
5   Walford, E. 'Hanover Square and its neighbourhood', in *Old and New London*, Vol. 4, p. 314
6   Ibid., p. 314
7   ed. Sheppard, F. H. W. *Survey of London: Volumes 31 and 32, St James's Westminster, Part 2*, 1963, pp. 442–55
8   ed. Sheppard, F. H. W. *Survey of London: Volume 39, the Grosvenor Estate in Mayfair, Part 1*, 1977, p. 7
9   Ibid., p. 11

10   Ibid., p. 7
11   Reed, C. 'The Damn'd South Sea', *Harvard Magazine*, May 1999
12   See ed. Sheppard F. H. W. 1977, plate 2
13   Quoted in Kennedy, C. 1986, p. 37
14   Schlarman, J. 'The social geography of Grosvenor Square: mapping gender and politics, 1720–1760', *London Journal*, Vol. 28, no. 1 (2003), p. 16
15   ed. Sheppard, F. H. W. 1977, p. 17
16   Longstaffe-Gowan, T. 2012, p. 52
17   Ibid., p. 15
18   ed. Sheppard, F. H. W. 1977, pp. 13–16
19   Thorold, P. 1999, p. 112
20   Summerson, J. *Georgian London, revised edition*, Yale University Press, 2003, p. 94
21   Ibid., p. 95
22   ed. Sheppard, F. H. W. *The Social Character of the Estate*, London County Council, 1977, fn.1, pp. 83–6
23   Schlarman, J. 2003, p. 26
24   'Sir Robert Grosvenor', History of Parliament website, http://www.historyofparliamentonline.org/volume/1715-1754/member/grosvenor-robert-1695-1755

Afterword

1   'Who owns central London?', Who Owns England? website, https://whoownsengland.org/2017/10/28/who-owns-central-london/
2   Jenkins, S. *Landlords to London*, Constable, 1975, p. 4
3   Atkinson, R. *Alpha City: How London Was Captured by the Super-rich*, Verso, 2020, pp. 17–18
4   'Selling England (and Wales) by the Pound', *Private Eye*, September 2015, https://www.private-eye.co.uk/registry
5   Midolo, E. 'Who owns London?', *Property Week*, 16 March 2017, https://www.propertyweek.com/data/who-owns-london/5088280.article
6   'The UK's 50th biggest landowners revealed', Lovemoney website, https://www.lovemoney.com/gallerylist/72713/the-uks-50-biggest-landowners-revealed
7   Wynne Rees, P. 'London needs homes, not towers of "safe-deposit boxes"', *Guardian*, 25 January 2015
8   Barbon, N. 1685, p. 1
9   Barbon, N. ed. Hollander, J. A. *A Discourse on Trade*, Baltimore, 1905, p. 16
10   Allen, K. 'Speculative investors head for the exit in Nine Elms Development', *Financial Times*, 10 July 2015
11   'Living cities', Grosvenor, 2012, found here: https://www.grosvenor.com/Grosvenor/files/8c/8c11529e-ae66-414d-9e8e-ace94f70453b.pdf
12   Grosvenor Square website, https://www.grosvenorsquare.org/
13   Jacobs, J. *The Death and Life of Great American Cities*, Modern Library, 1993, p. 50
14   Davis, J. P. 'The resilience of a London great estate: urban development, adaptive capacity and the politics of stewardship', *Journal of Urbanism*, Vol. 11, no. 1 (2018), p. 109

15 Ibid., p. 111
16 UK House Price Index, Land Registry website, https://landregistry.data.gov.uk/
17 Piketty, T. *Capital in the Twenty-first Century*, Harvard University Press, 2014
18 Christophers, B. 2018
19 Monbiot, G., Grey, R., Kenny, T., Macfarlane, L., Powell-Smith, A., Shrubsole, G. and Stratford, B. *Land for the Many*, 2019, https://landforthemany.uk/

Index

References to images are in *italics*.

abduction 76
Albemarle, Duke of 120, 121
Alexander, Mr 175
Alston, John 243, 257
America 48, 73, 77–8, 189
American Embassy (London) 256
Andrews, Mr 168
Andrews, Richard 237, 248
Anglicanism 24, 101, 102, 106, 109
Anjou, Philippe, Duke of, *see* Philip V of Spain, King
Anne of Great Britain, Queen 89, 114, 147, 175, 229
anti-Catholic sentiment 101–5
architecture 30, 73–4, 82–3, 92–3, 226, 254–5
Ariès, Philippe 60–1
aristocracy 30, 50, 68, 115–16, 120–1, 252–3
Arlington, Lord 50, 79, 113
Arthur, Mr 2, 4, 153, 156
    and Hôtel Castile 158, 159, 160, 164
asylums 220–1
Atkins, Thomas 143
Atkinson, Rowland 252
Atkyns, Edward 54
Aubrey, John 141
Audley, Hugh 14–16, 20–1, 23–7, 31, 33, 247

    and Goring House 49
    and Manor of Ebury 22
Axtell, Anne 181–2, 183, 208
Ayres, Dr 4, 158, 159–60, 162–3, 176, 195–6, 204

Baker, Robert 30
banking 15, 112
Barbon, Nicholas 117–20, 122
    An Apology for the Builder 254–5
Barlow, Thomas 237, 240, 243
Barnaby, Bryan 35
Becket, Thomas à 209
Bedlam, *see* Bethlem Hospital
Behn, Aphra 89
Belgravia (London) 10, 32
Berkeley, Lady 121–2
Berkeley, Lord 67, 72–5, 85, 113
Bethlem Hospital (London) 134, 135, 220
Blake, Sir William 49
Blencoe, Sir John 212
Bloomsbury (London) 115–17, 232
Blount, Lady Anne 96
Boghurst, William 36
Bond, Sir Thomas 121, 122
Bonfroy, Nicholas 25–6, 27
Bonfroy, Thomas 25–6

Bonnie Prince Charlie, *see* James Francis Edward Stuart
Booth's Uprising (1659) 80, 100
Bossy, John 106–7
Bowtell, John 143
Bracey, Anne 178, 213
Bradshaw, John 185
Brerewood, William 138, 139, 144, 197–8
Britannia Illustrata (Kip/Knyff) 225–6, 227
Brough, Dorothy 169
Browne, Thomas 113
Buckingham, Duke of 21, 79–80
Buckingham Palace (London) 22, 49
Burlington, 1st Earl of 67
Burlington, 3rd Earl of 234, 235
Burlington House (London) 234
Burnaby, Richard 181, 182, 183, 189, 208
Burton, Robert: *The Anatomy of Melancholy* 135–6
Burton, Thomas 94–5
Bury, Sir Thomas 212
Byerley, Joseph 150, 151, 177, 180

Cadogan, Lord 233
Campbell, Colen 234, 235, 244
capitalism 19–20, 78, 112, 247
Carew, Thomas 249
Carlos II of Spain, King 150
Cartwright, Dr Thomas, Bishop of Chester 107, 110, 129
Catherine of Braganza, Queen 101
Catholic Church 18, 90, 101–5, 109
    and Grosvenor, Dame Mary 105–6, 107–8
    and Rome 152–3
    see also Jacobites
Cavendish, Margaret 89
Cavendish Square (London) 238, 240, 245
Chancery 217
Charaz, Frederick 177–8
Charles I of England, King 20, 23, 72, 73, 92–3
    and execution 186
    and London 66
Charles II of England, King 24, 29, 30, 50, 77, 120
    and death 108
    and Great Fire 54, 56

and heir 101, 104–5
and London 65
and plague 39
Charles VI, Holy Roman Emperor 150, 151
Chester 79, 80, 83, 84, 91–6, 99–100
    and anti-Catholicism 102, 103, 104
    and James II 110
Cheyne, George: *The English Malady* 137
childbirth 125–6, 127–8
children 60–4, 130
Chirk Castle (North Wales) 248
Cholmondeley, Charles 96, 98, 221, 222
Cholmondeley, Francis 93, 143, 207, 218–19
    and Fenwick 172–3, 180
    and Grosvenor children 211–13, 214–15, 221–2, 225
Cholmondeley, Robert 100
Cholmondeley, Sir Thomas 85, 134, 143, 144, 168, 172
Christophers, Brett 7
    The New Enclosure 259
churches 69, 232, 237
Churches, Christine 46
Civil Wars 25, 27, 30, 49, 72–3
    and Catholic Church 102
    and Chester 99–100
    and Grosvenors 80
    and Westminster 185
    and women 91
Clarendon, Earl of 20, 22, 67–8, 113, 120–1
class 63, 70, 191, 217
Clement XI, Pope 152, 153
common land 18–19
Compton, Henry 212
Cook, John 35
Cookson, Mrs 146, 152, 198
Corsellis, Nicholas 52
Cotton, Lady 138
Court of Chancery 173
Court of Delegates 209–10, 212–14
Court of Wards and Liveries (London) 16, 20, 22–3, 24, 216, 217
couverture 45, 247
Cowper, William 233
Cox, Sarah 76
Cranfield, Lionel 21–2, 31, 48
Cromwell, Oliver 23, 29, 32, 47, 80

and head 185
and London 66
and matrimony 70
Crown, the 16–17, 18, 22, 32, 254
Culpeper, Nicholas 126
Cutler, Sir John 13

Dahl, Michael 2, 147
Daniell, Peter 80
Davies, Alexander 24, 25–6, 27, 30–1, 49
    and death 40–4, 60, 64
    and inheritance 32–4, 35
    and land 78
Davies, John 25
Davies, Mary, *see* Grosvenor, Dame Mary
Davies, Thomas 25–6, 27, 33, 43, 44, 48
Davies, William 43
Davis, Juliet 257–8
Davis, Rob 134, 197
De Worde, Wynkyn 14
Defoe, Daniel 220, 241, 244
    A Journal of the Plague Year 36, 39,
        40, 42
Delaval, Robert 91
Delaval, William 150, 177
Denham, Sir John 234
Dissolution of the Monasteries 18, 22,
    32, 45
Doblen, John 53
Dockwra, Richard 167
Dockwra, William 145, 167, 168, 203
Dorchester Hotel (London) 22
Drake, Judith: *An Essay in Defence of the
    Female Sex* 88–9
Dubois, Nicholas 235
Dufief, Madame 159, 176, 177, 200, 201–2
Dukeson, Dr Richard 24, 27, 85
Dutton, Thomas 103

Earle, John 102
Eaton Hall (Chester) 79, 82, 83, 84, 91–6,
    97, 169–70
    and *Britannia Illustrata* 226, 227
    and Grosvenor, Sir Richard 225
Ebury Manor, *see* Manor of Ebury
Eccleston 99, 140–1, 249
education 61, 62–4
Egerton, Elizabeth 128
Elizabeth I of England, Queen 29, 36, 89
Ellis, Bishop 155, 179–80

Enlightenment 8, 112, 137
environmentalism 256
Erickson, Amy Louise 45, 46
Errington, John 149
Europe, *see* Grand Tour; Paris; Rome;
    Spain
Evans, Catherine 197
Evelyn, John 50, 95, 61–2, 73–4, 116, 121
    Fumifugium 29–30
    and Great Fire 53, 56
    and London 68, 69
Exclusion Crisis 101–5, 106, 116, 185

Fairchild, Thomas: *The City Gardener* 243
Fallowes, Thomas 220–1
Faversham, Earl of 108
Fawkes, Guido 185
Fenwick, Edward 2, 4–5, 6–7, 146,
    147–8, 179
    and Court of Delegates 210,
        212–13, 214
    and estate 168–9, 181–3, 208, 209
    and Hôtel Castile 158, 159, 160–5
    and marriage 173–5
    and Paris 154–5, 156, 177
    and trial 180, 189–206
    and Westminster 170–1
Fenwick, Sir John 189
Fenwick, Lodowick 1, 4, 130–1, 139, 142
    and Court of Delegates 212–13
    and Ellis 179–80
    and Hôtel Castile 158, 159, 160, 161,
        162, 163–4, 178
    and travel 144, 152, 154, 155, 156
    and trial 190, 192, 193, 195, 196, 198,
        199, 203
fire insurance 117, 122
Fitzwilliams, Michael 103
Fleet Street (London) 57–8
Flitcroft, Henry 235
Foucault, Michel 216, 217, 220
Franklin, Thomas 181–2, 183, 208
Frith, Richard 122, 123
Fuller, Thomas 19
Fulwood, Roger 76
funerals 140–2

gardens 243, 257
Gatty, Charles 26
Gay, John: *The Beggar's Opera* 44

Gehl, Jan 256
George I of Great Britain, King 230, 232, 233, 243
George of Denmark, Prince 147
ghost houses 258
Glorious Revolution (1688) 111
Godfrey, Sir Edmund Berry 101
Goodchild, John 33, 34
Goring, Lord 49
Goring House (London) 32, 48–9, 50, 65, 72, 79
   and Arlington 113
Grand Remonstrance (1641) 22–3
Grand Tour 81–2, 211, 226
Grange (Dorset) 92
Great Fire of London 50–8, 69
Grosvenor, Anne (daughter) 144, 167, 207–8, 219, 237
Grosvenor, Dame Mary 1–2, 207–8, 210–11, 248–9, 250
   and Berkeley 72, 74–5
   and birth 34, 35
   and care 218–20, 221, 222–4
   and Catholicism 105–6, 107–8
   and childhood 60–1, 63, 64–5
   and Court of Delegates 212, 213, 214
   and Eaton Hall 91–2, 93, 94–5
   and Fenwick, Edward 4–5, 6–7, 168–70, 171–3, 174–6, 177–8
   and Fenwick, Lodowick 130–1
   and first marriage 8
   and Hôtel Castile 158–65
   and inheritance 3–4, 9–10, 45, 46–8, 50, 58
   and Manor of Ebury 123–4
   and marriage 84–6, 87–8, 90, 96, 98
   and mental health 131–2, 133–4, 137, 138–9, 155–6, 167–8, 215–16
   and Millbank 166–7
   and motherhood 125–7, 128–30
   and Paris 149, 150, 151–2
   and portrait 2–3
   and widowhood 140, 142–3
   and Rome 153–5
   and travel 144, 145–8
   and trial 179–81, 182–3, 189–206
Grosvenor, Richard, Earl (grandson) 249
Grosvenor, Sir Richard (son) 79–81, 143, 145, 207–8
   and death 249

and Grand Tour 211
and Grosvenor Estate 242, 243, 246, 247
and inheritance 214–15, 221–2, 225
and marriage 228–9
and politics 230
and portrait 226, 228
and speculating 235–6, 237
Grosvenor, Sir Robert (son) 143, 207–8, 230–1, 236–7, 249
Grosvenor, Sir Thomas (husband) 8, 79, 81–2, 83–6
   and death 139, 140–4
   and Eaton Hall 94–5
   and Exclusion Crisis 101–2, 104, 105
   and James II 108–10
   and land 112–13
   and marriage 87–8
   and politics 98–9, 100–1, 124–5
   and religion 107, 108
Grosvenor, Sir Thomas (son) 143, 207–8, 230–1, 249
Grosvenor Square (London) 240–7, 251, 256–8
Guy, Thomas 220
Gwynne, Nell 68

Hale, Sir Matthew 201
Hamilton, Duke of 204
Hanover Square (London) 232, 245
Harcourt, Simon 190–1
Harvey, Robert 25–6, 27
Hawksmoor, Nicholas 232, 235
Hay Fair 114–15
Henri IV of France, King 48
Henry II of England, King 186, 209
Henry VIII of England, King 18, 20, 47
Hermannides, Rutger 28, 29
Hill, Emery 35
Hinde, John 121–3
Hodges, Nathaniel 37, 39
Hollar, Wenceslaus 184, 185
Holt, Lord Chief Justice John 6, 188–9, 194, 205–6
Hooke, Robert 56, 57, 116, 134, 137
Hooper, Mr 193–4, 195, 196, 197
Hopper, George 212
Hôtel Castile (Paris) 1–2, 4, 6, 10, 156, 157, 158–65
   and Fenwick's story 174–5
   and Middleton 176, 177

housing 7, 30, 57, 68, 69, 258
  and Barbon 118–20
  and gardens 243
  and Grosvenor Square 246
  and London 234–5
Houston, R. A. 137–8
Hubert, Robert 55
Huguenots 48
Hyde Manor (London) 31
Hyde Park (London) 66–7

Innocent XII, Pope 152, 153
insane, *see* madness
Ireland 23, 74, 75, 100, 102
Ireton, Henry 185

Jacobites 148, 149, 150, 151, 189
  and rebellion 229, 230, 231, 249
Jacobs, Jane 257
James I of England, King 20, 21, 22, 36, 48
James II of England, King 2, 72, 73, 101,
    108, 109–11
  and Catholic Church 153
  and death 178
  and the law 188
  and Paris 148, 149–50
  and Rye House Plot 116
James Francis Edward Stuart 150, 178,
    230, 249
James, John 232
Jenkins, Simon 8, 259
  Landlords to London 252
Jennings, Will 146, 152, 198
Jerman, Edward 69
Jermyn, Henry 68, 115
Jones, Inigo 67, 82, 92
Jonson, Ben 14

Kensington (London) 10, 55
Kent, William 235
Kip, Johannes and Knyff, Leonard:
  Britannia Illustrata 225–6, 227

Lammas Ground 19
land 7, 8, 10–11, 138, 258–60
  and America 77–8
  and aristocracy 252–3
  and Audley 21
  and common 18–19
  and compound fine 23–4

and control 16–18
  and Davies 32–3
  and Grosvenors 112–13
  and London 113–14, 115–16
  and suburbs 68, 69
  and women 45–7
  see also property
law, the 17, 18, 209–10, 212–14
  and women 45, 46, 90
*Lawe's Resolutions of Women's
    Rights, The* 90
Le Brun, Charles 149
Le Cleve, Thomas 178
Le Vau, Louis 149
Leicester Square (London) 30
Lely, Sir Peter 83–4, 147
Leoni, Giacomo 235
Leopold I, Holy Roman Emperor 150
Lewis, Mr 4–5, 164–5
Lilly, William 35
Lincoln's Inn Fields (London) 34, 35
Livingston, Elizabeth 91
Lloyd, Nathaniel 171, 172
Locke, John 255
  *An Essay Concerning Human
    Understanding* 62
  Fundamental Constitutions of Carolina
    77–8
Lockwood, Marie 25
Lodge, Tom 146, 154, 155–6, 163–4, 165
  and trial 199–200, 204
Londinum London (map) 28, 29
London 6–8, 10–11, 65–70
  and anti-Catholicism 102
  and Audley 15–16
  and Barbon 117–19
  and Bloomsbury 115–17
  and Burlington Estate 234–5
  and Davies 32–4
  and Evelyn 29–30
  and expansion 113–14, 115–16, 231–2
  and Great Fire 50–8
  and Grosvenor Estate 235–8, 240–7,
    256–8
  and housing 119–20
  and maps 27–9, 30–2
  and Mayfair 251–2
  and ownership 252–4
  and Pepys 13–14
  and plague 36–43, 47

and property prices 259
and South Sea Bubble 238, 240
and speculators 121–3
and squares 232–3
Louis XIV of France, King 148, 149, 150, 151, 178
Luttrell, Narcissus 206
Lyon 155–6, 176, 177

Macclesfield, Earl of 105
Mackay, John 239, 240
Macky, John: *Journey through England* 235
Mad House Act (1774) 217, 221
Maddison, Charles 138, 139, 198
madness 132–3, 134–8, 216–18, 220–1
Magna Carta 17
Mainwaringe, Dr Everard 32
Manchester, Lady 150
Mandeville, Geoffrey de 22
Manor of Ebury (Westminster) 9, 10, 19, 31–2, 48, 56
    and Audley 21, 22, 26–7
    and Fenwick 181–2, 208
    and Grosvenor, Dame Mary 123–4
    and Grosvenor, Richard 222
    and Parliament 229–30
    and tenants 173–4, 211–12
maps 27–9, 30–2, *97, 157, 239, 240*
Market Meadows 32, 33, 35, 44
Marlborough, John Churchill, Duke of 108
marriage 70–2, 76, 90–1, 209, 213–14
Marriage Acts:
    1653: 70
    1753: 214
Mary II of England, Queen 111, 131
Massey, Edward 100, 103
Massey, William 103, 104, 106
May, Hugh 73–4, 82
May Fair 114–15
Mayfair (London) 8, 10, 251–2
melancholy 135–7
Mercator, Nicholas 82
Middleton, George 171, 172, 173, 176–7, 178–9, 180
    and imprisonment 191
Miège, Guy 232
Millbank (London) 5, 28, 29, 40, 44, 235–6
    and Great Fire 55

Miller, Tom 146, 152, 154, 155, 167, 213
    and Hôtel Castile 161, 162, 165
    and trial 192, 195, 199–200, 204
Mills, Peter 57
Misson, Henri 141, 142
Monbiot, George 260
moneylending 15–16
Monmouth, James, Duke of 104–5, 108, 109
Monument (London) 69, 102
Moore, Francis 150
More, Thomas: *Utopia* 19
Morris, Dr 62–4
Myddleton, Sir Richard 143, 221, 237–8
Myddleton, Robert 248
Myddleton, Thomas 85

Neate House (London) 31, 32
neoclassicism 226, 234, 244
New World, *see* America
Newton, Sir Isaac 238
Nicholls, Dr John 138, 167, 197
Nicolson, William 212
Norman Conquest 16, 22, 79
North, Roger 118

Oates, Titus 101, 102, 185
Orton, John 181–2, 183, 208
Osbourne, Thomas 40
Oxford 23, 39
Oxford, Edward Harley, Earl of 238

Palladio, Andrea 226
Panton, Thomas 30
Papists, *see* Catholic Church
Paris 8, 148–50, 154–5; *see also* Hôtel Castile; Versailles
Parliament 17, 18, 22–3, 24, 99
    and churches 232
    and James II 109–10
    and land 48
    and Manor of Ebury 229–30
    and power 111
    and property 78–9
Parry, Henry 177
Pepys, Samuel 13–14, 50, 66, 68, 73
    and Great Fire 51, 52
Perrault, Claude 149
Peterborough, Earl of 34
Peterborough, Henry Mordaunt, Lord 72

Peterborough, Lady 168, 173
Peterborough House (London) *41,*
   168, 236
Pevet, Margaret 155
Philip V of Spain, King 150, 151, 167, 178
Phipps, Edward 181–2, 183, 208
Piccadilly (London) 30
Piggot, Mr 169, 170, 198, 230–1
Piketty, Thomas: *Capital in the Twenty-*
   First Century 259
Pimlico (London) 10
place-making 255–7
plague 36–43, 47
Plessington, John 103–4, 106
Poole, James 103
poor, the 18–19, 37, 40, 42
Powell, Sir John 212
Powys, Sir Thomas 189–90, 194,
   197, 202–3
Pratt, Roger 57, 82
   Certain Heads to be Largely Treated
      Concerning the Undertaking of Any
      Building 67
pregnancy 125–7
Price, Thomas 153–4
primogeniture 17, 247
Private Eye (magazine) 252
private property 8–9, 10–11, 24, 55–7, 259
property 16–18, 138, 117–20,
   181–3, 225–6
   and investment 258
   and London 252–4
   and marriage 71
   and ownership 77–9
   and women 45–7, 89
   see also housing; private property
Property Week (magazine) 253
Protestantism 107
psychiatry 132–3, 134–7, 216
public land 259–60
Purcell, Dr John 136

Qatar 253
Queen's Bench 180–1, 182, 188
Queen's House (London) 92–3
Questel, Robert 213

Radcliffe, Francis 4, 154, 164, 165, 213
   and trial 180, 204
Raleigh, Sir Walter 185

Ralph, James 245
rape 201, 203
Rea, John 24, 27
Rebuilding Act (1667) 57
rentier capitalism 78
Restoration 24, 29, 44, 49
Ridley, Mrs 204
Rippon, William 133, 197
Roberts, Hugh 80–1
Rolfe, Samuel 69
Rome 144, 151, 152–5
Roxburghe, Duke of 233
Royal Exchange (London) 69
Royal Society 136
Royalists 24, 26, 47, 49, 72–3
   and Chester 80
   and Cromwell 23, 32
Rue Saint-Dominique, *see* Hôtel Castile
Russell, Lady Rachel 116, 117, 215, 232
Russell, William, Lord 116
Rye House Plot 116

St James's Park (London) 50
St James's Square (London) 68
St Paul's Cathedral (London) 13, 25,
   69–70, 89
   and Great Fire 53, 54, 55
Samwell, William 82–3, 92–3
sanitation 242
Scarborough, Richard Lumley, Earl of
   232–3, 237
Schlarman, Julie 246
Second Anglo-Dutch War 50
Sedgemoor, Battle of (1685) 108
Selby, Mrs 146, 152, 154, 167, 213
   and Hôtel Castile 159, 160, 161–2,
      163–4, 165
   and trial 192–5, 199–200, 204, 205
Shaftesbury, Earl of 77, 101, 109–10
Shakespeare, William 70
Shepherd, Edward 245
Sherrington, Grace 63
Shireburn, Sir Richard 102
Showalter, Elaine 137
Shrewsbury, Earl of 124
Simmons, John 244–5
slavery 108, 188–9, 238
Sloane, Daniel 191, 194, 203
Smith, Judge John 212
South Sea Bubble 238, 240

Spain 150–1
Spanish Succession, War of the 178, 231
Sprat, Thomas 212
squares 232–3, 240–7
Stanley, Rowland 103
Stawker, Robert 33, 34
Strype, John 116–17, 123–4
Stukeley, Dr William 136
suburbs 38, 56, 68, 69, 119
Summerson, Sir John 245
Sydenham, Thomas 37
syndicates 121–3

Taswell, William 50, 52–3, 54
Tate, Francis 141
Temple, Sir William 71, 75
Test Act (1678) 101, 103
Thomas, Cadogan 122, 123
Thornton, Alice 127–8
Tonkin Liu 257
trade 13–14, 16, 100, 113
Tregonwell, John (stepfather) 47–8,
    49–50, 64, 74, 78–9, 85
Tregonwell, Mary (mother) 6, 43–5, 47–8,
    169, 180, 222
    and daughter 144, 145, 166–7, 168,
        218–19
    and death 236
    and Manor of Ebury 123–4
    and motherhood 59–61, 63, 64, 70, 71
Trelawney, Charles 124
Trial of the Seven Bishops, The (Herbert)
    187, 188
true mile 18
Turnour, Mr 139, 146, 147, 191–2
Turnour, Mrs 129–30, 139, 145, 147, 151
    and trial 174, 189

urban planning 57
usury 15–16
Utrecht, Treaty of (1713) 231

Versailles 82, 149, 150, 151
Vincent, Thomas 37, 52, 53
Vitruvius Britannicus (Campbell) 234

Ward, Sir Edward 212
Ward, Ned 65–6
Watts, William 35
wealth 252
Weights and Measures Act (1593) 18
West End (London) 115–16
Westminster, Dukes of 10, 249
Westminster Abbey (London) 22, 32
Westminster Diocese 170–1
Westminster Hall (London) 5–6,
    184–8
Whigs 101, 105, 109–10, 124
widows 43, 44–5
William II of England, King 185–6
William III of England, King 111, 131,
    150, 153, 178
Willis, Thomas 136–7
women 43, 44–7, 88–9
    and childbirth 125–9
    and education 63–4
    and Grosvenor Estate 246–7
    and marriage 71, 90–1
    and mental health 137–8, 217
    and religion 106–7
Wood, Ellen Meiksins 19–20
Wood, Ralph 19
Worcester, Battle of (1651) 32
Wren, Christopher 56, 57,
    68, 69–70
Wright, Nathan 173
Wyndham, Jane 229
Wyndham, William 229, 230
Wynne Rees, Peter 254

York, James, Duke of, see James II of
    England, King
York, Robert 191

LEO HOLLIS is the author of two acclaimed history books: *The Phoenix: The Men Who Made Modern London* and *The Stones of London*, and the international bestseller *Cities are Good for You*. He has written for the *New Statesman, Guardian* and *Financial Times*. He lives in London.